What's in the Bible for Women

Georgia Curtis Ling

Larry Richards, General Editor

BETHANYHOUSE

MINNEAPOLIS, MINNESOTA

Published by Bethany House Publishers
11400 Hampshire Avenue South
Bloomington, Minnesota 55438

Bethany House Publishers is a division of Baker Publishing Group, Grand Rapids, Michigan.

Originally published by Starburst Publishers. Now revised and updated.

General Editor: Larry Richards
Managing Editor: Lila Empson
Associate Editor: Natasha Sperling
Scripture Editor: Deborah Wiseman
Assistant Editor: Amy Clark
Design: Diane Whisner

Printed in the United States of America

ISBN-13: 978-0-7642-0383-1
ISBN-10: 0-7642-0383-5

Library of Congress Cataloging-in-Publication Data

Ling, Georgia Curtis.
   What's in the Bible for women : life's questions, God's answers / Georgia Curtis Ling ; Larry Richards, general editor. — Rev. and updated.
      p. cm. — (What's in the Bible for—)
   Summary: "Bible-based information relevant to today's women. Arranged topically, material includes Scripture and analysis, character studies, personal application, illustrations, quotations, and more. Suitable for individual or group study"—Provided by publisher.
   Includes bibliographical references and index.
   ISBN-13: 978-0-7642-0383-1 (pbk.)
   ISBN-10: 0-7642-0383-5 (pbk.)
 1. Christian women—Religious life. 2. Christian life—Biblical teaching. 3. Women in the Bible. I. Richards, Larry, 1931- II. Title.

BV4527.L56 2007
220.6'1082—dc22

                                                                                    2006101338

07 08 09 10   10 9 8 7 6 5 4 3 2 1

Introduction

INTRODUCTION

The journey of life—what a trip! What woman doesn't desire to live a successful, simple, stress-free life? We all have hopes and dreams for success in this journey, and yet we sometimes choose to limit ourselves by failing to search for God's best in our lives. We choose to clutter our lives with chaos instead of peace, overcommitment instead of balance. We settle for spiritual complacency instead of spiritual abundance. But don't lose heart. There is a simple solution!

God is concerned with your living the best possible life, and that's why he gave us a simple, step-by-step guide to living a fulfilled life. He gave us a map for every aspect of our lives so that we can live a better life than we could dream of as we travel on our journey.

This book is about finding answers to life's questions through the Bible. It's about discovering meaning and purpose in your life. It's about developing an intimate relationship with God and the ones you love. It's about making sense of uncertain times, suffering, and loss. It's about family, friendships, and faith. It's about balancing work and home, your budget, and your time. It's simply about being the best woman God wants you to be. We'll open the pages of the Bible and see what secrets are revealed as you find and live God's best for your life.

Why Look to the Bible?

Several years ago, *Writer's Digest* magazine carried a feature in their seventy-fifth anniversary Special Edition entitled, "75 Books Every Writer Must Read." These books were chosen by published authors, an exclusive list of "must-reads" to update your own bookshelf. According to these literary professionals, the number one book every writer must read was . . . the Bible! Yes, the Bible. One writer commented, "Lay your chosen faith aside and experience this beautifully written book."

The Bible has been the number one bestseller of all time, and it's no wonder—it has the answers to all of life's questions. Contrary to popular belief, Freud did not write the book on human relationships, nor did Dr. Spock write the book on raising kids. Someone else did: God, our Creator. Of course it's the world's greatest book! Our Father knows best!

Scripture opens the door to understanding. It is living and active. Once you discover the truth, you will understand its relevance for your life and be able to apply it each day. The Word of God offers hope when a crisis hits, comfort in time of grief, encouragement when you are weary, and guidance in relationships. The Bible's timeless advice for women has guided countless lives across the millennia.

Women of the Bible

God gave us snapshots of women's lives in the Bible to give us a wealth of inspiration, wisdom, and encouragement. Though separated by thousands of years, drastic cultural differences, and divergent customs, the ancient Bible woman and the modern woman still share the same joys, sorrows, anxieties, disappointments, pains, and dreams of a safe, stable life. Just as we do, Bible women longed for an intimate faith in their Creator and struggled to develop rewarding relationships. Because these women looked to a loving God during confusion, disappointment, and suffering, they lived rewarding inner lives no matter what the external circumstances were.

Enjoy their stories. May these newfound friends step out of the pages of the Bible and walk alongside you as you reflect on how relevant their examples are for today's modern woman.

A Word About Words

As you read *What's in the Bible for Women*, you'll notice some interchangeable words: *Scripture, Scriptures, Word, Word of God, God's Word,* etc. All of these terms mean the same thing and come under the broad heading of "the Bible."

In most cases the phrase "the Scriptures" in the New Testament refers to the Old Testament. Peter indicated that the writings of the apostle Paul were quickly accepted in the early church as equal to "the other Scriptures" (2 Peter 3:16). Both Testaments consistently demonstrate the belief that is expressed in 2 Timothy 3:16, "All Scripture is God-breathed."

One Final Tip

There's a wonderful promise given when we turn to the Bible to answer life's questions. As we read the inspired Word of God, he himself promises that his Word will make a distinct difference in our lives, and he is present whenever we read it.

As you read, pray, and open your heart to God, ask him to speak to you. You will find your life enriched and changed forever as you find out what's in the Bible for women.

About the Author

Georgia Curtis Ling is a bestselling author, an award-winning writer, and a well-liked speaker who touches the heart and tickles the funny bone as she writes about faith, love, and life. She has been teaching and helping women find answers through the Bible to life's questions since she graduated from Kentucky Christian University with a major in Bible in 1979. She and her husband, Phil, have one son and live in a log cabin in Kentucky.

About the General Editor

Dr. Larry Richards is a native of Michigan who now lives in Raleigh, North Carolina. He was converted while in the Navy in the 1950s. Larry has taught and written Sunday school curriculum for every age group, from nursery through adult. He has published more than two hundred books, and his books have been translated into some twenty-six languages. His wife, Sue, is also an author. They both enjoy teaching Bible studies as well as fishing and playing golf.

What's in the Bible for You?
This Series Will Help You Find Out

For every situation you face and for every stage of life, there's no better place than the Bible to turn for answers and advice. This book in the What's in the Bible™ series guides you from life's questions to God's answers by tackling the topics that matter to you most. Its organization allows you to quickly and easily find the godly wisdom you need to be your best in every area of your life.

You can start with chapter 1 and read straight through the whole book, or, if you prefer, you can go right to the Table of Contents to find the topic you're looking for. The friendly format in each chapter includes:

- Perspectives on the topic, examples from the Bible, and real-life stories
- In-depth snapshots that let you see the true character of men, women, couples, and teens from the Bible in situations just like yours
- Quick definitions of key words and concepts
- Helpful insights and additional information from experts on the topic
- Examples of God's power and promises throughout history
- Ways your topic fits into context with the rest of the Bible to give you the bigger picture
- How-to suggestions for putting biblical truths into action
- End-of-chapter reflections and questions

On page after page, you'll meet real people just like you who dealt with real issues just like yours. So take heart and take hope. You're about to find out that the Bible has everything you need.

Special Features for Each Topic

sovereign
Psalm 141:8

More information is at your fingertips! Look up the Bible verse listed in the margin to better understand the <u>underlined</u> word in the text you just read. The underlined words are key concepts that will help you build your faith.

When you see this icon, you'll know you're about to read something especially important for your mind, your heart, your soul, your whole life.

This icon is a signal for you to take time to consider the ideas in the passage. You'll want to savor the insights and consider how you can live out the truths and practical suggestions.

The Bible is full of wisdom you'll want to take to heart. But how do you move it from your heart to your life? This icon gives you guidelines and encouragement for jump-starting your faith into action.

How does God work in people's lives? Look for this icon to see encouraging examples of God's power and promises throughout history.

It's often in those moments over a cup of coffee that hearts are shared, pain is relieved, and comfort is found. Author Georgia Curtis Ling collects those tender times here with stories that will inspire and empower you.

Want to make your day better? Insights and stories come alongside you like an old and trusted friend, and they offer timely advice for putting biblical truths into daily practice.

What else is there to read on the topic? Look for this icon at the end of each chapter for the author's recommendations for further reading on the topic.

Think of this as the moment to build up your marriage. This tried-and-true advice from someone who's been there will motivate and equip you to make your marriage stronger and better than ever.

There's nothing like a good example to drive home an important point. Biblical examples of the godly and the ungodly will empower you to respond wisely to the situations and relationships you face each day.

Snapshots of Women in the Bible

The Widow of Zarephath (1 Kings 17:1–24)

The widow of Zarephath was no stranger to pain and suffering. But God rescued her from eternal suffering by showing her his power through the prophet Elijah.

Who were the men, women, couples, and teens of the Bible? Informative snapshots give you a close, personal look into their minds, hearts, and lives so you can be inspired to live in a way that pleases God.

What do others have to say about the topic? This icon highlights the opinions and perspectives of others to increase your understanding of the topic.

Chapters at a Glance

Part Two: Family Ties

Part One

Wisdom for the Journey

Chapter 1: Spiritually Fit

Renewing and Strengthening Your Intimate Walk With God

What's in This Chapter

- Is the Doctor In?
- Spiritual Fitness Checkup
- Give God the Controls
- Snapshot: Mary of Bethany
- Exercise Your Way to Fitness
- Where Did I Put That Exercise Bike?
- Nurture Your Soul With Worship
- It's Just the Two of Us
- Let's All Get Together
- Snapshot: Elizabeth
- What's for Dinner? My Soul's Famished!

- Scripture-Based Diet
- The Parable of the Squirrel
- Supplement Boost
- Snapshot: The Queen of Sheba
- The Purest Water on the Market
- Snapshot: The Samaritan Woman
- Get Some Rest
- How Do You Spell Relief? I Spell It P-R-A-Y-E-R
- "We Just Don't Talk Anymore"
- What's My Goal?
- Enjoy a Healthy Spiritual Life

Here We Go

David
I Chronicles 11–29

statutes
established customs
precepts
directions for daily living
ordinances
authoritative commands

PSALM 19:7–11 *The law of the Lord is perfect, reviving the soul. The **statutes** of the Lord are trustworthy, making wise the simple. The **precepts** of the Lord are right, giving joy to the heart. The commands of the Lord are radiant, giving light to the eyes. The fear of the Lord is pure, enduring forever. The **ordinances** of the Lord are sure and altogether righteous. They are more precious than gold, than much pure gold; they are sweeter than honey, than honey from the comb. By them is your servant warned; in keeping them there is great reward.*

We all have questions about life. Among those questions may be this one: Can I have an intimate relationship with God? The key to finding the answer and strengthening your connection with God is in listening for him as you read the Bible, often referred to as "God's Word."

<u>David</u>, who wrote most of the Old Testament book of Psalms, was the most famous king of Israel and ruled his kingdom under God. He points out in Psalm 19:7–11 what is special about God's Word:

1. It is perfect and true.

2. It makes us wise.

3. It brings joy in life if we follow its guidelines.

4. It leads us only to do what is right.

5. It is a treasure better than gold and sweeter than honey as it satisfies the appetite of our souls.

Our search for an intimate faith is fulfilled first and foremost in discovering what's in the Bible for women. Just as God created ways for our bodies to stay physically fit, he also gave us ways to become spiritually fit using his Word.

One of the questions I'm asking when I make it to heaven is this: "Why do women have to constantly fight the battle of the bulge?" Good grief! With raging hormones, pregnancies, water retention, menopause, no hormones, and hot flashes—what was God thinking?

It seems like every so often for a New Year's resolution I declare the "year of the body." The most amazing results occurred four years after our son was born. In that lovely pregnancy I had gained several pounds. (Let's be honest, I gained more than several; to be exact, it was sixty.) Those extra pounds were with me for quite some time, so I gave them a pet name: Baby Fat. That year I decided to say farewell to Baby Fat. I declared war. I laid out a strategic plan, set goals, and obtained advice from diet and fitness experts. Realizing "friendly fire" could help me, I shared my plan with my family and enlisted them in my personal battle of the bulge.

Let me tell you, it was a long, hard battle. It took commitment, discipline, and hours of physically demanding work. But as the months passed I reached my weight goal, going from a size sixteen dress back to a size six. I felt like a new person!

To get physically fit, I went back to the basics and followed five steps. I'm sure you know them by heart; we're bombarded with them every day:

1. Have a regular checkup by a physician.

2. Exercise regularly—at least three times a week.

3. Eat a proper diet.

4. Drink plenty of water.

5. Get adequate rest.

Hang on! Don't put this book down! This is not a "mini-fat farm" book. In this chapter, I use basic health and fitness principles as guidelines to show us how to shape up and become fit spiritually.

psalmist
an author of the book of Psalms
Jerusalem
home to the Jewish people
children of Israel
God's chosen people; the Hebrews
exile
a period of seventy years that the Israelites were held captives

Is the Doctor In?

MATTHEW 9:20–22 *Just then a woman who had been subject to bleeding for twelve years came up behind him and touched the edge of his cloak. She said to herself, "If I only touch his cloak, I will be healed." Jesus turned and saw her. "Take heart, daughter," he said, "your faith has healed you." And the woman was healed from that moment.*

In the culture of first-century Jews, women who bled as this woman did were ceremonially unclean. That meant she could not participate in worship at the temple in Jerusalem, and against her will was counted out of other activities that faithful Jews enjoyed. The gospel of Mark tells us, "She had suffered a great deal under the care of many doctors and had spent all she had, yet instead of getting better she grew worse" (Mark 5:26). Her illness was not just a health problem. It grew into a social problem and a financial problem. No wonder she fought through a large crowd for a chance at healing. I've done as much just to snag a great bargain at a sale!

When Jesus healed her, the healing touched every aspect of her life the illness had touched. In the same way, when we open our hearts to Jesus, he can transform every aspect of our lives. That's why he's called the "Great Physician." But first this determined woman had to put forth effort. So must we.

David the **psalmist** knew a thing or two about brokenness. He declared in Psalm 147:1–3, "How good it is to sing praises to our God, how pleasant and fitting to praise him! The Lord builds up **Jerusalem**; he gathers the exiles of Israel. He heals the brokenhearted and binds up their wounds."

David gives praise to God for his ability to heal. He is gracious not only to see to the physical needs of his **children of Israel** as he rebuilds their city, he also sees to their spiritual needs and heals their hearts that were broken from their suffering in **exile**.

dead to sin and alive in Christ
Romans 6:1–12

personal relationship
John 1:12–14

accepted Christ
John 3:16

Eve
Hebrew for "mother of all living"

Sarah
"mother of nations"

Isaac
"son of promise"

Mary
"loved by Yahweh"

Jesus
"the Lord saves"

Examples From the Bible

The pages of the Bible are filled with women of faith who put their trust in God to heal their hearts or build their lives:

- **Eve,** the first woman God created, disobeyed his commands, but turned back to God as he renewed their relationship. (Genesis 3:1–8, 20)

- **Sarah** put her faith in God as she followed her husband, Abraham, and waited upon God's promise of the miracle birth of her son **Isaac.** (Genesis 21:1)

- The extraordinary faith in God by **Mary** the mother of **Jesus** enabled her to surrender herself to God as he chose her to give birth to his Son Jesus. (Luke 1:35; Matthew 1:18–25)

- **Rahab**, a prostitute, put her faith in a God she didn't know when she hid the Israelite spies in Jericho. Her faith saved not only his nation, but it also saved her family and transformed her life. She is listed in the genealogy of Jesus. (Joshua 2; Matthew 1:5; Hebrews 11:31)

- **Mary Magdalene** experienced healing when Jesus cast out demons. Her tormented life was transformed into a new beginning. She became a faithful follower of Jesus. (Mark 16:9)

Spiritual Fitness Checkup

If you are like most women, you have a way of putting off or just not surrendering to the good old annual checkup with your physician. It's against our nature to surrender, but spiritual healing begins when we surrender to the lordship and loving guidance of Jesus Christ as we become dead to sin and healthy and alive in Christ. We need to have an encounter of the closest kind with God in order to have a personal relationship with his Son Jesus Christ.

Give God the Controls

I've always considered myself to be a "spiritual person." I don't have a dramatic testimony of deliverance. I grew up in a Christian family. If the church doors were open, we were there. I accepted Christ at the age of eleven. I attended youth groups, summer church camps, and even graduated from college with a major in Bible.

I served as a missionary intern and even married a minister. I showed all the signs of faith and I felt like I had a relationship with

*Jesus, but not until I fully **submitted** myself to God did I encounter him on a personal level. Twenty years ago, it looked like I had it all: a successful career, a wonderful husband, and a baby on the way. I thought I was in control. Then we relocated, I left a successful business behind, and we lost our baby. I was spiritually, physically, and emotionally sick until I turned it all over to Jesus Christ, the <u>Great Physician</u>. That was a defining point in my life. Many writers refer to it as "brokenness." It took total surrender of every aspect of my life, my marriage, my career, weight, children—I had to yield everything to God every day. I allowed God to have control, and he took this broken woman and made her whole. "Draw near to God and He will draw near to you" (James 4:8 NASB). Once I put God in the driver's seat, my life's journey became amazing.*

No matter where you are in your spiritual walk with God, you're not as close as you can be. As we use basic physical health steps to symbolize spiritual fitness, our first step is to have a regular checkup with the Great Physician. The first step may be the hardest because it is built around the verb **surrender**.

think about it

Snapshots of Women in the Bible
Mary of Bethany

The first snapshot we have of Mary of Bethany finds her at the home of Martha, her sister. Martha had opened her home to Jesus and his disciples as they traveled. Mary, Martha, and their brother Lazarus were friends of the Lord. We find Mary sitting at the <u>feet</u> of Jesus, listening to his every word. She not only knew the Savior as a friend, she knew and understood how important it was to know his heart. Her sister, who evidently was doing all the work, complained to Jesus and told him to order Mary to help her. Jesus replied with that double-name singsong, "<u>Martha</u>, Martha." (You know the tone. It's that "I'm disappointed in you" tone. I can easily picture him shaking his head.) He said Mary had chosen what was important, and he wouldn't ask her to leave.

Mary surrendered her time and attention. Nothing was more important than being with Jesus.

In the next snapshot, we find Mary with Jesus. Lazarus was gravely ill. The family had sent for their friend and healer Jesus, but he came too late. By the time Jesus arrived, Lazarus had been dead for four days. When Mary saw Jesus, she questioned his methods, but she still <u>fell</u> at his feet and

check this out

called him Lord. In her time of sorrow, Mary surrendered her suffering soul to her Great Physician for healing. He not only comforted and wept with her, but also raised her brother from the dead. There is no such thing as "too late" for Jesus.

The third snapshot of Mary occurs as Lazarus hosted a dinner in Jesus' honor. I'm sure it was a celebration to honor the man who gave him life. Mary, who listened to Jesus' teachings, understood because she listened with her heart. The men did not understand; they only listened with their ears. She knew Jesus talked of the day that his death would come. During the dinner as Jesus reclined around the table, she surrendered all she had by breaking a costly bottle of imported perfume (see Illustration #1). For the third time she was at Jesus' feet, this time anointing him for burial. If the perfume was like the perfume of a separate story in Mark 14:3–9, she <u>poured</u> away a year's worth of wages. She surrendered her most precious possession as a **sacrifice** to the One who would soon be sacrificed for the world. As the perfume lingered in the air, the **disciples** complained of the waste of money, saying it could have been given to the poor. But Jesus commended her, saying she'd done a beautiful thing. Imagine the stirring of her soul as Mary heard her Master speak those words.

Power & promises

Illustration #1
Spikenard—The plant from which Mary's perfume was made. The sweet-smelling ointment made from this plant was imported, at great expense, from India to Israel.

check this out

poured
John 12:1–11

sacrifice
an offering

disciples
followers; in this case followers of Jesus

How Others See It

Jill Briscoe

Jesus loved Mary. He loved her because she was discerning, disciplined, and delighted with him. He loved her through her periods of doubt and despair, and he loved her for her grand display of adoration as she poured upon him her costliest sacrifice, putting her future in his hands.[2]

Jesus is the Great Physician—get checkups regularly. When Mary's heart broke in the face of death, Jesus removed her sorrow. Similarly, he will heal your broken heart and give you a fresh outlook, a revived hope, and an inner image of a new faithfully fit life.

Exercise Your Way to Fitness

PSALM 86:11–12 *Teach me your way, O Lord, and I will walk in your truth; give me an undivided heart, that I may fear your name. I will praise you, O Lord my God, with all my heart; I will glorify your name forever.*

In Psalm 86, David prays to God during a time of crisis. David is running for his life as King Saul, jealous of David, attempts to kill him.

David asks God to teach him how to live and pledges to trust and walk in the path of God's truth. He wants his heart united with God's, and David **pledges** to **worship**, **obey**, and **praise** God forever.

As we exercise our way to spiritual fitness, like David we need to pledge to worship, obey, and praise God daily.

pledges
promises
worship
to revere, honor, or be devoted to
obey
to follow God's commands and instruction
praise
to express admiration or appreciation

How Others See It

Anne Graham Lotz
A changing world needs the Word of God to stabilize it. You and I, living in a changing world, need the Word of God to stabilize us! We need God's wisdom and guidance and comfort and hope that He offers through His Word. And we need to be in a right relationship with Him in order to not only survive the rapid changes and challenges but to seize the opportunities to make our changing world a better place.[3]

My friend was having a hard time battling the bulge. I asked if she had a regular aerobic exercise program. "Yes," she said with a sly grin. "I walk a few feet to the mailbox every day."

The biggest complaint about exercise is that it takes too much time. There are even programs with just ten minutes of exercise a day designed for the hurried woman. But experts tell us if we want to make a difference in our health it takes a minimum of thirty minutes of aerobic exercise at least three times a week. Our spiritual fitness also needs an aerobic workout as we walk with God.

Three Ingredients for Spiritual Fitness

	Scripture	Description
Worship God	Exodus 20:5	• Worship God only.
	Psalm 29:2	• Worship the Lord in the splendor of his holiness.
	Hebrews 12:28	• Worship God acceptably.
Obey God	1 Chronicles 21:19	• David obeyed.
	Hebrews 5:7–9	• Jesus obeyed.
	Romans 5:19	• Obedience of Jesus brings righteousness to all.
Praise God	Hebrews 13:15	• Offer praise to God.
	1 Peter 1:7	• Trials come so that praise, glory, and honor will go to God when Jesus is revealed.
	Psalm 111:10	• To God belongs eternal praise.

Where Did I Put That Exercise Bike?

Years ago, on our son's fourth birthday, he received his first real bike. He thought he was big stuff. No more Big Wheel toys! He had moved on up to a manly two-wheeler (with manly training wheels), where he could ride faster, weave in and out of obstacle courses, and ring his bell as he passed by. He said his bike was "really cool."

We spent many hours out on the driveway. To make those minutes productive, I decided to join the bicycling ranks and pull out the old exercise bike. (You may be familiar with this bike; it's usually the one in your den that serves as a coatrack.)

Tucked away in the dark shadows of the garage, the bike weighed a ton as I struggled to pull it out. Finally I climbed on. I tried pedaling but it wouldn't budge. I turned the bike upside down and began tinkering. When I looked at the tension pads, they were rusted to the metal wheels. Does that give you a clue as to how long it had been since that bike had a good workout?

Have you found yourself wanting to get spiritually fit only to find that when you turn to your first exercise of reading the Bible the pages are rusted shut? Maybe you start to pray but since you're out of the habit, you're spiritually short of breath and you quit early. Have you dropped out of regular worship and can't remember the church service times? Don't worry, help is on the way. You are not alone if you turn to God and <u>rely</u> on his promises and great power.

rely
Ephesians 1:19–20
Ten Commandments
Exodus 20:1–17;
Deuteronomy 5:4–21

wisdom
having knowledge and the ability to apply it to life
Ten Commandments
the ten laws God gave Moses at Mount Sinai for Israel

Examples From the Bible

In our "spiritual aerobics," what is special about walking with God? One who walks with God . . .

- is blameless. (Psalm 15:2)
- walks continually in truth. (Psalm 26:3)
- is happy and blessed. (Psalm 89:15)
- walks in freedom. (Psalm 119:45)
- has guidance in life both day and night. (Proverbs 6:22)
- walks securely in **wisdom**. (Proverbs 10:8)
- learns God's ways and walks in God's paths. (Isaiah 2:3)
- walks in the newness of life in Jesus. (Romans 6:4)
- walks by faith, not by sight. (2 Corinthians 5:7)
- lives and walks by the Spirit. (Galatians 5:25)
- walks in love, just as Christ loved us. (Ephesians 5:2)

As with physical fitness, spiritual fitness requires regular exercise. I encourage you to loosen and turn those pages—give your Bible a workout. Strengthen your stamina by communicating longer with God in prayer. Don't let anything keep you from worshiping God with others as you gain encouragement from believers. Discipline yourself. Make the effort, and you'll reap the rewards. If you seek God daily, walking with him becomes easier. "I will instruct you and teach you in the way you should go; I will counsel you and watch over you" (Psalm 32:8).

Nurture Your Soul With Worship

PSALM 95:6–7 *Come, let us bow down in worship, let us kneel before the Lord our Maker; for he is our God and we are the people of his pasture, the flock under his care.*

Worship is so important it ranks number one and number two on God's Top Ten List—that would be the **Ten Commandments**.

By having "no other gods" before him, we are to trust in God alone. By worshiping "no other idols," we are to worship God alone. Worship is an essential part of a Christian's life. Through worship we give praise, honor, and respect to God. Not only does this nourish your soul when you take

delights in our praise
Psalm 149:1–4
King David
1 Samuel 16:1–3

the time to thank and praise God for the ordinary and extraordinary parts of your day, but it is also good for God. Yes, you read it right. It's good for God. He loves to hear our thanksgiving, and he <u>delights in our praise</u>.

Worship is practiced throughout the Old and New Testaments:

- God gave the Israelites instruction on worship. (Deuteronomy 12:1–32)

- Hannah went to the house of the Lord to worship. (1 Samuel 1:1–20)

- David and the house of Israel celebrated and worshiped. (2 Samuel 6:14–22)

- Blessing is appointed to those who rejoice in God all day long. (Psalm 89:16)

- David longed to worship God. (Psalm 42:1)

- Jesus attended worship. (Matthew 12:9; Mark 1:21)

- Children worshiped at the temple. (Matthew 21:16)

- The early believers worshiped. (Acts 2:42–47)

- The church of Antioch met to worship. (Acts 13:1–3)

- Paul and Barnabas worshiped regularly. (Acts 14:1; 17:2)

- Lydia was a worshiper of God. (Acts 16:11–15)

It's Just the Two of Us

PSALM 146:1–2 *Praise the Lord, O my soul. I will praise the Lord all my life; I will sing praise to my God as long as I live.*

<u>King David</u> is one of the most famous kings of Israel, and he is one of the most famous men in the Bible. I believe those accolades came because he was known to be "a man after God's own heart." Wouldn't it be wonderful to be remembered as a woman after God's own heart?

In the Old Testament, the book of Psalms is a collection of worship songs written by David. It's probably one of the most quoted and famous books of the Bible. Every time I open the pages of Psalms, I feel as though I'm reading David's most private and personal journal. The book of Psalms is filled with the everyday highs and lows of life as he takes me on a journey to the highest mountaintop and then to the lowest valley. All the while and with every step, David praises and worships his Creator.

Worship is not confined in four walls on the weekend. It's an everyday thing. We are to be women of worship—living worship every day of our lives. "Offer your bodies as living sacrifices, holy and pleasing to God— this is your spiritual act of worship" (Romans 12:1).

You can be worshiping and walking as you speak praise and thanksgiving to God. You can be worshiping, driving, and singing praises to God with your favorite praise-and-worship CD. You can be working and praying as you multitask. Multitasking is second nature for women; you can use it for worship.

Nothing is more worshipful than praising God through prayer. If you're new to this thing called prayer, I have a suggestion. Do what Jesus did. <u>Jesus prayed the psalms</u>. Start your morning by praying David's songs of praise. Use a modern Bible version—it will read like your own thoughts and words. It's a great way to jump-start your worshipful prayer life.

check this out

Jesus prayed the psalms
Hebrews 2:12–13;
10:5–7

> ## How Others See It
> ### Dee Brestin
> Psalms remind us to seek God in all kinds of situations and to trust Him. When we pray the psalms with our mind and heart, we connect with God. When we pray Scripture, we know we are praying within the will of God.[4]

Let's All Get Together

ACTS 2:42 *They devoted themselves to the apostles' teaching and to the fellowship, to the breaking of bread and to prayer.*

Just as important as living a daily life of personal worship is being with others in corporate worship. Without the encouragement and support that Christians gave one another during the infancy stage of the early church, the persecution of the early Christians could have hampered Christ's message of new life and hope. But because of the Christians' obedience through corporate worship, Christ's message spread like wildfire and ignited the flame that still burns today in the hearts of men and women like you.

I have a suggestion. Don't get caught up in the "worship wars." If you're a seasoned veteran of church, you know what I'm talking about. If not, worship wars are a result of people in the pews disagreeing on the style worship should take, whether hymns or contemporary choruses, traditional services or contemporary, hands lifted or kept at the sides.

everyday insights

priest
Leviticus 21:1–7
childless
Luke 1:7

priest
mediator between
God and others
epitaph
an inscription on a
gravestone

Worship has changed throughout the generations. Music has evolved into something the musician King David probably never imagined. The architecture of modern buildings is far from King Solomon's temple. I would suggest that you choose a place of worship that preaches God and Jesus alone and uses Scripture as its road map. Choose a place where you feel the freedom to worship as you need to show praise and adoration to God. Remember, we are not the spectators at church; God is the spectator as we worship him.

Essentials of Worship in the Early Church

Element of Worship	Scripture
Leaders, paid professionals, and people not belonging to a religious profession took part in the worship of the early church.	1 Corinthians 14:26 1 Timothy 4:13 2 Timothy 3:10–4:5
Songs of praise were offered in worship.	Acts 4:24–30 Ephesians 5:14 1 Timothy 3:16
The Scriptures were read, taught, and studied.	1 Corinthians 10:6 Romans 15:4
Prophecies and gifts were used during worship.	1 Corinthians 12:1–12
The Lord's Supper was remembered.	1 Corinthians 11:17–34
Prayer was an essential part of worship.	1 Thessalonians 5:17
An offering of financial gifts was gathered.	1 Corinthians 16:2
The early church prayed for the sick.	James 5:14–15

Snapshots of Women in the Bible
Elizabeth (Luke 1:8–25, 29–45)

This snapshot of Elizabeth records one of the most flattering descriptions I think any woman of the Bible ever received. She, along with her **priest** husband Zechariah, were described as "upright in the sight of God, observing all the Lord's commandments and regulations blamelessly" (Luke 1:6). Wow! What a compliment! I think the greatest **epitaph** on a tombstone would read, "She walked with God." If there had been tombstones in that era, that's what Elizabeth's would have read.

Elizabeth and Zechariah suffered greatly as a couple because they were childless, a condition that was humiliating in their culture. Elizabeth may have questioned God: Why had he not blessed them with a child? What had she done wrong?

As Zechariah performed a once-in-a-lifetime priestly duty of burning incense to God (see Illustration #2), the angel Gabriel appeared to him. Zechariah was "startled and was gripped with fear" (Luke 1:12). Every reference in Scripture to <u>Gabriel</u> follows with the fear factor. I wonder if he discussed this with other angels: "Why are they so afraid? Is it my looks? My voice? What?"

Gabriel shared the good news that the prayers of Elizabeth and Zechariah would be answered—they would have a son, who should be named John. We know him as John the Baptist, who was the forerunner of Jesus Christ.

Gabriel
Daniel 8:17;
Luke 1:30

Illustration #2
Burning Incense—
Zechariah probably
used incense holders
such as these when he
performed his priestly
duty of burning
incense.

Zechariah questioned and doubted Gabriel's message. The old priest wanted proof. That didn't sit too well with the angel. In modern terms Gabriel asked, "Don't you know who you are talking to?" Gabriel gave "proof" by striking the priest mute. Zechariah would not be able to speak until the birth of John.

After Zechariah went home to Elizabeth and wrote out his story of Gabriel's visit, she conceived and went into seclusion for five months. Scripture doesn't give her reasoning, but I think she secluded herself from the world to study, to pray, to praise God for answered prayer, and to prepare herself for raising a child who would bring the world one step closer to God. Elizabeth was a woman of intimate faith who walked with God. Jesus later said, "I tell you the truth: Among those born of women there has not risen anyone greater than John the Baptist" (Matthew 11:11).

How Others See It

Kathy Troccoli
Our time with Him—our adoration and worship—deeply moves the heart of God. The scent of our worship stays with Him always. Whenever I hear

John the Baptist
Isaiah 40:3–5

tempted
Matthew 4:1–11

manna
Exodus 16:31–32

baptism
a religious ceremony
in which a spiritual
leader uses water to
show that a person
belongs to God

John the Baptist
prophet who foretold
the coming of the
Messiah

fast
to willingly give up
food for a time

Satan
"adversary," or enemy;
Satan is the enemy of
God and his people

tempted
to lure, entice, or coax
to sin

manna
food God provided for
Israelites in the desert

the beloved Christmas carol "O Come, All Ye Faithful," I can't help but lift my face toward heaven. It is so easy to lift my hands in worship when I sing this song. It really does make me want to give all to God and to give Him the praises He is due.[5]

Today one out of five couples is infertile or has trouble conceiving. In Elizabeth's time, without modern medicine, I'm sure the numbers were even worse. We can learn from Elizabeth and her husband as they remained faithful in their service and prayers during their time of suffering and questioning. (We'll talk more on this subject in chapter 2.)

God chose Elizabeth for a special blessing. She remained faithful to God during her entire life as she walked with him. What blessings and rewards he showers on the faithful! As you gain strength and stamina in the Lord, he will transform you from a wheezing jogger to a marathon runner. He can cause you to endure when you face life's challenges of heartache, grief, suffering, and change.

What's for Dinner? My Soul's Famished!

MATTHEW 4:4 *Jesus answered, "It is written: 'Man does not live on bread alone, but on every word that comes from the mouth of God.'"*

After the **baptism** of Jesus by <u>John the Baptist,</u> Jesus immediately went into the desert for forty days to pray and **fast**. Baptism indicated the beginning of his ministry, and even God's Son sought strength from his Father, choosing the solitude of the desert.

There in the wilderness **Satan** <u>tempted</u> Christ, testing his inner spiritual strength during a time of physical weakness. Satan's first temptation dealt with Jesus' hunger by telling him to turn a stone into bread to prove he was the Son of God.

Jesus replied with an Old Testament story. When the Israelites wandered in the desert they survived on God's miraculous provision of <u>manna</u>, a bread from heaven. Jesus quoted Deuteronomy 8:3: "Man does not live on bread alone but on every word that comes from the mouth of the Lord." The Israelites learned there was more to life than filling their stomachs. They needed God to satisfy their souls. The way Jesus broke the power of the temptation was by meeting it with God's truth from the Scriptures.

How Others See It

Bill Hybels

You can barely read a page in the Bible without encountering a situation where God is guiding someone. <u>Noah</u> was told to build a boat, and he was told exactly how to do it. <u>Abram</u> was instructed to leave his country and go to a land that God would show him. God guided Abraham's <u>servant</u> so that he could locate a wife for Isaac. Israelites were led on their <u>journey</u> out of Egypt by a pillar of fire by night. The most productive, and most effective, way to receive God's guidance is the Bible. Almost all that we need to know is right there. Often the only things missing are the details. God has already told us in general terms how he wants us to live.[6]

We are so confused by contradictory experts telling us what we can and can't eat that we're starving ourselves for fear of eating the wrong thing. We know we're to eat a proper diet, but what does it consist of? I recently read that years after the media blitz declaring bran the "cure-all" food, it's been proven to have no major effect on cholesterol. (That's okay by me. I wasn't real crazy about bran muffins anyway.)

From now until eternity, experts will disagree on what our lips should or shouldn't touch for the overall health and fitness of our physical bodies. But nine out of ten religious experts would agree that the best diet for spiritual fitness is the Bible. The Scripture holds the answers to all of life's questions. It serves as our handbook to becoming faithfully fit. It is food for the soul.

Scripture-Based Diet

This Scripture-based diet is the only diet I recommend you consume in large quantities. I'm particularly fond of the fruits of the Spirit: "love, joy, peace, patience, kindness, goodness, faithfulness, gentleness and self-control" (Galatians 5:22–23).

What is special about the fruits of the Spirit? The fruits of the Spirit are an outward expression of Christ's love in us as we walk in the Spirit.

- *Love*—the love of Christ that united man with God and man to man. "My command is this: Love each other as I have loved you. Greater love has no one than this, that he lay down his life for his friends" (John 15:12–13).

- *Joy*—the expression of celebration of God's love. "I have told you this so that my joy may be in you and that your joy may be complete" (John 15:11).

- *Peace*—live in harmony with God and man. "Peace I leave with you; my peace I give you. I do not give to you as the world gives. Do not let your hearts be troubled and do not be afraid" (John 14:27).

- *Longsuffering*—the patience of God toward man and man's patience toward others. "Love is patient, love is kind" (1 Corinthians 13:4).

- *Kindness*—gentleness, the outward expressions of our heart as we grow in Christ. "Therefore, as God's chosen people, holy and dearly loved, clothe yourselves with compassion, kindness, humility, gentleness and patience" (Colossians 3:12).

- *Goodness*—our love is to be an action, our lives filled with acts of goodness. "We constantly pray for you, that our God may count you worthy of his calling, and that by his power he may fulfill every good purpose of yours and every act prompted by your faith" (2 Thessalonians 1:11).

- *Faithfulness*—trustworthy; our faith and trust in God. "Let us hold unswervingly to the hope we profess, for he who promised is faithful" (Hebrews 10:23).

- *Gentleness*—submitting to be like the gentle, kind spirit of Christ. A gentle spirit gives us strength and power as we teach and serve others. "For the kingdom of God is not a matter of talk but of power. What do you prefer? Shall I come to you with a whip, or in love and with a gentle spirit?" (1 Corinthians 4:20–21).

- *Self-Control*—the disciplines of our heart and actions to protect us both physically and spiritually as we follow God's teachings. "'Everything is permissible'—but not everything is beneficial. 'Everything is permissible'—but not everything is constructive. Nobody should seek his own good, but the good of others" (1 Corinthians 10:23–24).

The Parable of the Squirrel

Suppose you were a squirrel. What would your basic survival kit consist of? (If it took you more than two seconds to answer this, you're not cooperating with me.) Ask any local squirrel—nuts, nuts, and more nuts! Now, if you're wondering if I've gone nuts, just hang with me for a few more sentences.

The trees behind our house are filled with furry little critters scurrying here and there. Up the branches, down the branches, and dig, dig,

dig. When we first moved into our house, one morning we watched from our kitchen window as a little brown squirrel dug and dug until his head disappeared. He popped back up, looked around cautiously to make sure there weren't any evil commando squirrels lurking in the woods, then he quickly hid his stash of nuts. In a flash he filled in the hole and covered it, camouflaging it with leaves. He ran like lightning up the tree and out of sight.

His basic survival kit consisted of nuts, nuts, and more nuts, hidden away for a future time of need. And sure enough, in winter we saw him (well, it looked like him) return to his nut stash for sustenance.

This story from Mr. Squirrel is a life lesson, or a **parable**. Our Basic Survival Kit should consist of Scripture, Scripture, and more Scripture. The only truth we can rely upon is the Word of God. You might be battling poor health, mending relationships, facing grief, or seeking guidance in pressing decisions. Whatever it is, turn to your basic survival kit and dig, dig, dig.

We have to constantly read God's Word and squirrel it away in our hearts, so in our time of need we have his help to survive. "I have hidden your word in my heart that I might not sin against you" (Psalm 119:11).

Supplement Boost

Proverbs 4:5–7 *Get wisdom, get understanding; do not forget my words or swerve from them. Do not forsake wisdom, and she will protect you; love her, and she will watch over you. Wisdom is supreme; therefore get wisdom. Though it cost all you have, get understanding.*

The Proverbs were wise sayings collected to train young men for leadership in governing Israel's **twelve** <u>tribes</u>. **Solomon**, the author and compiler of Proverbs, looked back on the guidance and **wisdom** he received as a young boy from his father, King David. He also recalled the tender loving care and <u>teaching</u> of his mother, **Bathsheba**.

Wisdom and understanding provide the essential ingredients to succeed in everyday life as we overcome struggles, endure heartaches, and face life-changing decisions.

If we want wisdom, Proverbs says we need to start with a healthy intake of "the **fear** of the Lord" (Proverbs 1:7). God doesn't want us to dread him. Rather, he wants us to seek his perspective about all areas of life.

Like vitamin supplements that give our bodies an extra boost, we can add supplements to our daily Bible study by gaining wisdom from others who

tribes
Genesis 49:1–28
teaching
Proverbs 1:8

parable
a story teaching a moral lesson
twelve tribes
descendants of the twelve sons of Jacob
Solomon
"peaceful" third king of Israel
wisdom
good sense; insight; understanding
Bathsheba
committed adultery with David; later married him
fear
reverence or worship

visited
Luke 1:39–40
**wisdom and faith
were known**
I Kings 10:23–25

walk with God. When Mary the mother of Jesus found out she would be pregnant with God's Son, she immediately <u>visited</u> her relative Elizabeth for guidance. There she found comfort, wisdom, and understanding of her divine calling as Elizabeth ministered to her. You'll find a wealth of resources in this book's "How Others See It" sections and in the "Read On" section at the end of each chapter. I encourage you to read devotional thoughts and dive into Christian women's magazines that are based on Scripture. To energize spiritually, I highly recommend that you attend a Christian women's conference. I always return home encouraged and renewed by the different perspectives and insights I find at such conferences. We are not meant to follow God alone. Hey, even the Lone Ranger wasn't really "lone"—he had Tonto! We can gain wisdom from others who have walked with God.

Snapshots of Women in the Bible
The Queen of Sheba—Searching for Truth
(1 Kings 10:1–29)

The Scripture offers a snapshot of royalty who searched for something more. The queen of Sheba had all the wealth and luxury her heart desired, yet, she had a longing in her heart for more. Armed with intelligence, questions, riddles, and extravagant gifts, she embarked on a long, dangerous journey to visit this King Solomon, whose <u>wisdom and faith were known</u> throughout the world.

In awe of Solomon's wisdom and wealth, the queen of Sheba was breathless. How magnificent it must have been. As planned, the queen was granted time with Solomon. The Scripture says she spoke with him about all that was in her heart. That might not mean much to "just give me the facts" men, but we women know what "all that was in her heart" truly meant. I believe she was searching for God. Being royalty, cost was of no concern; she sought out the only man she knew who could answer the questions on her heart. The Bible records that Solomon gave the queen of Sheba all she desired, whatever she asked, besides what was given to her according to the royalty generosity, and she returned to her own country.

Truly wise women search for God. We long for an intimate relationship with him. The story of the queen of Sheba ends there. It's not recorded if she found faith in Solomon's God. I think the reason of this snapshot of royalty was revealed when Jesus spoke of her in Matthew 12:42, "The Queen of the South will rise at the judgment with this generation and condemn it; for she came from the ends of the earth to listen to Solomon's wisdom, and now one greater than Solomon is here." He referred to her as a seeker and commended her search for truth. Never stop searching <u>God's Word,</u> and seeking <u>Jesus—the Way, the Truth, and the Life</u>.

The Purest Water on the Market

JOHN 7:37–38 *Jesus stood and said in a loud voice, "If anyone is thirsty, let him come to me and drink. Whoever believes in me, as the Scripture has said, streams of living water will flow from within him."*

During the last days of Jesus' ministry, he faced <u>opposition</u> from the religious leaders. In the middle of the celebration of the **Feast of Tabernacles** Jesus went to the temple courts and began to teach. The Jews were amazed at his knowledge and wondered if he was the **Messiah**. Many believed and put their faith in him, but because of envy the **Pharisees** sent guards to arrest him. But no one laid a hand on him.

Traditionally, on the last day of the feast the priest would draw water and take it to the temple to be poured out. This represented the abundant supply of water God <u>provided</u> the Jews in the wilderness. Significantly, that was the day Jesus proclaimed that he was the <u>Rock</u> out of which the only water flowed that could quench the spiritual thirst of humanity.

check this out

God's Word
Psalm 119:160;
Galatians 2:5;
2 Timothy 2:15

Jesus—the Way, the Truth, and the Life
John 14:6; 1:14

opposition
John 7:1

Feast of Tabernacles
Leviticus 23:36

Messiah
Isaiah 53:1–12

provided
Exodus 17:7

Rock
1 Corinthians 10:4–6

Feast of Tabernacles
an annual celebration of God's past care for his people

Messiah
Hebrew word meaning "anointed one"

Pharisees
self-appointed Jewish leaders who often opposed Jesus

suppressant
subdue; restrain; conceal

How Others See It

Joyce Meyer
God alone can water a thirsty soul. Don't be deceived into thinking that anyone else can satisfy you fully and completely.[7]

everyday insights

Water is a must for weight loss and weight management. You can go without food for up to sixty days, but you can't live without water. It's life-giving, it replenishes, and it purifies. Water serves as an appetite **suppressant.** *It helps eliminate waste and removes fat. It helps maintain proper muscle tone. Since water is natural, your body knows exactly what to do with it.*

I had been out of town for a few days attending a conference, and when I got home, wilted plants greeted me. I had forgotten to ask my husband to water the plants. My husband had to pass by one large plant every time he went in and out of our bedroom. I'm surprised he didn't hear the plant screaming, "Water, water, I need water!" It looked like

purified
James 4:8
thirst
Psalm 42:1–2
cleanses
Psalm 51:1–2
Living Water
John 7:37–39

purified
make clean
cleanses
make holy and pure

it wouldn't survive, but I watered it heavily. The next morning the plant looked so good that I suspected my guilt-ridden husband had run out in the middle of the night and replaced it with a new plant. (He hadn't.)

Like my poor neglected houseplant, when we go without being replenished and __purified__ by the Living Water that Jesus gives, we become wilted and weary, barely hanging on to life.

When we drink the Living Water that Jesus gives, it quenches our <u>thirst</u> for righteousness. "For he satisfies the thirsty and fills the hungry with good things" (Psalm 107:9). He **cleanses** and removes waste from our polluted souls. Living Water is a metaphor for God's Holy Spirit, who gives us strength and stamina to stretch ourselves beyond what we think is possible. <u>Living Water</u> is the purest, most natural ingredient our spirits know.

Snapshots of Women in the Bible
The Samaritan Woman (John 4:4–26)

In the story of the Samaritan woman, we have a snapshot of an empty vessel being filled. Ordinarily, the daily task of drawing water from a well was a social event as women gathered in the cool of the morning for the chore. But the Samaritan woman was an outcast. Having failed at five previous marriages, she now settled for an illicit live-in partner. She either was not welcomed or chose not to endure the disapproving stares of the village women, forcing her to come in the dusty heat of the day to fill her pitcher.

Seeing a weary man seated at the well, she approached with caution. When he asked her for a drink, his accent gave him away. He was a Jew in Samaria. The Jews and the Samaritans hated one another, bitterly divided over religious issues that dated back centuries. She asked him why he would even speak to a woman, let alone an outcast Samaritan woman.

In their short conversation, not only did Jesus reveal the secret sins of her life and heart, but for the first time he revealed himself as Christ, the Messiah—the One both the Samaritans and Jews had long awaited.

The meeting with Jesus transformed the woman. She ran back to the village, unashamed, telling everyone about him. Because of her enthusiastic testimony, Jesus and his disciples stayed in Samaria for two extra days. Many believed in him.

An empty vessel allowed herself to be filled with Living Water. The Samaritan woman was filled with Living Water by believing Jesus. A life, a village, and a world were changed forever as they quenched their spiritual thirst.

Get Some Rest

MATTHEW 11:28–29 *Come to me, all you who are weary and burdened, and I will give you rest. Take my yoke upon you and learn from me, for I am gentle and humble in heart, and you will find rest for your souls.*

During this time in Jesus' ministry, even though he performed many **miracles**, the Jews rebelled against him. Still he held open the invitation to come rest in him. He knew how weary the people were.

The Pharisees, who had burdened the people with strict laws, did not practice what they preached. They knew the letter of the Law, but not the spirit behind it. The people felt they were saved by sheer obedience to the Law. They grew weary because keeping all of the Law as the Pharisees interpreted it was a hopeless task.

Jesus offered to lift their burdens, for only through the **grace** of Jesus are people saved. Only through resting in what Jesus has done for us will we find peace with God and man.

miracles
Matthew 11:20
Pharisees
Matthew 23:1–5
grace
Acts 15:10–11

miracles
acts done by God's power
grace
the special favor of God; God's free gift of salvation

What wakes you up in the morning? I have a new alarm clock that beeps at me. I liked the tone in the beginning. It wasn't as alarming as a foghorn blast. But sometimes when I wake, I have this sudden fear a garbage truck is backing over me, until I realize it's my alarm clock.

Earlier in my life, I didn't need an alarm. I had an internal clock that woke me up at the same time every morning, bright and early. Over the years, marriage, schedules, and childbirth seemed to change my internal clock forever. In fact, I think it broke.

I admit the real reason I have such a hard time getting up is quite simple: I'm not getting enough sleep!

Do you find yourself not only a physical but also a spiritual zombie? Are you not getting enough spiritual rest through prayer, Scripture reading, and meditation? Maybe this is your wake-up call.

I promise I'll hit the pillow earlier and rest more in him. How 'bout you? "Rest in the Lord, and wait patiently for him" (Psalm 37:7 KJV).

Evidently I'm not the only one lacking sleep. A recent cover story in Life magazine read, "Why 70 Million of Us Are Sleepless in America." Did you know there are 3,000 sleep disorder clinics across America? According to the article, they've sprung up in response to a national nightmare—"an epidemic of sleeplessness."

apostle
Mark 3:14–19
Paul
Acts 9:1–42
worry
Philippians 4:6–7;
Luke 12:26–32
prayer
Romans 12:12

apostle
a person who received
instructions from
Christ to plant
churches
Paul
Christian who traveled
throughout the Roman
Empire sharing the
Gospel
worry
to be torn apart; to be
anxious
prayer
talk to God

One congressional study determined we are a nation of zombies, and the cost to society is stunning. The article says nearly two-thirds of Americans claim sleep deprivation affects their work, which translates into a $70 billion loss in productivity.[8]

The problem harks back to 1879, when a famous short-sleeper named Thomas Alva Edison perfected the lightbulb. Over time, downtowns began to bustle after dark, shift-work burgeoned, and reading into the night (later, listening to the radio, watching TV, and surfing the Internet) became part of American life.

Hey, it's Edison's fault! Actually, it's not his fault. It's our own choice. It's called responsibility. You can turn a lightbulb off, you know.

How Do You Spell Relief? I Spell It P-R-A-Y-E-R

PHILIPPIANS 4:6–7 *Do not be anxious about anything, but in everything, by prayer and petition, with thanksgiving, present your requests to God. And the peace of God, which transcends all understanding, will guard your hearts and your minds in Christ Jesus.*

The **apostle** **Paul**'s simple message to the church at Philippi was don't **worry**. As we make our requests known to God through continual **prayer**, we experience the peace of God. As your heart and mind are torn in the struggles of living, God will guard your thoughts in Christ as you turn your worries over to him.

> ## How Others See It
> ### Stormie Omartian
> God wants us to want Him. And when we realize that it's Him that we want, we become free. We are free to identify the longings, loneliness, and emptiness inside of us as our signal that we need to draw near to God with open arms and ask Him to fill us with more of Him. But this deep and intimate relationship with God that we all desire and can't live without doesn't just happen. It must be sought after, prayed for, and nurtured. And we must continually seek after, pray for, nurture, and treasure it![9]

"We Just Don't Talk Anymore"

Exercise is one of the greatest stress relievers. When we're stressed we often forget to exercise, even though that's when our body, mind, and soul need it the most. We can get so stressed out that we can't even sleep. Experts agree that the best exercise can be as simple as a stroll. Get as far away from the source of your stress as possible.

slow
Psalm 46:10
rest
Psalm 116:7

I would add to that stroll a more powerful solution: Make it a prayer walk. Prayer is a discipline that lets us escape this world and turn our stress over to God. Prayer nurtures your relationship with God. You <u>slow</u> down to meet him, <u>rest</u>, talk, and walk with him. The biggest complaint we women have in marriage is, "My husband won't talk to me." We don't want God to have the same complaint about us.

Even God's Son took time away to be with him in prayer. If Jesus relied on its power, we should immerse ourselves in daily prayer.

Prayers of Bible Women

Old Testament Scripture Reference	What Women in the Bible Prayed For
1 Samuel 2:2–10	Hannah, the mother of Samuel the prophet, prayed in the temple.
Genesis 29:31–30:21	Leah, the wife of Jacob, bore six sons of the twelve tribes of Israel. She poured out her sorrows in prayer, for she was unloved by her husband.
Judges 13:1–24	Samson's mother had a visit from an angel as she meditated and prayed in a field. The angel predicted Samson's birth and instructed her how to raise him.
2 Kings 22:1–20	Huldah, a Hebrew prophetess, spent time with God as she prayed and listened to his message she delivered to the king.
Esther 4:15–16	Esther requested Mordecai to ask all the Jews in Susa to fast for her, as she and her maids fasted as well. Fasting and prayer go hand in hand.

New Testament Scripture Reference	What Women in the Bible Prayed For
Luke 2:36–38	Anna, an aged widow who lived and served in the temple at Jerusalem, prayed both day and night. As Jesus' parents brought him to the temple for consecration after his birth, Anna declared he was the promised Messiah.
Acts 16:14	Lydia, a wealthy businesswoman, met with women to pray. She opened her home as a house church.
Luke 1:46–55	Mary the mother of Jesus prayed and praised God for the wondrous miracle virgin birth of Christ.

changed
Acts 9:1–42

faithfulness
loyal belief, trust

endurance
to continue, to remain
firm

Prayers of Bible Women (cont'd)

New Testament Scripture Reference	What Women in the Bible Prayed For
Matthew 15:22	The Syro-Phoenician woman came praying to Jesus for help and healing for her daughter.
Acts 12:12	Mary the mother of John gathered with others to pray in her home.

What's My Goal?

1 TIMOTHY 1:12 *I thank Christ Jesus our Lord, who has given me strength, that he considered me faithful, appointing me to his service.*

In the letter the apostle Paul wrote to Timothy, his co-laborer and unofficial son in Christ, Paul testifies of his personal relationship with Jesus and how God <u>changed</u> his life from a persecutor of Christians to a proclaimer of the Gospel of Christ. Through the Lord, Paul gained strength to carry out his mission.

There are two themes you read frequently in Scriptures: **faithfulness** and **endurance**. That's what it takes to know God intimately.

Examples From the Bible

Faith is God's vehicle for bringing us closer to him. "Now faith is being sure of what we hope for and certain of what we do not see" (Hebrews 11:1). By faith

- Abel obediently brought an offering that pleased God more than his brother Cain's offering. (Genesis 4:4)

- Enoch trusted and walked with God so closely that God took him to heaven without an earthly death. (Genesis 5:21–24)

- Noah trusted and believed God's warning of a flood, prepared an ark, and saved his family. (Genesis 6:13–22)

- Abraham obeyed God's command to leave his homeland for land promised by God. He trusted that God would fulfill his promise of an inheritance. (Genesis 12:1–4, 7; Acts 7:2–4)

- Sarah in her old age believed that God would make her a mother. A whole nation came from Sarah and Abraham as God blessed them with Isaac. (Genesis 17:19; 18:11–14; 21:2)

- Isaac knew God would give future blessings to his two sons, Jacob and Esau. (Genesis 27:27–39)

- Jacob blessed each of the sons of Joseph and prayed and worshiped God. (Genesis 48:1, 5, 16, 20)

- Joseph, when he was dying, confidently spoke of God bringing the people of Israel out of Egypt. He was so sure, he made them promise to carry his bones with them when they left. (Genesis 50:24; Exodus 13:19)

- Moses' parents, when they saw God had given them a special child, hid him for three months, trusting that God would save him from the death the **pharaoh** commanded. (Exodus 1:16, 22; 2:2)

- Moses, when he grew up, chose to be mistreated along with God's people instead of living as the son of Pharaoh. By faith he left Egypt and did not fear Pharaoh. (Exodus 2:10–11; 12:50; Hebrews 11:25)

- Moses believed God's instructions and commanded his people to kill a lamb and sprinkle its blood on the door posts of their homes, so that God's Death Angel would not kill their oldest child. (Exodus 12:21–29)

- Moses led the children of Israel out of Egypt and walked through the Red Sea on dry ground. (Exodus 14:21–29)

Enjoy a Healthy Spiritual Life

1 TIMOTHY 4:7–8 *Train yourself to be godly. For physical training is of some value, but godliness has value for all things, holding promise for both the present life and the life to come.*

Our track to spiritual fitness is an ongoing process. A healthy spiritual life has to become a way of life. We have to make it a lifelong commitment.

Ask yourself this question: "What do I want to accomplish with my spiritual fitness program?" If you are spiritually healthy overall, you should raise your activity level. Dig deeper, aim higher, stretch yourself.

If you are just getting started, similar to the way fitness experts recommend light workouts for entry-level athletes, I recommend a moderate intensity of prayer and Bible reading for a total of thirty minutes a day. It will fortify your soul and help you attain your goal of being spiritually fit and drawing closer to God.

Final Thoughts

- On our quest to spiritual fitness, our first step is a regular checkup with the Great Physician. You must strive to develop an intimate relationship with him in order to become the woman he designed you to be.

- In order to stay in shape and remain healthy, spiritual fitness requires as much exercise, self-discipline, and good nourishment as physical fitness. You may have fallen out of the repetition of building your spiritual body, but there's no time better than now to commit to doing prayer, worship, and Bible study.

- Our money-back-guaranteed diet plan for spiritual fitness is: ingest the Scriptures. The Bible holds the answers to all of life's body questions. It serves as our handbook to becoming faithfully fit. It's the only diet where you should eat as much as you can.

- Jesus offers Living Water. He invites us to come and rest in him. Through prayer, allow God to minister to you, to guide you, to take away stress, and to quench your soul's thirst as you place your trust in him.

- Make it your goal to follow Jesus more closely.

Questions to Deepen Your Understanding

1. What is special about God's Word according to Psalm 19:7–11?

2. How did Sarah put her faith and trust in God?

3. What did Mary of Bethany surrender to Jesus?

4. As we exercise our way to spiritual fitness and commit to walking in God's truth, what three ingredients should be a part of our everyday life?

5. How did Elizabeth walk with God?

6. There is more to life than filling our stomachs with food. What does God offer that satisfies our souls?

7. What did the Samaritan woman find at the well?

8. According to Romans 12:12, how does prayer make a difference in your life and the lives of others?

read on

Some of Georgia's favorite books for renewing and strengthening your intimate walk with God:

- *Battlefield of the Mind,* Joyce Meyer, WarnerFaith

- *Believing God,* Beth Moore, Broadman and Holman Publishing

- *I Saw the Lord,* Anne Graham Lotz, Zondervan

- *Let Your Life Count: Only God Knows What He Can Do Through You,* Donna Partow, Random House

- *Live Like You Mean It,* Kathy Troccoli, WaterBrook Press

- *Look Great, Feel Great,* Joyce Meyer, WarnerFaith

- *The Power of a Praying Woman,* Stormie Omartian, Harvest House

- *A Woman of Worship Bible Study,* Dee Brestin, Cook Communications

- *Women of Faith Bible Study Guide Series, Living in Jesus,* Thomas Nelson

- *Women of Faith Bible Study Guide Series, Discovering God's Will for Your Life,* Thomas Nelson

- *Your Best Life Now,* Joel Osteen, WarnerFaith

Chapter 2: Rainy Days and Mondays

Loving God During Disappointments, Suffering, and Loss

What's in This Chapter

Here We Go

Pick up a newspaper in Anytown, USA, and you will find it filled with "rainy days and Mondays" stories any day of the week. (Even Monday.) "Rainy days and Mondays" stories tell of disappointments and suffering. Headlines bellow in bold print about uncertain times, terrorist attacks, natural disasters, murder, rape, violence, tragic accidents, death, bankruptcy, disease, and divorce. Behind the headlines are real people, just like you and me, who are in the storm of suffering.

In the 1960s Dr. Elisabeth Kübler-Ross wrote a book called *On Death and Dying*. Dr. Ross wrote of the five emotional stages a terminal patient experiences once he knows he is going to die. She gained her knowledge by talking with more than two hundred terminally ill patients. The first stage was denial, then anger, bargaining, depression, and finally acceptance.[1]

This chapter is not particularly about death. It's about living life during your suffering; it's about facing an uncertain future with confidence. But during our suffering we experience some of the same emotions Dr. Ross witnessed. We'll see what the Bible says about how we can handle our emotions when we suffer—and where to find recovery and the gift of hope.

sovereign
Psalm 141:8

message
Jeremiah 29:1–32

sovereign
supreme authority

prophet
a person who speaks
for God

idolatry
worshiping idols or
false gods

Nebuchadnezzar
king of Babylonia,
reigned from 605 to
562 BC

Examples From the Bible

Bad things do happen to good people, and the Bible is filled with "rainy days and Mondays" stories of men and women who encountered the storms of life and looked to God to calm the storm.

- Hannah was so distraught because of her infertility that she constantly wept and would not eat. (1 Samuel 1:7)
- When Michal helped her husband David escape the murderous wrath of her father King Saul, she was separated from her husband because she went against her father. (1 Samuel 19:11–17)
- The Canaanite woman suffered over the condition of her child who was demon-possessed. (Matthew 15:22–28)
- Jesus took pity on the mother who grieved over the death of her only son. (Luke 7:11–15)
- A sick, diseased woman who had been crooked and suffered for eighteen years came to Jesus for relief. (Luke 13:11–13)

How we respond to our rainy-day disappointments determines whether we spot the silver lining among the storm clouds. If you look at life from the perspective that God is <u>sovereign</u> and will love and protect you in the hard times, you'll find that surviving the wind and rain can actually bring you closer to him. Rain falls on both good and bad people. Run to God for shelter.

How Others See It

Anne Graham Lotz

While God doesn't always protect those He loves from suffering or answer our prayers the way we ask Him to, He does promise in His Word that He will be present with us in the midst of suffering and pain (Isaiah 43:1–4).[2]

When It Rains, It Pours

JEREMIAH 29:11 *"For I know the plans I have for you," declares the Lord, "plans to prosper you and not to harm you, plans to give you hope and a future."*

Jeremiah was a **prophet** called by God to deliver a <u>message</u> to the Israelites. Because Israel's leaders began practicing **idolatry**, God allowed **Nebuchadnezzar** to take the cream of Israel's society captive. Jeremiah wrote a letter to the captives, consoling those who were homesick and brokenhearted in exile. They may be suffering, he told them, but they shouldn't stop living. God wanted them to build houses, plant gardens, bear children, be good citizens, and not listen to false prophets. Speaking through Jeremiah, God promised that in seventy years he would free them, so they should be patient. They didn't know what the future held, but God did, and he knew they had a bright future—despite their current stormy times.

I'm sure disappointment has touched your life in some way. Like a crowd scattering to escape a downpour, we all get wet; but some get wetter than others. Suffering falls on the rich, the poor, the young, the old, the educated and uneducated, the saved and the unsaved.

There are times I think disappointment follows me and sets up camp in my living room. During a thunderstorm in my life (complete with deafening thunderclaps and terrifying bolts of lightning to my soul), my sister Connie said, "Georgia, I'm going to give you a new name. You've been through so much. I'm going to call you the Energizer Bunny. You just keep going, and going, and going."

I laughed and did my impersonation of the bunny marching around beating his drum. What else can you do but keep going? I used to ask God, "Why me?" But after suffering and growing closer to him with each storm, I now say, "Why not me?" Disappointment and suffering are another side of life. A painful side, yes, but one we all experience.

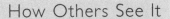

How Others See It

Joni Eareckson Tada

God's plan is specific. He doesn't say, "Into each life a little rain must fall," then aim a hose in earth's general direction and see who gets the wettest. He doesn't reach for a key, wind up nature with its sunny days and hurricanes, and sit back and watch the show. He doesn't let Satan prowl about totally unrestricted. He doesn't believe in a hands-off policy of governing. He's not our planet's absentee landlord. Rather, he screens the trials that come to each of us—allowing only those that accomplish his good plan, because he takes no joy in human agony.[3]

Like the Jewish exiles, we may feel as though we are trapped in a situation against our will. We can find hope in Jeremiah's message. Don't give up! Keep on living, for your God is the God of "hope and a future." Suffering is a part of life. God does not always remove suffering, but he fills it with his presence.

Zarephath
a city in the settlement
of the Sidonians

Hannah
the mother of Samuel

Samuel
earliest of the great
Hebrew prophets after
Moses

The Bible records many who did not give up when trials came their way. Jochebed was faced with the impending death of her baby boy, Moses, because Pharaoh had ordered all male Hebrew babies to be killed. Jochebed wove a basket boat, hid Moses in it, and trusted God to save Moses' life.

The starving widow of **Zarephath** did not give up when she faced a famine. She gave her last food to the prophet Elijah. Because she followed Elijah's directions, she and her son survived.

Remain Calm

The parting words of my physician as I left her examining room were, "Remain calm." I had already tried to "remain calm" for days preceding my office visit when I discovered a lump during a breast self-examination. After I saw my doctor, she advised further evaluation and a mammogram to be done the following week.

During the week of waiting my mind echoed her words: "Remain calm. Remain calm." But that's hard to do when your mind races with all the worst-case scenarios. Knowing that breast cancer is the second leading cause of death in women, my greatest concern was: If I died, who would help raise my then five-year-old son?

During my week of waiting, I spoke at a women's conference. My workshop title was, "Kids: Ya Gotta Love 'Em." I used 1 Samuel as my Scripture text, with Hannah as a model mother.

***Hannah** loved her son **Samuel** and trained him to know God, though she only had him for a short time. After he was weaned (which was three years or more, since the ancient East had no way to keep milk sweet), she had to release her son to Eli, the priest. She knew Samuel went to live in less-than-ideal circumstances, yet she offered beautiful worship as she released him to God.*

Hannah's example inspired me that day. As I led the workshop, I was supposed to be speaking to the audience, but I was actually speaking to myself. For the first time, I felt peaceful about my impending diagnosis. I knew that no matter what happened, I had trained our son to know and love God, and if I had to leave him before I wanted to, I was releasing him into God's hands. In fact, he had been in God's hands all along.

Visits with the radiologist, confirmed by biopsies, showed no sign of cancer, merely fibroid tumors. Praise God, it had been a false alarm.

*But even if it weren't, I still like my doctor's advice: "Remain calm." And in my times of waiting I will cling to the **exhortation**, "Wait for the Lord; be strong and take heart and wait for the Lord" (Psalm 27:14).*

exhortation
urgent encouragement

My Umbrella Will Protect Me

PSALM 34:18 *The Lord is close to the brokenhearted and saves those who are crushed in spirit.*

Across the eons, heartbreak is heartbreak. The psalmist felt his pain as deeply as you or I do now. Yet across those same eons, God has been near and comes to his children in their brokenness. When we call out to him in our time of need, God hears and rushes to our side just as a loving mother rushes to the bedside of her sick child to love and comfort him.

Webster's definition for *denial* reads, "a refusal to believe or accept." In times of disappointment and suffering, denial serves as a buffer. We pop up the protective umbrella of denial, believing that since we have an umbrella, we won't get wet.

Denial can seem to help for a short period of time, but the strong winds of reality turn our would-be umbrella inside out. Eventually, we are forced to face the truth of our tempest. The first step to calming the storm is to move beyond denial by calling out for God.

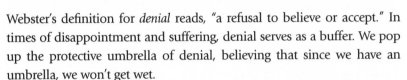

How Others See It

Gerald L. Sittser

Denial puts off what should be faced. People in denial refuse to see loss for what it is: something terrible that cannot be reversed. They dodge pain rather than confront it. But their unwillingness to face pain comes at a price. Ultimately it diminishes the capacity of their souls to grow bigger in response to pain. They make the same mistake as patients who, following major surgery, refuse to get out of bed and put damaged muscles back to work. They pretend nothing is wrong and tell everyone that they are feeling wonderful. But denial of their problems causes muscles to atrophy until they cannot get out of bed at all. In the end denial leads to a greater loss.[4]

In the days following the terrorist attacks of 9/11, an ordinary stay-at-home mom, Lisa Beamer, was thrust into the spotlight as a nation watched in horror. I'm sure you read the stories and saw the interviews of Lisa talking about her husband, Todd Beamer, one of the heroes of United Flight 93. We all remember his last words before fighting against the terrorist hijackers, "Let's roll."

Reading Lisa's *New York Times* bestseller, *Let's Roll*, I felt as if I were thumbing through her personal scrapbook as she gave glimpses of her life with Todd before 9/11, and then it became a memorial and journal of her life without her hero.

One week after the attacks on our nation, during an interview with Larry King, he asked Lisa, "How are you handling it?" Lisa responded, "Sometimes people look at me and wonder, 'Is she in shock? Or is she unrealistic about what the situation is?' They don't see me all the other times when I'm breaking down and losing my composure. Certainly, the faith that I have, like Todd's, helps me to understand the bigger picture here. And that God's justice will ultimately prevail. We have more to look forward to than just what we see here on earth."[5]

I'm Drenched in Pain

1 PETER 4:1–2 *Therefore, since Christ suffered in his body, arm yourselves also with the same attitude, because he who has suffered in his body is done with sin. As a result, he does not live the rest of his earthly life for evil human desires, but rather for the will of God.*

The apostle Peter wrote to the suffering church in **Asia Minor** with practical advice for their hardships. Persecution tested the believers, and they anticipated worse to come under Nero, the emperor of Rome.

Peter reminded the church that Christ also <u>suffered</u> in the body, so we should put on the spiritual attitude of Christ. As we turn away from sin and turn toward Christ, we no longer live for our own <u>wants</u> and desires; instead, we follow him. We live as Christ would have us live according to his <u>Word</u>.

The isolation of our pain brings us to God. During Christ's suffering before his **crucifixion**, he prayed to God. Though he had asked close friends for companionship, he prayed in isolation. Knowing what lay ahead, he asked God to "take this cup from me" (Mark 14:36). God did not remove the pain and suffering, but allowed his Son to suffer cruel death on a cross as a sacrifice for all humanity that we might have **eternal life**.

Our hope during suffering is in the intimate relationship we have with God. If we are <u>one</u> with him, we can enjoy life regardless of the suffering we experience.

Examples From the Bible

Suffering was a common experience for many people in the Bible:

- Job, a wealthy man of God, lost his children, his possessions, and his health when Satan took them all away. Yet he stayed true to God and praised him during his suffering. (Job 1:1, 21)
- The apostle Peter suffered the consequences and pain of his denying he knew Jesus. (Luke 22:55–62)
- Yet he recognized his failures and turned back to Christ, as he was the first apostle to run to Jesus' empty tomb. (Luke 24:12)
- Priscilla and her husband, Aquila, suffered mistreatment and loneliness as they and other Jews were expelled from their home in Rome. They risked their own lives and faced persecution as they helped spread the **Gospel** with their co-worker, the apostle Paul. (Acts 18:2; Romans 16:3–4)

The spiritual side of suffering is that pain can either turn you bitter or draw you closer to God. When mixed with patient faith, suffering can make your soul grow. Life-threatening events make our desires for earthly things vanish. The cars, the boat, the career—the trivial things of earth lose their luster. All you want is to feel God's ever-loving presence as he calms your soul, eases your pain, and renews your strength.

How Others See It

Jill Briscoe

A right theology of suffering brings comfort. Your theology deals with the fear factor, the frustration factor, and the future factor because of the Father factor. And the Father factor factors in all the factors you need to be God's man or God's woman in this present distress, whatever and whenever it might be. You can begin to see God and yourself in a new way, and you begin to see others around you with new eyes, too.[6]

Cradled in His Arms

The operating room was freezing. My body shook as nurses solemnly strapped me to the table for emergency surgery. With nowhere to look but up, I saw the brilliant lights form halos as my vision moistened and blurred.

"Mrs. Ling, I need you to count backward, starting with ten," instructed the anesthesiologist.

I begged the surgeon, "We want to have children. Please do whatever you can." His warm eyes assured me he would give me his best. Urgently, he repeated, "Mrs. Ling, please begin counting now."

Swallowing hard, I began. "Ten, nine, eight . . ." My speech slurred. I silently prayed for God's protection. "Seven, six, five . . ." My thoughts spun like a whirlwind, reliving recent events as darkness veiled the room.

We were a statistic. One out of five couples have trouble conceiving or are infertile. After nine years of marriage, I had my first positive pregnancy test. We were elated. The nurse scheduled my first prenatal visit three long weeks away, but I knew our out-of-town vacation would make the time pass quickly. I could hardly wait to visit my physician.

During our vacation I experienced extreme abdominal pain, bleeding, and soaring fever. We made frantic phone calls, and upon my doctor's instructions, I was rushed to an emergency room three hundred miles from home.

After several hours of examinations, ultrasounds, and concerned looks from attending physicians, we were finally informed I had lost the baby. My condition was life-threatening, and I needed emergency surgery.

Even though a curtain was all that separated my husband and me from the emergency room full of patients and medical personnel, we found privacy in our little stall. We clung to each other and sobbed as our hopes and dreams of a little one were snatched from our very arms. Our grief for the one we would never cradle here on earth began that very moment.

My surgery was successful. We thanked God for that, and for the encouraging news that chances were good for another pregnancy. Our love grew deeper as we began to pick up the pieces. But nothing prepared me for the emotions that surfaced after the loss of our baby. Kind souls trying to ease my pain with expressions like, "You're young, you can have more," "It was for the best," or "Just be thankful you were only a few months along," rubbed salt into my wounded heart. Days filled with silence but not understanding. Cards and phone calls were a wonderful blessing and comfort, but we grieved alone. Yet God drew me closer to him through the isolation.

My sense of loneliness prompted me to ask God to never let me forget my grief. I wanted to remain sensitive to the grief of others and to help comfort them.

God answers prayers. Over the years, from that deep corner of my heart, pain and grief emerge when I hear about the loss of a child. I track down the family's address, write them an encouraging note, offer my sympathy and prayers, and send them one of my favorite books on the subject. I want them to know it is natural to grieve and they are not alone in their heart-wrenching journey.

When facing the lonely and tragic death of a dearly wanted unborn child, I knew I could turn to God because he has also experienced the pain of losing a Son. He cradled me in his loving arms when I mourned over my empty arms—which God eventually filled. Two years later, I was in an operating room again, but this time I was able to cradle a scrunched-faced, squirming, healthy baby boy, my son Philip.

Snapshots of Women in the Bible
The Widow of Zarephath (1 Kings 17:1–24)

The widow of Zarephath was no stranger to pain and suffering. But God rescued her from eternal suffering by showing her his power through the prophet Elijah.

Elijah had appeared with a message from an angry God to **King Ahab** and **Queen Jezebel**. Ahab was described as one who "did more to provoke the Lord, the God of Israel, to anger than did all the kings of Israel before him" (1 Kings 16:33).

There were many reasons Ahab angered God, but one stood out: after he married Jezebel, a daughter of a king and priest of **Baal** (see Illustration #3 on page 40), Ahab not only allowed her to build temples to this pagan god, but he joined her in worshiping the god of sex, nature, and war. Baal worship required the horrific practice of child sacrifice.

Elijah's simple yet bold message was a prophecy that no rain or dew would fall in Israel until he said it could. This was God's scornful way of saying to Ahab, "See what your god of nature can do now!"

More than two years later, the drought continued, and Ahab considered Elijah Public Enemy #1. God directed Elijah to go to Zarephath (see Illustration #4), a great hiding place for him. It was Jezebel's hometown. No one would think Elijah stupid enough to go there.

At the city gate, Elijah saw the widow. I imagine her as a picture of suffering, an undernourished, hollow-eyed woman of skin and bones. I see her painstakingly bent over, gathering sticks from the parched ground to cook her last meal for her son. Led by God, Elijah asked her for food and water.

Elijah
prophet to the Northern Kingdom of Israel; famous for his defeat of four hundred false prophets at Mount Carmel

King Ahab
king over Israel in Samaria for twenty-two years

Queen Jezebel
wife of King Ahab and enemy of Elijah

Baal
the main god of **Canaanite** people

Canaanite
the ancient name of people living along the eastern shore of the Mediterranean

Illustration #3
Baal—A weather god associated with thunderstorms and fertility. Worship of Baal involved ritual prostitution and sometimes child sacrifice.

check this out

Exodus
Exodus 3:7–10
manna
Exodus 16:31–32
trust
Psalm 4:5; Isaiah 26:4; Hebrews 2:13
obey
Psalm 103:21;
Matthew 8:27;
Acts 5:29;
1 Peter 1:2

manna
Hebrew for "What is it?"; one of the foods God provided for the Israelites during the **Exodus**
Exodus
God's deliverance of the Hebrews from slavery in Egypt and their journey to a new land

Illustration #4
Elijah's Travels—Elijah ran from Queen Jezebel in Beersheba to the Kerith Ravine. Later he traveled to Zarephath, where he met the widow.

The widow openly shared her struggles and fears, and her plans for one last meal. Soon her family's suffering would end in death.

Elijah told her not to be afraid. He had a message from God. If she followed his instructions, there would be food for her household until the drought ended and the rain returned.

What did the widow have to lose? She obeyed Elijah. And it worked! Day after day she went to the jug of oil and jar of flour that she had emptied the day before. Day after day, jug and jar were again filled with enough to feed her household one more meal. It was just like the **manna** that God provided daily for the children of Israel in the wilderness. Her strength was renewed during her days of suffering.

Time wore on, and death surrounded her. Starvation swelled the bellies of children and claimed the lives of her neighbors. Her household was spared, until her son became ill and died.

Her disappointment and doubt returned. In her suffering and anger she asked, as we do, "Why me? I've done what you asked. What have I done to deserve this?"

Elijah, through God, miraculously brought her son back to life. The widow of Zarephath proclaimed that Elijah truly was a man of God.

By accepting and following the instructions from God, a widow survived her days of suffering and loss.

The Bible is our message from God. Turn to it in times of disappointment and suffering. Trust and obey, and God will be faithful to see you through, one day at a time.

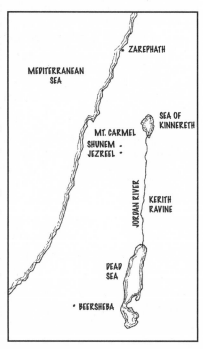

I like to journal my experiences during life's thunderstorms. Later, the journal jogs my memory, for when Jesus the Son shines, I can look back and see that God truly helped in times of crisis. "My God shall supply all your need according to his riches in glory by Christ Jesus" (Philippians 4:19 KJV).

Don't Pitch a Hissy Fit

EPHESIANS 4:26–27 *"In your anger do not sin": Do not let the sun go down while you are still angry, and do not give the **devil** a foothold.*

The apostle Paul wrote the church at Ephesus (see Illustration #13 on page 180) to give them guidance in their Christian walk. He advised them to control their anger. We can express our anger and frustration, but we are not to let anger turn to hatred and bitterness.

(see Illustration #13 on page 180)

devil
I Timothy 5:15;
Revelation 12:9

devil
Satan; "the adversary,"
enemy of God

Ninevah
capital city of Assyria,
east of Cilicia

Sarai
the name Sarah had
before God changed it

Abram
the name Abraham had
before God changed it

> ## Examples From the Bible
>
> The Bible gives us pictures of men and women who allowed anger to control their emotions and actions in a negative way:
>
> - Jonah, the Israelite prophet known for being swallowed by a big fish, is also known for throwing a tantrum and pouting. Jonah's preaching in the city of **Ninevah** paid off—they repented and turned to God, so God showed his mercy. Jonah was mad and embarrassed, for he had preached ruin and destruction, but God gave restoration and renewal. (Jonah 4:1–4)
>
> - **Sarai**, **Abram**'s wife, had no children (Genesis 17:16). After waiting ten years for the Lord to fulfill his promise of blessing her with a child, she gave up. As was the custom, she devised a plan for her Egyptian maidservant, Hagar, to sleep with Abram. Hagar became pregnant. Sarai became jealous, then bitter, then hateful. In anger she mistreated Hagar, who fled the camp. (Genesis 16:1–6)
>
> - The children of Israel were led out of captivity into freedom. Instead of celebrating their deliverance, they seized upon every hardship as an excuse to grumble against their leaders, Moses and Aaron. In anger they said they were better off as slaves in Egypt than starving in the desert. (Exodus 16:1–3)

When things don't go our way, we regress back to the "terrible twos" and, as my mother would say, "throw a hissy fit" with God. You've seen the red-faced, clenched-fist little toddler stamping his feet, whining and crying because he didn't get his way. When we act the same way in our hearts, I'm sure God isn't surprised. Like parents who let those toddlers get it out of their system, and then love them back into reality, God does the same for us.

We can allow anger to be a road to recovery or a path to destruction. If you express your anger without losing control, it can help heal whatever is upsetting you. Communicating your feelings lets others know what you need from them and releases the stress of keeping your feelings silent. But if you give in to anger by allowing it to consume your thoughts and actions, it can destroy your relationships and build a wall around your heart. I hope you choose the road to recovery and let anger reveal truth, but not destruction.

When All Your Days Seem Like Mondays

PSALM 42:1–6 *As the deer pants for streams of water, so my soul pants for you, O God. My soul thirsts for God, for the living God. When can I go and meet with God? My tears have been my food day and night, while men say to me all day long, "Where is your God?" These things I remember as I pour out my soul: how I used to go with the multitude, leading the procession to the house of God, with shouts of joy and thanksgiving among the festive throng. Why are you downcast, O my soul? Why so disturbed within me? Put your hope in God, for I will yet praise him, my Savior and my God.*

In this passage, the psalmist is in misery. He's depressed. He can't eat and he cries both day and night. His soul thirsts for God. He wants relief from his suffering and heartache. His enemy seeks to destroy him, and he wants God to deliver him.

In his loneliness and depression he reminisces about the good old days when he worshiped and rejoiced in the temple. As he reflects on God he asks himself, "Why am I depressed and discouraged? I have hope in God, who will deliver me."

check this out

forty days
Genesis 7:17

altar
place for sacrifices;
usually made from
stones
Noah
built the famous ark
that survived the
Flood
Flood
an ancient event when
God judged humans by
sending forty days of
rain to flood the earth

Examples From the Bible

Bible women faced depression as they dealt with sorrow and pain, but they also found relief and happiness:

- Noah's wife spent more than four months cooped up with her family and dozens of stinky, loud, hungry animals in the ark. But finally the floodwaters receded; they left the ark, built an **altar**, and praised God. (Genesis 8:20; Exodus 20:24–25)

- Hagar was mistreated and sent away by her mistress, Sarah. In the wilderness an angel comforted her and gave her strength and hope to carry on. (Genesis 16)

- Naomi grieved the deaths of her husband and two sons. She became bitter but stayed true to God as he blessed her with the company of her daughter-in-law Ruth. (book of Ruth)

Did you ever hear that it rains all the time in Seattle? Well, guess what—it's true! And I have proof: We lived under the misty skies of Seattle, and during one winter it rained a record of ninety-one straight days. Yes, ninety-one straight days. **Noah** only had a downpour for <u>forty days</u>. What gives?

It was depressing to say the least. I believe the statistic I heard that Prozac is prescribed more in Seattle than any other part of the country.

During times of disappointments and suffering, we feel as though all forecasts are for continuing gloom, and every day feels like a Monday. But there is hope in dealing with depression.

heart to heart

I love the testimony of Sheila Walsh, vocalist and featured speaker for the Women of Faith Conferences. In her book *Outrageous Love*, she talks candidly of her battle with depression and her treatment. She writes, "In that fall of 1992 when I was admitted into a psychiatric hospital diagnosed with severe clinical depression, I never could have imagined that this place of my undoing would be the beginning of a new life."[9]

Depression is nothing to be ashamed of. If necessary, seek professional help. As Sheila experienced, it can be the beginning of a new life.

Help, God! I'm Drowning!

> **PSALM 69:1–2** *Save me, O God, for the waters have come up to my neck. I sink in the miry depths, where there is no foothold. I have come into the deep waters; the floods engulf me.*

The psalmist feels the waters of depression threatening his life. As the torment and pain increase, his misery is almost more than he can bear. He cries out in desperation, "Help, God! I'm drowning!"

Most people usually bounce back from disappointments. But when the sadness persists and you feel like you are drowning under dark skies, when everyday mundane things become too difficult, maybe your problem is deeper than a blue mood. If you're experiencing any of the following symptoms, you may be suffering from depression:

1. Sad, anxious, or empty mood that lasts for two weeks or more.

2. Loss of interest or pleasure in most activities you once enjoyed.

3. Feelings of worthlessness, hopelessness, and quiet.

4. Significant change in weight or appetite.

5. Change in sleep habits.

6. Fatigue, loss of energy, agitation, and irritability.

7. Difficulty concentrating, making decisions.

8. Frequent thoughts of death or suicide.

By informing you of these medical conditions, I do not mean to frighten you. But if these symptoms describe you, I encourage you to seek medical advice.[10]

The first step to receiving help is being honest with yourself and admitting you are depressed. Go to God and cry out to him in prayer. He has not forsaken you. He will help you; he will send a lifeline in your time of despair. Seek help from a doctor, minister, or professional counselor. He or she can give you support and advice. There's nothing to be ashamed of—depression is not a sign of weakness, and you are not alone. Statistics show that as many as one in five Americans will be affected by depression in their lifetimes.

Get Out of the Rain

Judah
one of the twelve
tribes of Israel

ISAIAH 40:29 *He gives strength to the weary and increases the power of the weak.*

Isaiah the prophet addressed the children of **Judah** who were in exile. Gradually the captives had lost their hope of ever returning home. Discouragement and despair took over. Isaiah spoke of God's comfort and almighty power. He promised that God would renew their strength and give them the power they needed to walk the seven hundred miles back to their homeland.

Probably none of us will face a seven-hundred-mile walk home, but that doesn't mean Isaiah's message isn't for us. When we feel weary, whether from physical or emotional trials, God is always there, powerful beyond our understanding. When we seek his help, he gives us strength and renews our spirits for the journey ahead.

What the Bible Says About God's Comfort

What God Says	Scripture Reference
Even though I walk through the valley of the shadow of death, I will fear no evil, for you are with me; your rod and your staff, they comfort me.	Psalm 23:4
He has sent me . . . to proclaim the year of the Lord's favor and the day of vengeance of our God, to comfort all who mourn.	Isaiah 61:1–2
Blessed are those who mourn, for they will be comforted.	Matthew 5:4
Praise be to the God and Father of our Lord Jesus Christ, the Father of compassion and the God of all comfort, who comforts us in all our troubles, so that we can comfort those in any trouble with the comfort we ourselves have received from God.	2 Corinthians 1:3–4

What the Bible Says About God's Almighty Power

What God Says	Scripture Reference
Yours, O Lord, is the greatness and the power and the glory and the majesty and the splendor, for everything in heaven and earth is yours. Yours, O Lord, is the kingdom; you are exalted as head over all.	1 Chronicles 29:11
He who dwells in the shelter of the Most High will rest in the shadow of the Almighty. I will say of the Lord, "He is my refuge and my fortress, my God, in whom I trust."	Psalm 91:1–2
Holy, holy, holy is the Lord God Almighty, who was, and is, and is to come.	Revelation 4:8

everyday insights

I remember Mom's advice when she sent us off to camp or college. She would always say, "Take care of yourself, eat right, and get plenty of rest." Let me be your mom and echo those words.

*During struggles our whole lives are turned upside down. Schedules change and our routines elude us. Where calmness once ruled, chaos is now the order. We find ourselves so emotionally drained and weary we don't even want to think about eating, let alone actually take a bite. But in order to maintain strength, we must eat something, drink lots of water (tears and stress can cause **dehydration**), and try to sleep or at least nap.*

I know there are days you can't imagine crawling out of bed, but I need to mention one more word: exercise. It doesn't have to be a workout. Start with baby steps: maybe walk with a friend around the neighborhood, or play with the kids; anything to get you moving.

How Others See It

Verdell Davis

When a storm comes along of sufficient force to wipe out our livelihood, our health, our most treasured relationship, or perhaps our lifelong dreams, and we are left standing in the rubble of our shattered lives, we are in many ways reduced to infancy. So much has been lost and so much changed that we must essentially start over again. We must begin to walk before we can think about running or soaring. Indeed, we need help just to be able to stay on our feet.[11]

Physically, taking care of yourself during a time of crisis is crucial to maintaining a healthy attitude and gaining overall strength during your struggle. Spiritually, turn to Scripture for renewed strength as you place your trust in God.

Laughing in the Rain

PROVERBS 17:22 *A cheerful heart is good medicine, but a crushed spirit dries up the bones.*

The book of Proverbs is a book of wisdom, with wisdom being the key to understanding life, emotions, and relationships. The author, believed to be Solomon, often uses sayings to describe truths about human experience.

Proverbs 17:22 speaks of the joy of wisdom. Joy is a prescription to lift the spirits. Even faced with struggles and pain, a cheerful heart is like medicine. As believers we can be the most joyful people on the planet, for we know the Creator of joy. Laughter is a natural painkiller. Take large doses.

dehydration
the excessive loss of water

Joy From God and Joy for Believers

Joy From God

What God Says	Scripture Reference
You have made known to me the path of life; you will fill me with joy in your presence, with eternal pleasures at your right hand.	Psalm 16:11
Rejoice in the Lord always. I will say it again: Rejoice!	Philippians 4:4
May the God of hope fill you with all joy and peace as you trust in him, so that you may overflow with hope by the power of the Holy Spirit.	Romans 15:13

Joy for Believers

What God Says	Scripture Reference
Those who sow in tears will reap with songs of joy.	Psalm 126:5
I have told you this so that my joy may be in you and that your joy may be complete.	John 15:11
Be joyful always; pray continually; give thanks in all circumstances, for this is God's will for you in Christ Jesus.	1 Thessalonians 5:16–18
Though you have not seen him, you love him; and even though you do not see him now, you believe in him and are filled with an inexpressible and glorious joy.	1 Peter 1:8

Examples From the Bible

Even amid times of trial, people in the Bible found reason for laughter:

- At the age of ninety-nine when Abraham and Sarah heard from God that they would have a son, Sarah must've bitten her tongue to keep from laughing, because the Scripture says she laughed on the inside (Genesis 18:12). In the midst of grief over her barrenness, she got a chuckle out of imagining herself pregnant.

- Paul encouraged the early church to rejoice even though they suffered, because God uses suffering to change and mold our character. (Romans 5:2–4)

- After a desperate escape through the Red Sea, Moses and Miriam joyfully led the multitude in a song service in the desert. (Exodus 15:1–21)

When *Patch Adams* hit the movie screen, audiences laughed and cried as they watched Robin Williams portray a wacky, unusual doctor who touched hearts and made a difference in the lives of his patients with the medicine of laughter. The best part about the movie? Patch Adams is not just a fictional character; he is a real doctor whose charitable health work is called the Gesundheit Institute.

We Laughed All the Way Home

In one of my days in the fog of despair, I made a quick trip to the grocery store with my sister Sherry. As we put the bags of food in the back of the van, I grabbed a banana to eat on the trip home. Before she unlocked the car doors, Sherry walked away to return our cart, so I waited in the parking lot clutching this banana. As a man walked by and smiled, I realized it looked like a gun, so I pointed my weapon at him and said, "I've got a banana and I'm not afraid to use it!" He immediately put up his hands and backed away laughing. He saw my sister as she headed back to the van and said, "Look out for that lady! She's got a banana and she's not afraid to use it." The joke surprised me as much as it did my "victim."

We may go through misery, trials, and difficulties on this earth, but remember the words of Jesus: "Now is your time of grief, but I will see you again and you will rejoice, and no one will take away your joy" (John 16:22). So laugh with a friend; watch an old *I Love Lucy* show; have your kids tell you some jokes; whatever . . . just have a good ol' belly laugh.

What You Can Do

If life isn't so funny and you have to manufacture some laughs, try a few of these:

- Pick up a new humor book and read it when you're down.

- Pop in a funny video. (Liz Curtis Higgs and Chonda Pierce are two of my favorite comediennes. They always make me laugh, and you can buy their material as books or videos.)

- Watch a funny movie.

- Play a board game with your kids.

- Put on some music and dance with your kids.

- Try a new sport. (I took up in-line skating during a "not so funny" time in my life. My family got several great laughs, but probably not as many as my watchful neighbors.)

- Look for the absurdity in your situation. (Sometimes our difficulties pile so high, we can't help but laugh.)

Just Call My Name; I'll Be There

1 CORINTHIANS 12:25–26 *So that there should be no division in the body, but that its parts should have equal concern for each other. If one part suffers, every part suffers with it; if one part is honored, every part rejoices with it.*

In the preceding verses, Paul compares the church body to our physical bodies. To be whole, we need all the parts of our bodies. If you were one big eye, you wouldn't be able to hear. Just as our bodies depend upon all parts, to be whole we need to depend upon others. Let others minister to you. It's their gift to you.

When close friends offer help during your disappointment, learn to say yes. We were designed to help one another.

Examples From the Bible

Friends in need and friends in deed in the Bible:

- When Job's friends Eliphaz, Bildad, and Zophar heard that Job was in the pit of despair, they immediately went to comfort him. (Job 2:11)
- Abram received the news that his nephew Lot had been taken captive in a battle. He rounded up a posse of 318 men and rescued Lot in his time of despair. (Genesis 14:14)
- Jonathan came to his friend David's aid and helped him run to safety away from the threatening hand of King Saul. (1 Samuel 20:4–42)
- Four friends of a paralytic heard Jesus was healing. They dug through a roof to lower their paralyzed friend down to where Jesus taught. Jesus took pity upon him and healed him. (Mark 2:1–12)

Our initial response to suffering is the oft-mistaken notion that we can handle it on our own. We think we can manage the house, manage the children, manage our marriage, manage the office, and manage our emotions all while our life is falling apart. I call it the Superwoman Syndrome. But the fact is, Superwoman usually can't find her cape during chaos. She needs help from her super friends and family.

Friends and family want to minister to you during your struggles. Allow them to help even in little ways, like grocery shopping or fixing meals. (Sometimes I almost look forward to being incapacitated, because two of my friends are such great cooks.) Each thing your friends do for you is that much unspent energy you can store in your reserve tank to use in days ahead when you can find your cape and face the world again.

Sue Buchanan

Gather up the gifts people offer one by one and put them in a big basket (figuratively speaking, of course). You'll find the gifts that are brought have a marvelous variety of intangible, indisputable qualities, such as humor, joy, acceptance, crying, listening, surprise, prayer, and perhaps the greatest gift of all—time. That basket, that source, will provide everything you need to get through an illness—or through life, for that matter.[12]

Somewhere Over the Rainbow, Skies Are Blue

HEBREWS 10:23–24 *Let us hold unswervingly to the hope we profess, for he who promised is faithful. And let us consider how we may spur one another on toward love and good deeds.*

The teacher of Hebrews encourages the believers to hold tight, or fasten down, their hope. When trouble comes our way we are not to get off balance. We are to hold on, keeping our eyes fixed on Jesus and the hope he offers. God's waiting room is a safe place to be. If we grow weary and wavering, we are to encourage each other to hang in there and not give up. Biblical hope is inseparable from reliance upon God.

Examples From the Bible

Bible examples of hope and encouragement:

- While the children of Israel were in the wilderness, the Amalekites attacked them. The power of God was in Moses' **staff**. When he held the staff aloft, the Israelites were winning the battle. If Moses lowered his hands, the Amalekites were winning. When Moses grew weary, Aaron and Hur knew the hope of victory was in the raised staff, so they helped Moses hold up his arms. (Exodus 4:1–5; 17:8–13)

- Deborah, Rebekah's maidservant and nurse, comforted and encouraged Rebekah as she waited in agony to deliver twins. Deborah helped raise the twins. Deborah must've encouraged not only Rebekah, but also her entire family, for when Deborah was buried they placed her under a tree and called it the "Oak of Weeping." (Genesis 24:59; 25:23–35:8)

Hope is a necessity in surviving our disappointments. We cannot live in the land of hopelessness for very long—it will destroy us.

My message of hope is that God loves you. Your days may be rainy and dark, but don't lose hope. For as each day dawns, they will get brighter, the storm will let up and turn to a mist, the sun will shine, and you can look to the sky for the brilliant colors of the rainbow. Just as God made a **covenant** with Noah giving him hope for the future and sealed it with a rainbow, God gives you hope in him, even through your suffering. "We also rejoice in our sufferings, because we know that suffering produces **perseverance**; perseverance, character; and character, hope. And hope does not disappoint us, because God has poured out his love into our hearts by the **Holy Spirit**, whom he has given us" (Romans 5:3–5).

Jesus knew his arrest and crucifixion were fast approaching, and he went to the Garden of Gethsemane to pray. He was so distressed he said, "My soul is overwhelmed with sorrow to the point of death" (Mark 14:34). But Jesus didn't give up. He knew the Resurrection awaited him.

Do not give up. The gift of hope is in God's Word and his Son Jesus Christ. There truly are blue skies awaiting you beyond the rainbow, both here and in eternity. God has made a covenant with you just as he did with Noah, and he will not break his promise.

covenant
Genesis 9:16
Holy Spirit
John 14:26

covenant
binding promise
perseverance
to keep trying despite difficulty
Holy Spirit
"the Paraclete," a Greek word translated as "Comforter" or "Helper"

God's Business Card

Several years ago my parents visited me, and I wanted them to see the Pacific Northwest in all its splendor. Sometimes our beautiful snow-capped mountains outline the clear blue skies, but the weather didn't cooperate with my plans for my parents. Split, splat, drip, drop . . . sometime you should come on out for the Pacific Northwest Rain Festival, which runs from July 1 to June 30.

Now as you well know, you can't have your mom visit and not go shopping. So we donned our raincoats, grabbed our trusty umbrellas, and headed to a great outlet mall. There, we became separated. My dad and son gave up on Mom and me and were waiting in the car. I was in a dress shop. Mother was roaming around a china shop. We had agreed to reunite at a specific time and location. When I went outside for our rendezvous, I beheld one of the most spectacular sights I have ever witnessed. The sky cradled a magnificent double rainbow. The colors glistened in the sunbeams. Stores emptied as everyone came out to view this phenomenon with necks bent back, mouths dropped open, and fingers pointed to the sky.

As we drove home our conversation turned to the rainbow. Even though we were all in different locations, each of us witnessed this spectacular event. Mom commented that she was humored by the clerks who, moments before they saw the rainbow, acted as if it were a chore to assist

virtue
Galatians 5:22

you. But each clerk who had a turn viewing the magnificent rainbow returned to the store transformed and excited, making sure everyone she encountered, friends and strangers alike, stepped outside to see the glory.

Whether they realized it or not, all who witnessed the rainbow had a close encounter with God (well, at least they were touched by his handiwork and saw his signature). I've always said that if God had a business card, it would have a rainbow insignia in the background.

When the hand of God touches you, your life is transformed, your personality is changed, and you have a new, exciting outlook on life to share with friends and even strangers.

God has wonderful ways of reminding us of his eternal promises. Only he can turn gray skies into a rainbow, glowing like an opal. And only he can give hope and transform dark lonely lives into vibrant glowing personalities. "I have set my rainbow in the clouds, and it will be the sign of the covenant between me and the earth" (Genesis 9:13). Have a rainbow promise day!

Give Me Patience, Now!

PSALM 27:13–14 *I am still confident of this: I will see the goodness of the Lord in the land of the living. Wait for the Lord; be strong and take heart and wait for the Lord.*

As opposition surrounded David, he continually looked to God for deliverance. He wanted to learn God's ways. David had the faith and hope that he would see his rescue in the present "land of the living," not far off in the distant future. Even as David ran for his life when King Saul wanted to kill him, David took time to pray and wait on God. David learned patience as he waited for God to answer his prayers. In the lonely nights as David hid from Saul, I imagine he was glad he had practiced patience years earlier while tending his father's sheep.

Waiting is hard, especially when you're not sure what you're waiting for. And when we pray for relief from our sufferings, we're not sure if that relief will come immediately or much later. It's easy to become frustrated and anxious. That is why patience is a <u>virtue</u>. Take heart. Your patience will be rewarded in the future, when you see its effects in your life. "No discipline seems pleasant at the time, but painful. Later on, however, it produces a harvest of righteousness and peace for those who have been trained by it. Therefore, strengthen your feeble arms and weak knees" (Hebrews 12:11–12).

In our fast-paced, fast-food, no-wait, next-day-delivery society, we are programmed to expect immediate attention to our wants and needs. It's no wonder when we shoot up a crisis prayer to God that we want him to answer immediately. We fail to realize that our rescue will come all in God's timing—not ours—and we can grow in our spiritual walk if we patiently wait on him.

When our son Philip was younger, he fell while running. I had to restrain him while the doctor inspected and cleaned a long, dirt-filled laceration. Philip's tears flowed down his cheeks, and his expression seemed to say, "How could you do this? How could you hold me still while they inflict pain?" It tore at my heart. I only hope he remembers the tears of love that welled up in my eyes as I held him. He didn't understand: despite his pain, I had to restrain him so he could receive the treatment he needed to get well.

Our heavenly Father weeps as he sees his children suffering, but he knows we gain faith in him, become stronger, and live closer to him if we cling to him during our time of waiting.

Snapshots of Women in the Bible
Sarah and Hagar (Genesis 21:1–21)

Sarai gave up a life of luxury to become a **nomad**, joining her husband as he followed God's command. But obedience had its rewards.

Sarai and Abram were childless. God had promised heirs to them, but time was running out—the biological clock was ticking. A decade had passed since the promise, and Sarai was tired of waiting. She took matters into her own hands.

Hagar, an Egyptian slave girl, became a trusted servant to Sarai. The custom of the day allowed **maidservants** to bear children for a childless couple. Sarai thrust the responsibility of childbirth on her slave. Sarai departed from God's principle of <u>**monogamy**</u>, trusting her own wisdom over God's.

Abram went along with the plan. Hagar became pregnant. True to form, Sarai's ungodly acts bred seeds of discontentment as she watched Hagar's belly swell with life. Sarai suspected that Hagar now expected a share in Abram's wealth. In her jealousy, Sarai treated her slave so cruelly that Hagar ran for her life into the wilderness.

monogamy
Genesis 2:24

nomad
one who moves from place to place
maidservants
female slaves of wealthy families in Old Testament times
monogamy
the practice of marrying only once during life

promise
Genesis 12:1–4

Sarah
Hebrew for "princess"

In Hagar's suffering, loneliness, fear, and confusion, an angel of the Lord met her in her time of need. He called out her name. She must have been terrified at first, but then she was comforted to know that Abram's God knew her name. He knew her personally.

God gave her hope as he shared that her son would be called Ishmael, meaning "whom God hears." He promised a great nation would spring from Ishmael. She was able to return to Abram's camp with a renewed hope because she found God in the wilderness.

Time passed, and God fulfilled his promises to Sarai (now called **Sarah**) when she became pregnant and bore a son, Isaac. But when Sarah had her own son, once again she let the seeds of bitterness take control. She cast Hagar and Ishmael out into the desert.

Hagar found herself suffering in the wilderness once again, but this time she held the hand of her son—the son with which God had promised to make a great nation. Had God forgotten his promise? How could he fulfill it if Hagar and Ishmael perished in the desert?

As they came close to death she could not bear to watch her son die. She laid him under a bush, walked away, and began to sob. She must have thought she was delusional when she first heard her name. Then she remembered that familiar, comforting voice, the same voice she'd heard before in the wilderness.

God heard Hagar and her son cry for help and sent an angel that whispered her name and ministered to them. He provided a well of water and saved their lives, just as he promised. Scripture records, "God was with the boy as he grew up. He lived in the desert" (Genesis 21:20).

This snapshot is a study in contrasts. Sarah and Hagar, two different women who were forced to be in God's waiting room, both learned that God is always faithful. Neither behaved ideally, yet he kept his promises to them. "Never will I leave you; never will I forsake you" (Hebrews 13:5).

The Sun Will Come Out Tomorrow

PHILIPPIANS 3:12–14 *Not that I have already obtained all this, or have already been made perfect, but I press on to take hold of that for which Christ Jesus took hold of me. Brothers, I do not consider myself yet to have taken hold of it. But one thing I do: Forgetting what is behind and straining toward what is ahead, I press on toward the goal to win the prize for which God has called me heavenward in Christ Jesus.*

The apostle Paul wrote the Scripture above in his letter to the church at Philippi (see Illustration #13 on page 180). Imprisoned in a dark, lonely cell, saturated in suffering, Paul found joy during misery—a ray of hope in Jesus. He uses the **metaphor** of a highly competitive athlete to illustrate that as Christians we should want to do all we can for God's kingdom. Paul said he was in no way <u>perfect</u>, yet he continued to strive toward the goal of doing God's <u>will</u>—his good, pleasing, and perfect will.

Paul forgot his past, his failures, his successes, and his suffering as he looked forward to his future of receiving heavenly <u>rewards</u> from God.

perfect
Matthew 5:44–48
will
Romans 12:1–2
rewards
Hebrews 11:6

metaphor
symbolic story; image
prostitute
to sell oneself for sexual intercourse
Jericho
the first city taken by the Israelites during the conquest of Canaan
adultery
sexual intercourse between a married man and a woman that is not his wife
godly
devoted to God; holy; devout

Examples From the Bible

Others who forgot the past and became what God wanted:

- Rahab, a **prostitute** in the city of **Jericho**, harbored two spies from Israel's army and saved her family from destruction. She left behind her immoral life and believed in God as she joined the Israelites. The New Testament commends her for her faith. (Joshua 2:1–21; 6:17; Hebrews 11:31)

- David rose above his moral failures of **adultery** and murder and became a **godly** king. (2 Samuel 11:1–16, 26)

- Joseph suffered the injustice of his brothers' selling him as a slave, was wrongfully accused, and sent to prison. Yet he forgot the past, relied and waited on God, and became a ruler under the Egyptian pharaoh and saved the nation during a famine. (Genesis 37:27; 39:1–23; 41:46–49)

Paul reminds us of what really matters: knowing Christ and forgetting the past that holds us back from becoming what God wants us to be. Forget your pain, hurt, bitterness, and suffering. Look forward to a rewarding life today and inner sunshine tomorrow—whatever the outward circumstance may be.

How Others See It

Jan Silvious

Are you holding on to events that were too painful or things that people have done to you that have left you bleeding? Do you see yourself as a certain kind of person because of something unfortunate that has happened in your life? If so, today might be a good day to put that event behind you and, with God's help, go on. Don't allow yourself to continue to be identified by the past. If you want to move to the next level of maturity and insight, it's time to look at your circumstances differently. Start by telling yourself: Whatever happens, it is one event in a lifetime of events. I must go on![13]

consolation
comfort; relief

It's Your Turn

2 Corinthians 1:3–4 *Praise be to the God and Father of our Lord Jesus Christ, the Father of compassion and the God of all comfort, who comforts us in all our troubles, so that we can comfort those in any trouble with the comfort we ourselves have received from God.*

Instead of wallowing in his trials and sorrows, Paul encourages the Christians in Corinth (see Illustration #13) to comfort one another in their sufferings even as God has comforted them in their time of need.

We don't have to walk in the same shoes of suffering in order to comfort, but those who've been there can offer great **consolation** to others. Paul alludes to "the fellowship of sharing in [Christ's] sufferings" (Philippians 3:10). The "fellowship of sufferings" is a club with a steep entrance fee. Yet it is no exclusive clique. Many of us are inducted despite our best efforts to stay out. Once you're in, though, no one can comfort you like a fellow member. This ability to help fellow sufferers adds great dignity and meaning to our anguish. In Christ, we never suffer without reason.

Yes, your life has meaning. Your steps have led you down a road of hardships, yet through the power of God, you've survived. Your faith has been stretched. You have a new understanding of life. You know what's really important. You've weathered the storm. Now it's your turn to help others through their tempests; to share the comfort that Jesus ministered to you.

When tragedies are brought into our homes via live satellite TV, there seems to be a connection with the individuals and families left behind. We all mourned the Columbia space shuttle tragedy of 2003. In the days that followed that tragedy, we were introduced to Columbia's commander, Rick Husband, and his profound faith in God.

Rick's wife, Evelyn, shared his journey of faith in the book High Calling. *Describing a very difficult interview with Katie Couric, she writes, "The most difficult part of the interview came when Katie said, 'Let's listen to what Commander Rick Husband had to say about this mission.' For the first time since Rick's death, I could hear his voice in my earpiece. I held my breath to keep from crying. At the end of the interview, Katie asked how I would like Rick to be remembered. I said, 'When Rick autographed pictures for people, he always put a Scripture on it that was Proverbs 3:5–6, which says, "Trust in the Lord with all your heart and lean not on your own understanding; in all your ways acknowledge him, and he will make your paths straight." And that has been a blessing [for] me and Rick. And now it's a tremendous blessing to me because I don't understand any of this, but I do trust the Lord. And so that's been a tremendous comfort.'"*[14]

Through this tragedy, Rick Husband's lifelong journey of faith became a light and witness to the world. The watching world saw first-hand what his Creator accomplished in his life and death.

God has plans for your life, far greater than you can imagine. Embrace him, embrace life, be a **testimony** of his unfailing love. Choose to trust him on the rainy days as well as when the sun is shining. The love and joy he gives you will shine through the clouds and draw others to the source of your hope.

testimony
any declaration that a thing is true

How Others See It

Gerald Sittser

Suffering can lead to a simpler life, less cluttered with nonessentials. It is wonderfully clarifying. That is why many people who suffer sudden and severe loss often become different people. They spend more time with their children or spouses, express more affection and appreciation to their friends, show more concern for other wounded people, give more time to a worthy cause, or enjoy more of the ordinariness of life.[15]

Final Thoughts

- Life's storms of disappointment, suffering, and loss hit everyone. How we respond to the situation is what is important. After the initial shock, we must move beyond denial to calm the storm in our lives. If we run to God, rather than away from him, our souls will grow through the suffering.

- It makes sense to express anger rather than repress it. However, we cannot allow anger and bitterness to lead us into wrong behavior.

- Feeling down? Depression can be more than just the blues and may require treatment. God has provided Christian men and women who specialize in the field. Take the first step by crying out to God; then seek a Christian counselor who can give you emotional, mental, and spiritual support and advice. Take care of yourself during this time. Maintain your strength by eating, remembering to drink water, and trying to get physical exercise. Allow your friends and family to help out during your crisis, and find something to laugh about.

- God has not forgotten you. Do not give up! Be patient. Turn to Scripture and prayer for comfort, guidance, and strength. God loves you. Cling to him during your time of waiting.

- Your life has meaning, though it may not be the meaning you expected. There is a rewarding life available to you today and tomorrow. Live life to its fullest one day at a time and share with other suffering souls how God has helped you survive your struggle. Your life will be a comfort and blessing to others.

Questions to Deepen Your Understanding

1. During the captivity of the children of Israel, what message of hope did Jeremiah deliver?

2. When drenched in pain, who can we turn to who knows our suffering? How does this change our approach to suffering?

3. How did the widow of Zarephath save herself and her son from starvation?

4. What advice on dealing with anger did the apostle Paul give the church at Ephesus?

5. Bible women faced sorrow and pain, but also found relief and happiness. How did Noah's wife, Hagar, and Naomi find relief and happiness?

6. When depressed, what was the first step the psalmist took in receiving help?

7. According to Proverbs 17:22, how can you find relief for your heart when you are in the pit of despair?

8. The apostle Paul compares the church body to a physical body needing all its parts to be whole. When we suffer, how can we gain relief from others?

9. How did Rahab overcome her past and become what God wanted her to be?

read on

Some of Georgia's favorite books for loving God during disappointments, suffering, and loss:

- *A Grace Disguised*, Gerald Sittser, Zondervan

- *High Calling*, Evelyn Husband, Thomas Nelson

- *Is God Really in Control?* Jerry Bridges, NavPress

- *Let's Roll*, Lisa Beamer, Tyndale House

- *Look at It This Way*, Jan Silvious, WaterBrook Press

- *The New Normal*, Jill Briscoe, Multnomah

- *Outrageous Love*, Sheila Walsh, J. Countryman

- *31 Days Toward Overcoming Adversity*, Joni Eareckson Tada, Multnomah

- *Unveiling Depression in Women: A Practical Guide to Understanding and Overcoming Depression*, Dr. Archibald Hart and Catherine Hart Weber, Baker Books

- *Why?* Anne Graham Lotz, W Publishing Group

Chapter 3: From Burnout to Balance

Setting Priorities to Balance and Simplify Your Life

What's in This Chapter

Here We Go

With uncertain times, terrorist attacks, and natural disasters, churched and unchurched people alike are continually searching for meaning and purpose in their lives. We're stressed out, burned out, and put out with lives spinning out of control. It's no wonder Rick Warren's *The Purpose Driven Life* has sold tens of millions of copies and Pastor Joel Osteen's *Your Best Life Now* remains on the *New York Times* bestseller list. And then there are Oprah Winfrey's all-day Live Your Best Life workshops that have produced sold-out crowds since her tour began in 2001.

We women are desperately searching for significance, direction, and simple steps to living a balanced life. In our fast-paced, overscheduled, complicated lives, women continue to search for the simple life.

God has great advice on managing stress and balancing your life. Let's take a look and see just what the Bible has to say about setting priorities, balancing, and simplifying your life.

How Others See It

Rick Warren

It's not about you. The purpose of your life is far greater than your own personal fulfillment, your peace of mind, or even your happiness. It's far greater than your family, your career, or even your wildest dreams and ambitions. If you want to know why you were placed on this planet, you must begin with God. You were born by his purpose for his purpose.[1]

worried
Luke 10:39–42

I Want a Simple, Stress-Free Life

MATTHEW 6:25–27 *Therefore I tell you, do not worry about your life, what you will eat or drink; or about your body, what you will wear. Is not life more important than food, and the body more important than clothes? Look at the birds of the air; they do not sow or reap or store away in barns, and yet your heavenly Father feeds them. Are you not much more valuable than they? Who of you by worrying can add a single hour to his life?*

Jesus taught his disciples to trust in God. As the old song goes, "Don't worry, be happy!" He wanted them to let go and let God be in control of the driver's seat (or chariot seat).

Worrying is a waste of time and energy and causes stress as it complicates our lives. We think we are in control, but we really can't control what happens from day to day. So Jesus gives us a simple stress-free plan; live one day at a time in him.

Years ago I had a writing assignment dealing with the topic of striving for a simpler life. When you start writing about specific topics sometimes it really hits home. I stepped back and looked at my juggling act called life. I accepted the fact that my life was way too busy, our son's life was too cluttered, and life in general was way out of balance. I worried where I would find the time to squeeze in just one more thing. I was stressed out! I longed for a good night's rest, a cup of tea with a friend, and a night alone with my husband. I wanted a simple, stress-free life.

Maybe it had something to do with my impending fortieth birthday as I reflected on what was important in life, but whatever fueled the fire, I made some changes. I recruited my husband, and we even went so far as to sell the 3,200-square-foot house that took me five hours to clean. In its place we bought a 1,400-square-foot little cottage that I could whip through in minutes. I yanked the smothering unwanted weeds of over-commitment out of my schedule, slowed down, and limited our son's extracurricular activities (i.e., sports) to one per season. I actually began to breathe as I slowed my pace, turned everything back over to God, and put him back where he belonged: first.

When Martha complained to Jesus that her sister Mary was too busy listening and not helping her serve his dinner, Jesus told her she was <u>worried</u> about too many secondary things. She was caught up in the things of least importance while Mary had chosen the thing of most importance: time with Jesus.

A simple life has its advantages. It has less stress, it's more rewarding, and it makes room for God and family. Paradoxically, if you leave more empty spaces in your schedule, your life can fill with simple pleasures.

Defining Your Top Priority

PHILIPPIANS 1:9–10 *And this is my prayer: that your love may abound more and more in knowledge and depth of insight, so that you may be able to discern what is best and may be pure and blameless until the day of Christ.*

The book of Philippians was written by the apostle Paul when he was in a jail cell in Rome about AD 63. Talk about a stressful life! Paul's life was threatened on a regular basis; he was wrongfully accused and arrested, shipwrecked, imprisoned, and plagued with an unknown affliction. (And that's just listing a few of his problems.) Yet through it all he spread the Good News of Christ more than any other person recorded in the New Testament.

Paul's letter was a thank-you note written to his friends in the church at **Philippi**, thanking them for their encouragement, friendship, and support of his ministry. He also shared the secret of living above the stresses of life as he instructed them on living a good Christian life and making Christ first in your life. He said, "I want to <u>know Christ</u>."

As we discussed at length in chapter 1, knowing Christ is the number one priority in our lives. When we seek his way of living, we automatically set up boundaries, priorities, and limits for our lives. We don't just make it up as we go; it's already laid out for us in the Scripture to follow as we start accessing what is and isn't important in our lives. We start viewing our lives through the eyes of Jesus. Paul wrote: "All of us who are mature should take such a view of things. And if on some point you think differently, that too God will make clear to you" (Philippians 3:15).

know Christ
Philippians 3:10

Paul
apostle of Christ
Philippi
city in the Roman
province

The world has many distractions that knock us off balance. When you are faced with choices of something you say yes or no to, ask yourself if it is a priority in God's plan for your life. When you know God's Word, it gives you a special insight and discernment in making tough decisions—like knowing which direction you need to take in your life. God doesn't just want what's good for your life; he wants what is best for your life. Praying for guidance, looking to God's Word, and seeking his advice are the starting points in defining your priorities and living a balanced, stress-free life.

> ## How Others See It
>
> ### Joanna Weaver
>
> When our lives are overbooked, it's easy for us to become spiritually dry and undernourished. We can barely hear God's voice above the busy noise, let alone say yes to what he is asking. In this case, we need to learn how to say no, but only so we are able to say yes to God when he wants to give us an assignment.[3]

Publishers Can't Lose

Publishers can't seem to lose with books exploring spirituality. Books that focus on spirituality are the industry's fastest-growing category. Over the past few years, if you put the word soul *in the title, you've got a bestseller on your hands.*

Some attribute the success to different interests that range from New Age philosophies to the search for purpose in this crazy world. I agree, but I also feel it is the age-old desire to know and communicate with one's Maker. Communication with God and knowing his will for our lives is fulfilled through this thing called prayer.

Throughout Jesus' ministry, his example of praying to God in seclusion and in groups plainly shows the importance of seeking him. Prayer preceded every life-changing event in Jesus' life.

The ultimate example of praying in God's will was Jesus at the Garden of Gethsemane, the night before the Crucifixion.

No one would want to suffer the agonizing, humiliating death on a cross. Knowing the time was drawing near, he sought God's will: "He knelt down and prayed, 'Father, if you are willing, take this cup from me; yet not my will, but yours be done" (Luke 22:42).

He agonized the decision.

There are times in our lives when it hurts to be in God's will. We ago-

nize over decisions for our own lives, the lives of our children, and even the lives of friends, family, strangers, and the church.

It's no wonder books that focus on spirituality are the industry's fastest-growing category. The awesome power of prayer that gave enduring hope and renewed faith to believers in the early church is the same unchanging power that we have free access to today.

This thing called prayer keeps us in an intimate communication with God. If we can tap into this power individually and collectively, it can do for us what it did for the early church, as we too strive to turn the world upside down for his glory. "I glorified You on the earth, having accomplished the work which You have given Me to do" (John 17:4 NASB).

How Others See It

John and Stasi Eldredge

The vast desire and capacity a woman has for intimate relationships tells us of God's vast desire and capacity for intimate relationships. In fact, this may be the most important thing we ever learn about God—that he yearns for relationship with us. "Now this is eternal life: that they may know you, the only true God" (John 17:3). The whole story of the Bible is a love story between God and his people. He yearns for us. He cares. He has a tender heart.[4]

Examples From the Bible

God offers promises for those who seek his advice.

- "Call to me and I will answer you and tell you great and unsearchable things you do not know," says the Lord. (Jeremiah 33:3)

- "The Lord is near to all who call on him, to all who call on him in truth." (Psalm 145:18)

- "The Lord is with you when you are with him. If you seek him, he will be found by you, but if you forsake him, he will forsake you." (2 Chronicles 15:2)

- Jesus said, "Ask and it will be given to you; seek and you will find; knock and the door will be opened to you. For everyone who asks receives; he who seeks finds; and to him who knocks, the door will be opened." (Luke 11:9–10)

- "Trust in the Lord with all your heart and lean not on your own understanding; in all your ways acknowledge him, and he will make your paths straight." (Proverbs 3:5–6)
- "If any of you lacks wisdom, he should ask God, who gives generously to all without finding fault, and it will be given to him." (James 1:5)
- "Those who know your name will trust in you, for you, Lord, have never forsaken those who seek you." (Psalm 9:10)
- "I will guide you in the way of wisdom and lead you along straight paths. When you walk, your steps will not be hampered; when you run, you will not stumble," says the Lord. (Proverbs 4:11–12)
- "And without faith it is impossible to please God, because anyone who comes to him must believe that he exists and that he rewards those who earnestly seek him." (Hebrews 11:6)
- "The wisdom that comes from heaven is first of all pure; then peace-loving, considerate, submissive, full of mercy and good fruit, impartial and sincere." (James 3:17)

Unclutter Your Life

PHILIPPIANS 4:8 *Finally, brothers, whatever is true, whatever is noble, whatever is right, whatever is pure, whatever is lovely, whatever is admirable— if anything is excellent or praiseworthy—think about such things.*

I wish I were the genius behind *Real Simple* magazine. It knocked Martha Stewart's *Living* magazine out of the number one category and is now the top-selling women's magazine. It's all about offering easy solutions for everyday life—just what every woman needs.

Our lives get so cluttered with stuff. We buy plastic tubs to store stuff we'll probably never look at, let alone use again. We hire experts to organize our overstuffed, messy closets. We use computer programs to manage our stuffy bank accounts. Somehow, we're still cluttered with stuff.

Tips to Simplify Your Life

1. Slow down for a daily quiet time of prayer and Scripture reading.

2. Sit down and figure out how you spend your day, week, and month.

3. Evaluate and prioritize
   a. God
   b. Family
   c. Self

d. Career

e. Extracurricular activities

4. Learn to say yes to top priorities and no to low priorities.

5. Enjoy the simple pleasures with your family like taking walks, in-line skating, gardening, flying a kite, and cooking.

Unclutter Your Mind

Our minds sometimes mirror our clutter problems. We fill them with stuff that really doesn't need to be there. From time to time we need to take inventory of our hearts and minds and get rid of the clutter. We can determine what needs to go or stay by measuring them to Philippians 4:8. Ask the questions—Is it true, noble, authentic? Is it pure, lovely—not ugly? Is it the right thing? The best, not the worst? Is it something of excellence to praise? Is it God-honoring? The Scripture is all about offering easy solutions for everyday life—just what every woman needs.

It Follows Me Like a Plague

I did it again. I was so proud I made it through the holidays without an episode. With my checkered past, I knew it was bound to happen again. It seems to follow me like a bad plague.

It's really the tiny segment of my domestic side that caused it. I was merely disposing of long-overdue leftovers that did me in. I'm sure it was the combination of beef stew and rice that clogged my drain. With the look of disappointment from my husband and the elaborating of unpleasant reminiscing of days gone by, I was determined to unclog the sink myself.

My date for most of that evening was the toilet plunger—plunging up and down, up and down, and at the same time fighting with the drain cover, trying to keep one side down while I plunged the other.

It was quite a show.

The drain seemed to be really vocal as it burped, rumpled, and from time to time even spit gross items at me and all over the kitchen. My last resort was Drano.

I had faith it would work—the front cover of the bottle in bold type read: Opens drains fast! Works on kitchen clogs. Satisfaction guaranteed or your money back.

Well, guess what—I would be getting my money back—it didn't work. I had to call the professionals. When the receptionist asked if I had used their services, I laughed, gave her my name, and sure enough, I popped up on her computer screen as a loyal customer.

I really don't know what it is with me and kitchen sinks. Since the last plumber's visit I'd followed his advice—no potato peels, no eggshells, run water a long time while disposing, throw in some ice every now and then . . . I'd done it all. However, there was nothing mentioned about beef stew and the rice combo.

There are times when your life seems to get clogged. You know better, but somehow the black, nasty dirt of the world slips through. Your everyday life becomes filled with strife, stress, and wrong choices, and it all starts to build up. Before you know it you're at a standstill, frantically seeking help.

Take it from me, don't be stubborn and waste your time trying to solve the problem on your own—go to the Master Designer and the Scriptures, his ultimate Do-It-Yourself Handbook. With his help, your life can flow freely once again. Satisfaction guaranteed!

"He who believes in Me, as the Scripture said, 'From his innermost being will flow rivers of living water'" (John 7:38 NASB).

Stress—A Childhood Disease?

Mark 6:30–32 *The apostles gathered around Jesus and reported to him all they had done and taught. Then, because so many people were coming and going that they did not even have a chance to eat, he said to them, "Come with me by yourselves to a quiet place and get some rest." So they went away by themselves in a boat to a solitary place.*

As word spread about Jesus' teachings and miracles, people were always following him, some just watching, others pressing for a miracle. When the crowds grew so large that Jesus and the disciples couldn't even eat, Jesus knew what to do. Despite all the demands of the crowd, he took his apostles away to a "solitary place."

We can learn from Jesus. When our children's lives get too stressed, we need to help them find stress relief. Take a good long look and evaluate their schedules. Simplify them. If necessary, make your child slow down, step back, and get some rest.

Being "stressed out" is not reserved for adults only. This fast-paced world we live in is filled with a million and one things to do: nonstop Xbox games to play, organized sports from toddlers on up, pressure to excel in school, an avalanche of media. Result: Kids don't have much downtime. When I see kids on edge and angry, with dark circles under their glazed eyes, they have the look of stress. Physicians tell us we're growing our kids into unhealthy adults, giving them a head start on health-related problems such as ulcers, heart failure, and depression. Doctors advise us to look at our children's schedules and simplify their load. Do you understand your child's stressful world? Try simplifying it to relieve stress.

What You Can Do

Dr. Archibald Hart, author of *Stress and Your Child*, offers the following tips for helping your child ease the anxiety of excess stress at school:

- Don't put undue pressure on your child to make better grades than he or she is capable of making. Arrange for tutoring or counseling if your child seems unduly stressed about grades.

- Monitor the number of extracurricular activities your child is involved in.

- Let your child talk about anxiety. Sharing one's worries helps relieve them.

- Watch for signs that a very young child is under stress at day care. Typical symptoms: "clingy" behavior, an increase in temper tantrums, and other stress-related behavior.

- Be alert to security problems and be prepared to work with the school and other parents to solve these problems.[6]

Uncertain Times and Stress

ROMANS 8:15 *For you did not receive a spirit that makes you a slave again to fear, but you received the Spirit of sonship. And by him we cry, "Abba, Father."*

After 9/11 Laura Bush was featured on public-service announcements offering advice on comforting our children during uncertain times. She loves children, and her concern was evident as she spoke to our nation. With satellite TV, we bring the war into our homes. Even if we scurry children out of the room, they get glimpses of the images of war and overhear our conversations.

Time has a way of erasing memories of war. We somehow forget the war our Founding Fathers fought on American soil that brought us freedom, or even the horrific Civil War, where brothers fought against brothers. Fear of war has haunted children for centuries—it just lay dormant for a while. Our world has a "New Normal," which includes the stress brought on by fear.

everyday insights

We have to instill in our children the faith, security, and peace found in God's Word. I've never wanted to give our son the false hope that nothing bad would ever happen to him because, as we all know, bad things do happen to good people. When we prayed on our way to school, I would ask God to protect him, but that if harm came to him to give him strength to make it through the struggle. I would assure him that no matter what, we would get there as soon as possible.

When we lived on the West Coast, each year we would send Earthquake Disaster Kits to school for safekeeping. It had a blanket, flashlight, crackers, and juice box—just some creature comforts. The most important item was a sealed envelope with a letter from parents and a family picture that offered comfort and hope in a time of fear.

Stephen Arterburn and David Stoop, in their book *130 Questions Children Ask About War and Terrorists,* offer several things we can do to help alleviate fear in our children's lives. They suggest that we encourage our children to tell us about what they fear. And as parents we need to have an open dialogue with our children and talk about war, terrorism, or anything else that they want to discuss. Their book is an excellent tool for answering those tough questions.

As believers, God offers us hope and comfort in a time of fear. Share those Scriptures and prayers with your children. It will help ease their minds and calm their fears.

How Others See It

Stephen Arterburn

War teaches a child about spiritual things. During and immediately after wartime, a child thinks about prayer in a new way. It changes from a rote activity into a comforting time before bed at night. Children think about God more during a time of crisis, and that becomes an opportunity for you to talk to your child about Jesus and to read the Bible together.[8]

Examples From the Bible

Fear was a constant companion to women in the Bible. However, they turned their fear into faith as they trusted their God would carry them through their circumstance.

- Deborah, a judge of Israel, rose against fear and led the Israelite army into battle. (Judges 4:14)

- Jehosheba, sister of King Ahaziah, put her own life at risk when she hid the infant prince, Joash, in the temple, when Queen Athaliah overtook the throne and murdered her own grandchildren. Six years later Joash became king and restored the kingdom to David's line. (2 Chronicles 22:11)

- Esther, a Jewish woman, chosen queen of the Persian king Xerxes, feared losing her life but took a stand for her people and saved a nation. (Esther 4:16)

- Jochebed, mother of Moses, turned her fear into faith in God as she hid baby Moses and saved his life. (Exodus 6:20)

- Mary the mother of Jesus faced fear of rejection and stoning but recognized her purpose and willingly submitted her life to God and his purpose. (Matthew 1:18; Luke 1:26–30)

father
Acts 16:1
sensitive
Philippians 2:19–20
reserved
1 Corinthians
16:10–11

spiritual father
adopted father of faith
missionary
person sent out to
spread a religion
Gospel
Good News of Jesus
Christ

- Women did not allow fear to keep them from ministering to Jesus at the cross. (John 19:25)
- Priscilla, a leader and teacher in the early church, did not let fear of persecution keep her from spreading the message of Christ. (Acts 18; Romans 16:3–4)

Snapshots of Women in the Bible
Eunice (2 Timothy 1:1–6)

Eunice's heart must have swelled with pride when her son Timothy shared the apostle Paul's letter with her. What relief they felt to know that Paul had not yet been executed by the Romans.

Paul was like a father to Timothy. Timothy's own <u>father</u> was not known to be a Christian. In fact, scholars believe he died and Eunice raised Timothy alone. Timothy adopted Paul as his **spiritual father** and close companion. Between his travels with Paul and his pastoring a church Paul founded, Timothy ministered with Paul for over fifteen years.

I imagine Eunice and Timothy this way:

Following in the footsteps of her mother, Lois, Eunice passed her faith along to Timothy. Daily they studied the commandments and principles God set forth for his people. As she raised her son, she didn't know if he would ever share her faith, but day after day she continued to teach, encourage, and love him.

Eunice worried at first about Timothy's timidity. But she saw a boy who loved to learn—why, he drove her crazy with his meticulous details!—and she loved his tender heart. He was so <u>sensitive</u> to the needs of others. She had known God would use him in a special way; still, it surprised her when Paul asked young Timothy to join him on his **missionary** journey to spread the **Gospel**. She knew of the danger, but she knew he was safe in the arms of Jesus—either here or in eternity. She wondered how Paul and Timothy would work together—they were so opposite. Paul was bold and daring, while Timothy was quiet and <u>reserved</u>. But Timothy had proved to be the support, the detail man, and the strong right arm Paul needed to accomplish his mission.

Now, all these years later, tears trickled down her cheeks as she read Paul's words, "I have been reminded of your sincere faith, which first lived in your grandmother Lois and in your mother Eunice and, I am persuaded, now lives in you also" (2 Timothy 1:5). Her life had meaning. She had raised her son alone but had remained faithful to God. As a result, she and her mother had influenced not only her son, but now were instrumental in establishing the church and spreading the Good News of Jesus.

Stress Busters for Flying Solo

Holy Spirit
Luke 11:13;
I Thessalonians 4:8

ROMANS 5:5 *Hope does not disappoint us, because God has poured out his love into our hearts by the Holy Spirit, whom he has given us.*

As women of faith we can have confidence and hope in God. We have a free gift from God, the Holy Spirit, which fills our hearts when we accept Jesus as Lord of our lives. The Holy Spirit fills us with hope, confidence, and safety in God. No matter how bad the circumstance, no matter how much life has disappointed us, no matter how much we suffer, we can place our hope and trust in God to see us through. You may be stressed out from raising your children as a single mother. Perhaps a man has hurt you deeply. Remember that God is never a disappointment and he can heal the hurt.

Jealous Sarah cast out Hagar, a surrogate mother and Sarah's handmaiden, into the desert for the second time. This time Hagar was not alone; her teenage son, Ishmael, was rejected as well. Single, rejected, and dying of thirst, Hagar cried out to God. He heard her prayers and God provided a well to replenish Hagar and Ishmael. He gave her hope for her future.

God provides and gives hope to single moms and their children today just as he provided for Hagar and Ishmael.

How Others See It

Cynthia Yates

Pray for grace, single mom. Pray for the grace to stand firmly focused on the Lord. Pray for grace to be able to communicate His way of life to your children. Pray for grace to have patience without compromising God's values. Pray for grace to keep your home holy.[9]

words to live by

When you are parenting on your own, stress knocks on your door—and brings along some friends: loneliness, isolation, doubt, and a mountain load of other emotions.

Whether you have been divorced, widowed, or simply abandoned, don't lose hope. As we discussed in chapter 2, God is a God of hope. This is a solo flight you never asked to pilot, but with God's help and a hope for a better tomorrow, you can land safely.

What You Can Do

Even though you are flying solo as a single parent, you are not alone in a community of faith, family, and friends. Here are some tips on balancing life as a single mom:

- *Ask for help.* Extended family members are usually willing and able to assist you in helping out with the kids. After all, they are relatives! If you live away from family, ask friends from church to help. After all, they are friends! It may be a place for your children to go after school until you get home from work. Carpooling to school or sports, help with a leaky faucet, financial planning—whatever—just ask! CAUTION: Make sure you know the person you are leaving your child with. Also, know the man you are dating. Don't be afraid to check his background, and never leave your children with someone you just started dating.

- *Assign chores.* You can't do it all. If your children are old enough to help out with chores around the house, assign duties. Just so they don't forget, make a chart. Use a magnetic color-coded system in the kitchen so you can change the chart. Assign each member of the family a color. List all the chores on the chart. Place the color magnet on the assigned chore for the week. If the chore doesn't get done, have a consequence in place.

- *Extracurricular activities.* We've already talked about stress and kids, but it's a double whammy when you're single and trying to juggle multiple kids with multiple sports. If it fits into your budget, limit it to one per season.

- *Church activities for your children.* It's extremely important for your children to be involved in youth groups at church. Not only is it vital for spiritual growth, it's a safe place to make new friends and have other adults involved in their lives. Christian summer camps should be a high priority on your list. Not only is it great for them, it gives you a much-needed break. If your budget is too tight, talk with the camp or your church about a scholarship. Most camps have individuals who donate toward scholarships.

- *Church activities for you.* Hopefully your church has a ministry with single moms in mind. If not, you may want to find a church that ministers to you and your family. Make church a top priority for you and your family. Not only do you need the spiritual support offered at church, you need community. A place where everybody knows your name and is glad you came. It's also a wonderful opportunity for you to serve. When we're ministering to others, it has a way of easing our own pain.

- *Book club.* If you're struggling with a specific problem, read up on the solution. Your local library is free. Most churches have a library or bookstore. You have the computer at your fingertips . . . so you have no excuses. There are wonderful books out there for single moms just waiting for you to open the pages. (See *Read On* section at end of chapter.)

- *Circle of friends.* It's easy to be isolated and overwhelmed with life as a single mom, but don't let go of your friends. You need your "friendship breaks" to talk things out, have fun, do Bible studies, and a place where you can just be *you*.

How Others See It

Sheila Walsh

It takes a certain amount of internal fortitude to be able to ask for help, and perhaps even more to receive it. It's only as we are freed from the clutter in Wonder Woman's closet—the shame, fear, insecurity, and anger—that we reach a safe enough place to ask for help without dissolving into tears or rejecting the helper. So often we live such lonely lives, and we don't have to.[10]

Examples From the Bible

The Bible gives us examples of single women faced with adversity who influenced their children, households, and church:

- Huram's mother, a widow, whose son became a great artisan and cast metals for King Solomon's temple at Jerusalem. (1 Kings 7:13–14)

- A single mother whose oil was multiplied. A single woman left with debts had debtors demanding her sons in repayment. She went to Elisha the prophet for help. He performed a miracle through multiplying her oil, which she sold and paid her debts. (2 Kings 4:1–8)

- Widow of Nain: Jesus had compassion on the widow of Nain's son and raised him from the dead. It was the first person Jesus raised from the dead. (Luke 7:11–17)

Mild-Mannered Reporter by Day, Supermom by Night: Juggling Work and Home

PROVERBS 31:27–28 *She watches over the affairs of her household and does not eat the bread of idleness. Her children arise and call her blessed; her husband also, and he praises her.*

The ancient woman of Proverbs 31 appears to have a busy but balanced life. The writer describes her as a precious jewel—a rare woman we can all admire. The passage paints a beautiful, idealized portrait of a woman who has it all together. She works from dark to dark; she cooks, sews, quilts, buys and sells real estate, teaches her children and servants, takes care of the needs of her children and husband, has time for volunteer work, and she's prepared for the future. She basically "brings home the bacon and fries it up in a pan." (Oops, maybe not bacon. We need to think kosher here.)

At the end of Proverbs 31, the writer gives the secret of this ideal woman's balanced life: "A woman who fears the Lord is to be praised" (Proverbs 31:30). When she sets priorities, she honors God first and foremost, and her life has a way of balancing all of its busyness. A balanced God-centered life is one of the most important gifts you can give your family.

You look up from your desk and see the clock ticking away. How did that second hand get so fast? You realize you have another job to do and drop everything, run to the nearest phone booth, shut the door, and wham, bang, boom!—you fly out in your Supermom cape, racing home at the speed of sound to resume the job you left earlier that morning.

Nearly a third of all employed women in the U.S. have children under the age of thirteen, and 38 percent have children under eighteen. One study of two thousand managers reported that 11 percent of the women currently work part-time in order to spend more time with family. Fifty-six percent say they have a "nontraditional" work situation, meaning any variation from the standard 9 A.M. to 5 P.M., Monday through Friday. This is a good thing . . . finding balance between work and family.

What You Can Do

Gwen Ellis offers these simple tips for a balanced life in her book *Thriving as a Working Woman:*

1. Make your devotion or quiet time top priority. You must find that time to balance the rest. (You can read and pray while you relax in a hot bath with the door locked to ensure privacy.)

2. Keep everything simple. Complicated systems, tools, appliances, and clothing only take more time.

3. Divide big jobs into many smaller ones.

4. Stop trying to be perfect.

5. Get help from anyone who will help.

6. Buy duplicates of items that are in high demand—hair spray, toothpaste, toilet paper—to avoid emergency trips to the store.

7. Have special places for your keys, your purse, and any other items that are repeatedly being lost.

8. Try to do two things at once: Talk on the phone and cook supper; watch television and mend.

9. When you have shopping and errands to accomplish, make a night of it. Plan your route from one shopping place to the next so there is no backtracking.

10. Use delivery services as much as possible if your budget allows.[11]

Riding on Cloud Nine

I breathed a sigh of relief as the wheels touched the runway. So far, so good. I'd caught an early morning flight to attend a speakers' conference in San Diego. The sessions would begin in about an hour, so I knew I would cut it close if there were any delays.

As directed by the shuttle operator, I made my way across the street and found Cloud Nine Shuttle Service. The driver had room for one more in the backseat, so we loaded up and I belted in for the ride of my life.

Cloud Nine Shuttle Service was proud because they ran their vehicles on propane fuel. That fact was painted beneath their logo. But you couldn't fool me; by the way this guy drove, I knew it was jet fuel. He took off like lightning. Dodged in and out of traffic. Passed vehicles like they were sitting still. He must have been the cum laude graduate of Mr. Toad's Wild Ride Driving School.

With white knuckles clutching my shoulder belt, I knew the real problem I faced: I wasn't in control. It was a strange city, and I had no directions to the resort—just an address. I was strapped into a vehicle with a total stranger, traveling down the freeway at the speed of sound, and there wasn't a thing I could do about it. (Of course I could have jumped out at the first stop, but the clock was ticking—I had a session in less than an hour.)

I was the last passenger to be dropped off. We made it with a few minutes to spare, and I even had time to check into my room and grab a bite to eat.

Sometimes on life's road you feel as if you're on Mr. Toad's Wild Ride. Propelled by jet fuel and a busy schedule, you pass by people in your life as if they are sitting still. You can't sit down long enough to reach out and help someone in need. You dodge in and out of commitments, afraid to slow your pace. And there are those slippery "relationship" roads where our pell-mell drive feels especially treacherous.

We have to look to the One who is truly in control and relinquish the driver's seat to him. We need to let God strap us safely into the backseat (or, given the maturity level of some of us, the child seat). The ride won't always be smooth. There will definitely be bumps along the way. But with God in control, you'll feel like you're riding on Cloud Nine.

Final Thoughts

- If you long for a simple life, you can do much more than merely pine for it. It's out there waiting for you. Evaluate, prioritize, and look to God for guidance and wisdom in your life and the lives of your children.

- Jesus gave us a simple plan for living one day at a time in him. Keep your eyes focused on the important things in life—an intimate relationship with God and your family. Enjoy a life filled with simple pleasures.

- Take inventory of your life and start to unclutter not only your schedule but also your mind. Fill it with pure, lovely, God-honoring thoughts.

- Don't let stress take your family hostage. Get control of your family's schedule and take it easy—take a break—put your feet up. It's okay to relax.

- As believers, God offers us hope and comfort in times of uncertainties and fear. Share Scriptures and prayers with your children. It will help ease their minds and calm their fears.

- God gives hope and comfort for women who are parenting on their own. You are not alone during this stressful time in your life. God is there with you. Pray for his wisdom and guidance and look to your family, friends, and community of faith to help carry you through.

Questions to Deepen Your Understanding

1. In Matthew 6:25–27, what did Jesus instruct his disciples to do?

2. In Paul's letter to the Philippians, he shared the secret to living above the stresses of life. What was that secret?

3. When our schedules become overcrowded, how do we discern what to say yes or no to?

4. What is the litmus test for uncluttering our minds?

5. Stress is becoming a childhood disease. As a parent, what do you need to do to alleviate stress in your child's life?

6. How did Jesus relieve stress in his own life and the lives of his disciples?

7. How can we help calm our children's fears of terrorism, war, and uncertain times?

8. How did Eunice influence her son, Timothy, and the early church?

9. As a single mother, how did Hagar find hope in God?

Some of Georgia's favorite books for setting priorities to balance and simplify your life:

- *Balanced Living,* Focus on the Family Women's Bible Study Series, Gospel Light

- *Captivating,* John and Stasi Eldredge, Thomas Nelson

- *Cure for the Common Life: Living in Your Sweet Spot,* Max Lucado, Thomas Nelson

- *Having a Mary Heart in a Martha World,* Joanna Weaver, WaterBrook Press

- *I'm Not Wonder Woman: But God Made Me Wonderful,* Sheila Walsh, Thomas Nelson

- *Life Management for Busy Women,* Elizabeth George, Harvest House

- *Living Well as a Single Mom,* Cynthia Yates, Harvest House

- *130 Questions Children Ask About War and Terrorism,* Stephen Arterburn and David Stoop, Tyndale House

- *The Purpose Driven Life,* Rick Warren, Zondervan

- *Stress and Your Child,* Dr. Archibald Hart, Thomas Nelson

- *Stressed or Depressed: A Practical and Inspirational Guide for Parents of Hurting Teens,* Dr. Archibald Hart and Catherine Hart Weber, Integrity Publishers

- *Your Best Life Now,* Joel Osteen, WarnerFaith

Part Two

Family Ties

Chapter 4: Mom Factor

Realizing the Blessings, Power, and Responsibility of a Mother's Love

What's in This Chapter

Here We Go

The tide has slowly turned since the '70s, and it now seems back in vogue to be a mom. We no longer need to hide the fact; we can wear the "Mom Badge" with great pride. The problem is that between the *Leave It to Beaver* mom of the '60s and the *Desperate Housewives* mom of today, there was a huge void for mom role models. Today's mom needs a full-time coach to help "train a child in the way he should go" (Proverbs 22:6).

sow seed
I Corinthians 3:6

Sometimes we spend too much time and effort searching for the right books, psychologists, and experts to teach us how to be perfect parents. God designed a woman with a unique heart of love that not only opens to let her children in, but longs, yearns, and pulls her to be with her children. That God-designed "mother's heart" can take you a long way if you simply listen to it.

In addition, God gave us all the child-rearing principles we need in his Word. He gives us direction that helps us develop an everlasting love for our children while we focus on teaching them values, heritage, Scripture, and the simplicity of life without undue stress.

I realize that not every woman who picks up this book may be a mother, but this chapter is not just for mothers. Remember that it takes many workers to produce a harvest. Some <u>sow seed</u>, some cultivate the ground, some harvest the crops.

God's fellow workers
I Corinthians 3:9

Feast
Leviticus 23:1—4

return
Luke 2:41—51

memory
Luke 2:19

Mary
the mother of Jesus by
a miraculous virgin
birth

Jesus
Hebrew for "the Lord
saves"

Joseph
Mary's husband and
the earthly father to
Jesus

**Feast of the
Passover**
an annual celebration
of God's delivering the
Jews from Egypt

temple
God's "house"; a place
of worship

Jerusalem
capital of the Jewish
nation

Nazareth
a town in Galilee
among the southern
hills of Lebanon where
Jesus grew up

Not every woman is called upon to be a mother. But all of us are <u>God's fellow workers</u> in helping children become people of God. Every adult Christian should care enough about the next generation to take part in teaching and applying the Scriptures to young people.

Some will accomplish this through the role of leadership as a teacher, but most will simply do it in life, modeling attitudes and behaviors that are consistent or inconsistent with God's Word. Either way, we have the opportunity to teach some powerful lessons.

As we gain better understanding of our children and discover the unique way each child learns, we can encourage, build confidence, and bring out the best in them. Let's see what the Bible has to say to moms.

The Miracle of a Mother's Heart

LUKE 2:51–52 *[Jesus'] mother treasured all these things in her heart. And Jesus grew in wisdom and stature, and in favor with God and men.*

Mary, the mother of **Jesus**, and her husband, **Joseph**, had just celebrated the <u>**Feast** of the **Passover**</u> at the **temple** in **Jerusalem**. They were on their <u>return</u> trip home to **Nazareth**, traveling with a group of friends and family. During the long hike to and from Jerusalem, the women usually walked along and talked in one group as the men trailed behind in another informal cluster. The children ran back and forth between the groups just enjoying the trip, so it wasn't unusual for your child to be out of view for lengthy periods. Still, it came as a shock when, at the end of the first day's journey, Mary and Joseph could not find their twelve-year-old son, Jesus.

Mary and Joseph returned to Jerusalem and searched for three days. They finally found Jesus in the temple (see Illustration #5) sitting among the teachers, listening and asking questions. As frantic parents would, they scolded Jesus and asked, "Where on earth have you been? We've been worried sick! What got into you? Why did you do this?"

Jesus said he was about his Father's business. As an adolescent, he suggested to his parents that their business may not coincide with God his Father's business. Yet Jesus submitted to his parents and went home.

I think Mary knew that day that Jesus was separating himself from them. She may have sighed as she added another <u>memory</u> and new experience of motherhood to the treasury in her heart.

A mother's heart is a treasure box that gives splendid gifts to a child and is filled with joyful gifts from a child. Some mothers find their new heart as soon as their baby is born. Others discover this heart after they surrender to it. Sadly, some never discover this heart, or the God who designed it.

A mother's heart:

- is a treasure box of love;

- loves beyond measure;

- is created to have the same capacity of love that God has for his children;

- loves, gives, disciplines, protects, separates, heals, laughs, teaches, grieves, builds, shares, and suffers with a child;

- not only **transforms** a mother, but transforms her child as well;

- is a miracle.

transforms
changes the condition, nature, or function

C-section
Cesarean section; a surgical operation for delivering a baby by cutting through the mother's abdominal and uterine wall

Mother Love

*I'd heard about this thing called "mother love" for years. I thought it was the longing, the desire to be a mother. I yearned for years to fill my empty arms, but until I felt that first "butterfly" movement and heard the heartbeat of the life within me, I never knew the transforming power of mother love. Its primal strength took me by surprise. The surgeon said he had only performed a **C-section**, but I'd swear a heart surgeon must have worked alongside him too, because when they wheeled me out of surgery and laid that little bundle on my chest, my heart was different—larger. It was large enough to lodge this child for the rest of my life.*

We all know that men and women are different (thank goodness!). God gave women a special gift, a special design, a Designer Label Heart. The same heart that served as a lifeline to the child in the womb is still a lifeline to the child outside the womb.

coffee break

How Others See It

Brenda Hunter

Ah, the power of mother love. How it stretches and swells across generations, uniting mother and child, fleshing out the expectant mother's identity and femininity, shaping the personality and life of her child, and changing society in ways our culture has chosen to ignore. Mother love is ultimately a love song, a siren's call, luring women to new ways of being . . . to sacrifice and being turned inside out . . . to fulfillment.[1]

Illustration #5
Jesus at the Temple—
Jesus was among the
teachers in Jerusalem's
temple, listening and
asking questions, until
Mary and Joseph found
him after three days of
searching.

The Face Only a Mother Could Love

PSALM 127:3 (NASB) *Children are a gift of the Lord. The fruit of the womb is a reward.*

God created life, and children are the continuation of life. Our name is passed down from generation to generation as children are born and new life continues. God blessed us, his <u>creation</u>, with the gift of children. Children are not a burden; they are a blessing.

creation
Genesis 1:1, 28

contingencies
uncertain conditions

When the actress Kate Mulgrew called it quits a few years back, the headlines read, "Kate Mulgrew Plans to Abandon 'Voyager' Ship for Her Family." Kate may be better known to all Trekkies as Captain Janeway of the Federation Starship *Voyager*. The article quoted her as saying, "I'm so privileged and happy I had this job. But we're talking about a block of time that I've missed now with them; years in which nurturing was crucial to them, to their self-esteem, the kind of nurturing that comes without conditions or **contingencies**, the kind of nurturing that is so simple and basic to human nature regarding the relationship between mother and son. We missed it." The story told how her two teenage sons wanted her to come home, and how she wanted to make up for lost time with her boys before they finished growing and left home.

A young mother wrote me a thank-you note for some hand-me-down clothes I passed along to her son. The card read, "Your generosity comes at a great time. The at-home business I've been involved in hasn't made us the money we thought we would make, and going back to work began to look like our only alternative. But as the Lord has done so many times in my life, he **humbled** me and brought me to my senses. What price can I put on those tiny faces and innocent eyes? Suddenly a larger house, new toys, and self-indulgence just didn't seem that important to me anymore."

This is the mystery of motherhood: the mystical pull; the longing, yearning, loving heart that pulls you to the face only a mother could love—your child's.

humbled
James 4:10

humbled
not proud; to make meek

How Others See It

Oprah Winfrey

I believe the choice to become a mother is the choice to become one of the greatest spiritual teachers there is. To create an environment that's stimulating and nurturing, to pass on a sense of responsibility to another human being, to raise a child who understands that he or she is created from good and is capable of anything—I know for sure that few callings are more honorable.[2]

"You're Not a Woman . . . You're a Mommy!"

In the early days of my mommy odyssey, my then two-year-old son, Philip, revealed to me the hidden secret of mommyhood. It went something like this: Philip would make an elephant noise and say, "I'm an elephant." Then I would say, "You're not an elephant! You're a little boy." He would giggle and go on to the next sound and animal. I was happy to keep him occupied this way while I scrubbed pots and pans.

After we played a few rounds of our game, he decided that Mommy should take a turn. The bubbly suds must have taken his mind to the sea and The Little Mermaid, as he said, "You're a mermaid."

I replied properly, "I'm not a mermaid! I'm a woman."

To my surprise he yelled out, "You're not a woman . . . you're a mommy!"

Ouch! Out of the mouth of babes! He was on to something. I decided he was a blooming baby genius, a two-year-old psychiatrist! His declaration showed me why it's so hard to leave a career and be a stay-at-home mom. It feels as if everyone is secretly thinking you're no longer a real woman. You've changed into some lesser creature, a mommy.

I always said I would leave my career and raise my children until they were in school, and then maybe work part-time. I had waited eleven long years before Philip was born, and I was determined to stay home. Over the years I struggled to remain content with that decision. I even tried running a consulting business out of my home that first year. But it was hard to make phone contacts between diaper changes and screams, so I decided to "be content whatever the circumstances" (Philippians 4:11) and become the best mom I could be. Eventually my writing career took off and I worked from my home office. I burned the midnight oil writing away while my little man slept.

After some self-analysis, I think I know why I struggled at first with my decision. I am a very goal-oriented person and have always felt driven to be successful. I guess you could say I'm competitive. In business I seem to have the golden touch, and I enjoyed the praise and the perks that went along with it.

But as ever, if we are open to his sculpting, God uses every situation to help us grow and create something new. Over the years, I've learned some valuable lessons since I've been at home. For example: I really don't need adulation or a big paycheck to motivate me. I found out before Philip entered school that we really could survive without a second car. I don't have to have a closet full of the latest designer clothes or a house full of new furniture. I learned to enjoy the solitude of being at home, to slow down and get back in touch with God, and to appreciate what he blessed me with. I learned a new gratefulness for the "breadwinner" in our family and stopped taking him for granted. I reflected on my child-hood and reached a whole new perspective on my mother and the years of sacrifice, love, and nurturing she gave her children.

But the most valuable treasure I received from deciding to stay home was the gift of time—the time spent with our son. I'm glad I didn't miss any of his firsts: his first hugs, first kiss, first step, and first words. What a blessing. Time with your kids is a treasure.

According to Barna Research, 78 percent of women work outside the home. I don't think any less of full-time working moms. In fact, I pray for them to be the best they can be at work and home, because they have a hard row to hoe (that's a Kentucky gardening phrase). What I find interesting is a statistic that shows a "mini-migration is taking place as women who have been running hard on the career track take a detour onto the mommy track. The Harvard and Stanford business schools have done studies demonstrating the trend. Of the female business school graduates from the Harvard class of 1981, 1986, and 1991, only 38 percent are still working today."[3] Also, there has been a report that labor-force participation among new mothers dropped for the first time in nearly twenty-five years.

There's not a clear-cut commandment to spend twenty-four hours a day with your children. Each woman has to make her own decisions and ask God for his guidance in her life. (See chapter 8, "All I Do Is Work, Work, Work," for helpful hints for the full-time working mom.) But we are instructed to love, honor, and raise our children in the Lord. "Love the Lord your God with all your heart and with all your soul and with all your strength. These commandments that I give you today are to be upon your hearts. Impress them on your children" (Deuteronomy 6:5–7).

Over a decade has flown by and now as our son spends his days at school, I spend my time writing from my home office. I thank God for allowing me to be a stay-at-home mom with Philip. And I thank God for the gift of joy Philip brings me and the never-ending love I have for him. In the end, I'm proud to say I'm no mere woman. I'm a mommy.

Mom's Journal

Titus 2:3–4 *Likewise, teach the older women to be <u>reverent</u> in the way they live, not to be **slanderers** or addicted to much wine, but to teach what is <u>good</u>. Then they can train the younger women to love their husbands and children.*

In this passage **Titus**, a <u>co-worker</u> of the apostle Paul, is now on his own in a ministry in <u>Crete</u>. Paul is writing to give him specific guidelines on how to set up the new church.

As examples, or **mentors**, older women were instructed to teach the younger women. After living long lives, and learning by trial and error, older women were not to let their "wise old age" go to waste. No matter what age we are, God has a special plan and purpose for each of us!

Paul specifically instructed older women (you know who you are) to teach younger women to love their husbands and love their children.

This passage of life called motherhood is like a relentless roller coaster. Just when you get your children to stop playing and throwing things in the toilet and want to move to potty training, they lose the fascination this

reverent
Romans 12:1
good
Philippians 4:4–9
co-worker
Galatians 2:1
Crete
Acts 27:12–13

reverent
live as if worshiping God
slanderers
gossipers; spread stories that hurt
Titus
co-worker of Paul; church leader
Crete
a large island in the Mediterranean Sea
mentors
wise, loyal advisers

invention once held for them. You live through the terrible twos and pre-school years to face the independence and stubbornness of adolescence only to encounter the alien being that took over your teenager.

The journey of parenthood is a wild ride. Put God in the driver's seat, put love in the passenger seat, and the bumps in the road will seem much smoother.

I never completely understood the love my parents had for their children until I became a parent. I now have a glimpse of the worry, confusion, misunderstandings, bond, and love that only parents share. I can also remember those haunting words of my mother, "Someday your turn will come."

As I journal this adventure of motherhood, it seems a year goes by as fast as turning a page in a book. A few pages ago our son was only a baby, and I rocked him in my arms and whispered the poem "I'll Love You Forever."

I know before long I'll turn another page and he'll be moving out on his own. I'll be left with my journal and a heart filled with precious memories all tattered, creased, and stained, but as the apostle Paul instructed the women in Crete, I'll love him forever.

Journaling Tips

A mom's journal is a great way to store treasured memories of mother-hood as you record the joys and laughter, bumps and bruises, and incredible blessings of your children.

- Buy a journal or diary (or just any old notebook). Keep it just for your personal journal.

- Record something, even just a sentence, every day for twenty-seven days to get in the habit of writing in your journal. Then record in it as often as you can.

- Jot down events and color it with sights, sounds, smells, and emotions you remember. It will make it come alive in future years when you think about days gone by.

- Be sure to write your thoughts and insights gained from yours and your children's experiences.

Someday you can pass your journal down as a legacy to your children.

Examples From the Bible

persecution
Acts 8:1–3

There are many good models of parenting in the Bible:

- Though Samson's parents objected to his marriage, they still loved him. They were disappointed, yet they showed their love by attending his wedding. (Judges 14:3–5)

- Solomon knew his mother, Bathsheba, loved him, but she feared her son Solomon would not succeed King David on the throne. So she exposed a plot by Adonijah, David's son by Haggith, another wife, to become king. In her wisdom she pleaded her son's case before the dying King David, and Solomon was named the new king of Israel. (1 Kings 1:11–31; Matthew 1:6)

- It has been speculated that the blind person in John was a boy and that his mother and father brought him to Jesus in hopes of healing. They faithfully stood beside their son and watched as Jesus spat on the ground and placed the mud over the boy's eyes. Then they led the boy to the Pool of Siloam to wash away the clay just as Jesus instructed. The parents went home with a boy who could see their loving faces for the very first time. (John 9:2)

- One of Jesus' parables portrayed God's love for us by describing an ungrateful, insulting, **prodigal** son who demanded what was in his father's will before the father had died. The son wasted the money, but when he returned home, his father ran to him, kissed and hugged him, and celebrated his return, for his "son was dead, and is alive again; he was lost, and is found" (Luke 15:24 KJV). Implicitly, these stories commend parents who love their kids. It shows that they are acting like God.

prodigal
one who spends recklessly

persecution
to oppress for reasons of religion

Kids: Ya Gotta Love 'Em

2 Peter 1:5–8 *Make every effort to add to your faith goodness; and to goodness, knowledge; and to knowledge, self-control; and to self-control, perseverance; and to perseverance, godliness; and to godliness, brotherly kindness; and to brotherly kindness, love. For if you possess these qualities in increasing measure, they will keep you from being ineffective and unproductive in your knowledge of our Lord Jesus Christ.*

The apostle Peter wrote to the Christians of the early church who endured much suffering and **persecution**, but also overcame many trials. His theme throughout the book is don't give up. He weaves wonderful words of encouragement that can apply to almost any aspect of our lives, especially to our journey of motherhood. We must improve our loving skills to grow as parents, for "by this all men will know that you are My disciples, if you have love for one another" (John 13:35 NASB).

What You Can Do

Ingredients needed to be an effective mother:

- *Faith.* Our faith and trust in Jesus Christ is the foundation of our lives and the key to being effective moms. No matter what this journey of motherhood may hold, we can overcome any trial with Christ walking by our side. "Without faith it is impossible to please God, because anyone who comes to him must believe that he exists and that he rewards those who earnestly seek him" (Hebrews 11:6). "I can do everything through him who gives me strength" (Philippians 4:13).

- *Goodness.* Goodness is a product we produce in our lives when we obey God's teachings. "I myself am convinced, my brothers, that you yourselves are full of goodness, complete in knowledge and competent to instruct one another" (Romans 15:14). "As obedient children, do not conform to the evil desires you had when you lived in ignorance. But just as he who called you is holy, so be holy in all you do" (1 Peter 1:14–15).

- *Knowledge.* As we accept God's truths we can apply them in our lives and teach them to our children. "God our Savior, who wants all men to be saved and to come to a knowledge of the truth. For there is one God and one mediator between God and men, the man Christ Jesus" (1 Timothy 2:3–5).

- *Self-control.* We are to be under God's control as we strive to do good and control our conduct. It's easy to lose your temper and lash out at your children. But we can control our anger or other emotions or actions that cause harm if we have the knowledge of God's Word, the help of the Holy Spirit, and wise counsel. "Anyone, then, who knows the good he ought to do and doesn't do it, sins" (James 4:17).

- *Perseverance.* Continue in your Christian walk. Be patient. Don't give up. Keep praying. Don't give up on parenting. Hang in there and pray yourself through it. "And pray in the Spirit on all occasions with all kinds of prayers and requests. With this in mind, be alert and always keep on praying for all the saints" (Ephesians 6:18).

- *Godliness.* God lives within our hearts and souls, and we are to act like him and be devoted to him. As our children see how we live our lives, they will be drawn to God as they see God living in us. Our actions truly speak louder than our words. "Godliness has value for all things, holding promise for both the present life and the life to come" (1 Timothy 4:8).

- *Brotherly kindness.* Brotherly love for another believer is love that comes from the heart. Our children will learn how simple acts of kindness touch lives as we extend kindness to others. "Now that you have purified yourselves by obeying the truth so that you have sincere love for your brothers, love one another deeply, from the heart" (1 Peter 1:22).

- *Love.* As we love God, we are to love one another and our children— no matter what they do. We may approve or disapprove, but we still love them as God loves us. It's the greatest commandment. "Above all, love each other deeply, because love covers over a multitude of sins" (1 Peter 4:8).

As moms, we can't give up. We must keep on loving our children through the good and bad times, relying on God's instruction and help.

Years ago I was asked to conduct a workshop on loving your children. I went straight to the source and asked our five-year-old son, "When do you feel the most loved?" Without hesitation he answered, "When you give me hugs and kisses and when Dad wrestles me."

With age, his answer to that question will change. Later I'll probably hear answers like "When you let me do my own thing," or "When you give me my own credit card." But whatever stage you are in with your children, they need to know your love through word and action. We must balance the tender side of love and the tough side of love. We must learn our children's personalities and which of the **languages of love** each responds to. What makes them feel loved? How do they communicate their love? How do we communicate our love to them? Find the language of love your child understands and use it.

languages of love
person's preferred way to receive affection—a word, a touch, a present, a service
procreation
producing offspring

How Others See It

James Dobson

I should warn those who have not yet assumed the responsibilities of parenthood; the game of raising kids is more difficult than it looks. Parenthood is costly and complex. Am I suggesting, then, that newly married couples should remain childless? Certainly not! The family that loves children and wants to experience the thrill of **procreation** should not be frightened by the challenge of parenthood. Speaking from my own perspective as a father, there has been no greater moment in my life than when I gazed into the eyes of my infant daughter, and five years later, my son. What could be more exciting than seeing those tiny human beings begin to blossom and grow and learn and love? And what reward could be more meaningful than having my little boy or girl climb onto my lap as I sit by the fire, hug my neck, and whisper, "I love you, Dad." Oh, yes, children are expensive, but they're worth the price. Besides, nothing worth having comes cheap.[4]

Stitching Prayers

*I have a confession to make. I have a favorite blankie. Yes, I'm a closet cuddler. When I married, I had to give up my teddy bear. But I kept my blankie **incognito**, as an ordinary blanket at the foot of the bed, just in case it got too cold.*

It's a special, one-of-a-kind blanket. It's a quilt, handcrafted by my granny Curtis and my great-grandmother Mommy Duck (she waddled like a duck—hence, the nickname). It was a family tradition to make each grandchild a quilt when they were born. Their kids kept them busy with fourteen grandchildren.

To me, it's not just a quilt; it is a patchwork treasure chest filled with wonderful memories.

Both of these godly women are gone now, yet they seem close as I cuddle my soft, worn blankie. I can visualize them around the quilting hoop, hard at work as they chat about their family and the latest grand- child. Dreaming of what the future would hold for their grandchildren, and hoping to share many years with them, they said little prayers as they stitched away, stitch by stitch by stitch.

Hannah
I Samuel I and 2

incognito
with identity disguised

Nazirite
person who devoted his life to God; would not drink wine or cut his hair

It reminds me of <u>Hannah,</u> a godly childless woman, who year after year went to the temple and prayed for a son. In making deals with God, she vowed if God blessed her, she would give up her son, and commit him to be a **Nazirite**. At one temple visit, her downcast soul was lifted when the priest pronounced God's blessing upon her. Later, Hannah and her hus- band conceived a child. True to her vow, Hannah gave her son, Samuel, to the priest, to serve in the temple. Year after year, she made a special cloak for her son and journeyed to the temple to present it to him. You can imagine Hannah designing this coat in her mind, then spending long hours clipping the sheep, brushing the wool clean, crushing and boiling roots and berries to create brilliant colors, dyeing the wool, and then weaving the yarn so tightly. Perhaps with each stitch she prayed for her

WHAT'S IN THE BIBLE FOR WOMEN

son, stitch by stitch by stitch . . . stitching prayers, if you will, asking God's blessing on her son in her absence. With the help of his mother's prayers, Samuel grew to be the greatest Hebrew <u>prophet</u> since Moses.

Do we pray stitching prayers for our children and those we love? Anything we do needs to be stitched in prayer. It's the thread that holds our lives together. Prayer strengthens, comforts, encourages, heals, and gives us peace of mind, as we give everything to God. If a stitch in time saves nine, perhaps stitching prayers can save even the one in <u>99</u>.

I Never Wanted to Be a Teacher

1 KINGS 2:2–3 *"I am about to go the way of all the earth," he said. "So be strong, show yourself a man, and observe what the Lord your God requires: Walk in his ways, and keep his **decrees** and **commands**, his **laws** and requirements, as written in the **<u>Law of Moses</u>**, so that you may prosper in all you do and wherever you go."*

One of my favorite parental scenes in the Bible is in 1 Kings 2:2–4. Solomon is at his father's deathbed as King David is giving his final instruction to his son. Don't you find it interesting that David didn't dwell on the "Ten Management Tips for Running the Kingdom"? With his last breath, David was still teaching his son. I'm sure the charge to "walk in his ways" lingering in Solomon's ears was the key to his <u>success</u> as he ruled the kingdom.

"Walk in his ways." Those same words can be key to the success of our children in life too.

How many times have you heard little girls say, "I want to be a teacher when I grow up"? I don't think I ever said those words. When she was in grade school, my sister Sherry already knew she wanted to teach. She kept to her goal, and over the years she's taught them all—elementary through college. My sister Connie is a fabulous preschool teacher as well. She loves it!

Little did I know that parenting is all about teaching.

I am a researcher, by nature. I don't go into anything without knowing a little bit about the subject first. I remember when I was pregnant I read everything I could get my hands on about pregnancy. Then when our son was born I lived by the book *What to Expect the First Year*. But even with all the books and advice on the library shelves, we must always thank God for his instruction manual, the Bible, where we can find out how to raise our

prophet
Jeremiah 15:1
99
Luke 15:4, 7
Law of Moses
Exodus 20:1–17;
Joshua 23:6
success
1 Kings 10:1

decrees
laws that are declared publicly
commands
rules given by God applying to all people
laws
commands by God that tell people what they should or should not do
Law of Moses
the Ten Commandments and all related laws

children the way God wants us to. The most important aspect of this teaching profession called parenting is to instill in our children the Word of God.

What You Can Do

As David taught Solomon, what do we teach our children about walking with God?

- *Walk in INTEGRITY.* If we walk in God's ways, we will be surefooted and will not slip and fall into sin. "The man of integrity walks securely, but he who takes crooked paths will be found out" (Proverbs 10:9).

- *Walk in NEWNESS.* Don't live the way unbelievers live. They are far away from God. Your attitudes and thoughts must be different from theirs. Walk in goodness and holiness. "You were taught, with regard to your former way of life, to put off your old self, which is being corrupted by its deceitful desires; to be made new in the attitude of your minds; and to put on the new self, created to be like God in true righteousness and holiness" (Ephesians 4:22–24).

- *Walk by FAITH.* Trust that God's ways and teachings are true. "We live by faith, not by sight" (2 Corinthians 5:7).

- *Walk in LOVE.* As a child imitates his father, we are to follow the example of our heavenly Father and walk in love, just as Christ loved us. "Be imitators of God, therefore, as dearly loved children and live a life of love, just as Christ loved us and gave himself up for us as a fragrant offering and sacrifice to God" (Ephesians 5:1–2).

- *Walk in JESUS.* Just as you trusted Christ and made him Lord of your life, now walk in him, gain strength and truth from him. Just as a plant is nourished and rooted deep within the ground, you can build life on Christ's teachings. "So then, just as you received Christ Jesus as Lord, continue to live in him, rooted and built up in him, strengthened in the faith as you were taught, and overflowing with thankfulness" (Colossians 2:6–7).

The task of raising children is not so overwhelming when we realize that success in life will come when we teach them to walk in God's ways. We need not consume ourselves with dreams of having our children become rocket scientists or Nobel Prize winners. Our main responsibility is to help develop their inner lives and instruct them in the way of the Lord.

I asked a friend, Denise Nowery, to share her "thoughts from a mother's heart":

> *How do I begin with answering that one? I feel like I have been a mother since I was little and to know why, you would have to know my testimony of how I grew up. I'll spare you all the details for now, but I do feel that how I was raised has a lot to do with the journey that I am now on with the Lord.*
>
> *I have always loved every aspect of "caring for another," especially with children. Their lives are so dependent on others. And we, as adults, have that ability to add to or take away something special. Matthew, being the baby of the family, the last to leave home, tried really hard to come home on weekends for my sake. To make it even easier for me, Matthew moved back home for his last year of college. Out of my three children, I would have to say that Matthew kept me on my knees. He was the one child that did not openly express his commitment to God. It is said that people can tell what we love just by what we spend our time on. It has caused me to think deeply about how much time I have spent with my precious three, my family, others, and my Lord. Well, as any praying mother knows, we are to keep praying, because God is working all the time. Even when we sometimes wonder where he is. Matthew graduated in May 2006 from the Terry Business School at the University of Georgia. He was highly sought by some of the largest companies in the nation. He went to every interview but came home each time discouraged. He kept saying to his father and me that this was not the right place for him. Little did we know that God had a bigger plan for his life, a real "adventure" just for him. I say adventure because both of my boys are true adventurers. If they could go back in time and be Huckleberry Finn or Daniel Boone, they would.*
>
> *Just weeks after many turned-down offers, Franklin Graham called and asked to see Ashley, our daughter, and Matthew. Ashley and Matt had sent applications in to Samaritan's Purse unbeknownst to us. Within two days, we were sitting with Franklin Graham, listening to the stories of the great need of the people of Sudan.*
>
> *Of course they both went to Sudan, but Matt immediately was the one that said, "Sign me up." My heart instantly leaped for joy, for God had answered my prayers that I had prayed to him for many, many years. I was not as surprised as my husband, however, because God has always worked for me in the most unusual, mysterious ways, just like*

ordained
Exodus 28:41
encouragement
Philippians 2:19–20
timid
1 Corinthians
16:10–11

ordained
set apart

many other mothers I know. God has been so faithful! Matthew left ten days later, and I did not see him again for six months—the day after his twenty-fourth birthday. That was truly a gift for both of us.

I landed in the Sudan with his favorite cake in hand. Our celebration together was far greater than his being a year older. He was on the adventure of a lifetime. One I knew in my heart God had picked just for him. It was so obvious to see from the minute I landed that Matthew was in his element. The timing was God's. Every part of it was God's plan for Matthew's life. The acceptance of it from Matthew reassured my heart that prayers never go unanswered. He is always working, so there's no need to wonder.

Just last week Matthew called, and I asked him, "When are you coming home, son?" He answered, "Mom, home is where I am." With tears in my eyes, and quite choked up, I responded with, "Yes, home is where your heart is." Matthew's heart beats for those precious souls in Africa. Yes, he misses all of us terribly, but is there any greater joy or peace in a mother's heart than to know that her children are walking in the ways of the Lord? It is a precious promise for all of us. . . . He awaits for us to cling to it.

No mother knows when she may be raising another David or Nehemiah.

I Only Want the Best for My Child

2 TIMOTHY 1:6–7 *For this reason I remind you to fan into flame the gift of God, which is in you through the laying on of my hands. For God did not give us a spirit of timidity, but a spirit of power, of love and of self-discipline.*

In 2 Timothy, Paul writes his farewell letter from prison to Timothy, who had been his faithful partner in ministry for more than fifteen years. Paul encourages Timothy to "fan into flame the gift of God." This was the very gift Paul had prayed over and blessed when he laid his hands on Timothy and **ordained** him into ministry. Paul was reminding and encouraging Timothy to use his God-given gifts of <u>encouragement</u> and a sensitive heart. As we read between the lines of 1 and 2 Timothy, it appears Timothy may have been shy or <u>timid</u>. Paul exhorted him to carry on his mission in confidence.

We can use Paul's encouragement to Timothy as a model. As parents, we too want to encourage our children to discover their unique gifts and carry out their own special mission in life.

98 ———————— WHAT'S IN THE BIBLE FOR WOMEN ————————

Every child is different. Every child has unique gifts. You don't have to be a psychologist to notice that your child has his own individual quirks and is gifted in a certain area. But you do have to be a wise mother to understand your child and bring out the best in him or her.

In our son's class, each child has a different bent or gift. Lindsay loves ballet and excels in dance. Aubrey tries to take care of everyone's needs, always remembering to pray for them. Philip is a talented artist who sees life in intricate details. Jason is a math whiz and can build a Lego town in a flash. The world awaits this class of 2010 filled with Olympic medal winners, missionaries, artists, and inventors. I wonder how their lives will impact the world.

I highly recommend a fabulous author, Cynthia Tobias, who is an expert on the subject of **learning styles**. I became a fan of hers when Philip entered preschool. She has made a world of difference in how I appreciate, respond to, and nurture our son's special gifts and learning styles. She cuts through all the technical mumbo jumbo and helps you appreciate the different ways in which children receive, process, and respond to information. She can help you remove a lot of unnecessary frustration at home and at school while helping your kids achieve greater self-esteem.

As mothers we need to plant seeds of confidence and fan the flame in our children. We need to encourage our children in their area of giftedness. God has great plans for your child, just as he did for Timothy. He created each of us one of a kind. A child raised in an environment of encouragement and confidence may change the world. You can bring out the best in your children when you understand their unique giftedness.

How Others See It

Cynthia Tobias

Often the characteristics and behaviors that annoy us most about our children will be the qualities that make them successful as adults. You may feel your child talks too much or moves too much or takes too many chances, and yet those are some of the traits that are consistently found in successful entrepreneurs and business leaders. Although you must maintain bottom-line accountability and discipline, remember that the children who may be most inconvenient for you now may, when they grow up, turn out to be the best thing that ever happened to this world![5]

quiet
Judges 13:6
reverent
Judges 13:6
confronted
Judges 14:3

kosher
clean according to
Jewish dietetic law

Snapshots of Women in the Bible
Samson's Mom (Judges 13–15)

The Scripture gives her no name. She is only referred to as someone's wife and someone's mother. But there was a time when she felt no one would even call her mother. In her story, a barren, faithful woman and a barren, fallen nation come face-to-face.

An angel of the Lord appeared to Manoah's wife. It's not recorded where this first revelation took place. But in the glimpses Scripture gives us, I see a woman of character; <u>quiet</u>, obedient, and <u>reverent</u> to God's commandments while, in the sinking nation around her, "everyone did as he saw fit" (Judges 21:25). I believe she may have been alone in prayer, praising the Creator and calling on him to save the nation that now lived under the control of the Philistines.

The angel's message brought joy and hope. Her empty arms would be filled and her son Samson would begin to deliver Israel out of the hands of the Philistines. Her son had a religious mission, and thus was to be set apart as a lifetime Nazirite. The angel instructed her even in pregnancy not to drink wine or anything from the fruit of the vine and not to eat anything that was not **kosher**, so as not to defile the child in her womb.

Samson was born, and the Lord blessed him and his mother. She dedicated herself to God and raised her son for his mission.

Parenting didn't stop when Samson was grown and making choices on his own. When he chose to go against God's command by marrying a woman who worshiped other gods, Manoah and his wife <u>confronted</u> him and protested his choice. They reminded him of his vows.

I'm sure the heart of Samson's mother grieved as she watched her son, a miracle baby, a man with God-given strength, cave in to moral weakness. He gave himself over to passion, lust, and sin—sin that eventually ended his potential for becoming a great judge.

During Samson's last stand, when he was blinded and tied to the pillars (see Illustration #6), I wonder if he reflected on the women in his life. What sharp contrasts! Delilah, a sinful, deceitful woman he forsook all to have, betrayed him for silver. His mother, a woman of character, loved, understood, encouraged, and remained faithful to God. He must have thought of his mother, or at least remembered his mother's teachings; for he repented of his selfishness, and God gave him strength enough to bring down the building onto the Philistines—and himself. Though his life was cut short, he did begin the deliverance of Israel, just as the Lord foretold to his mother before his birth.

As mothers, we don't know how our kids will turn out. We are not called to be enforcers of the faith, but like Samson's mother, we are called to be obedient to the faith—to love, pray for, encourage, and instruct our children in the way of the Lord.

think about it

How Others See It

George Washington

My mother was the most beautiful woman I ever saw. All I am I owe to my mother. I attribute all my success in life to the moral, intellectual, and physical education I received from my mother.[6]

M-O-M-S (Moms Offering Moms Support)

1 THESSALONIANS 5:11 *Therefore encourage one another and build each other up, just as in fact you are doing.*

In Paul's letter to the believers in Thessalonica, he deals with the questions concerning the <u>second coming</u> of Jesus. They wanted to know: <u>What</u> happens to those who die before Jesus returns? <u>When</u> will he return? And in the meantime, how should we live?

Paul answers in verse 11 how we should live in the Christian community while we wait. As people <u>belonging</u> to God, we are to encourage one another in our daily lives. In our everyday walk as moms, we learn from both Paul and women of the Bible to encourage one another.

check this out

second coming
John 14:2–3
What
Luke 23:43
When
I Thessalonians 5:2
belonging
I Peter 2:1–10

John Mark
an apostle of Christ;
assisted Paul and Peter

Upper Room
the room where Jesus
had the Last Supper
with his disciples

Examples From the Bible

Women who offered support:

- After Mary the mother of Jesus found out she was pregnant, she spent three months with her cousin Elizabeth (who was pregnant with John the Baptist). They ministered to each other during her stay. (Luke 1:39–56)

- Lydia, a businesswoman of Philippi, encouraged and met with other women at the riverbank to pray and worship. (Acts 16:13–15)

- Mary the mother of **John Mark** supported her friends and the establishing of the church by opening her home to others to come and pray. (Acts 12:12, 25)

- Mary the mother of Jesus met with other women and the apostles in the **Upper Room** in Jerusalem. They came together to pray, encourage, and comfort one another after Jesus had ascended into heaven. (Acts 1:14)

heart to heart

My roots run deep in the foothills of the Appalachian Mountains in Kentucky. The area is known for its heritage in mountain crafts such as cane-bottom chairs, handcrafted dolls, and beautiful quilts. During the Depression, mountain moms made little corn-shuck dolls and hand-stitched quilts from colorful rags and sold them in New York City craft stores. That was how they provided desperately needed income for their families.

Isolation helped create these world-renowned mountain crafts. You didn't get out much in the back hills and hollows of the mountains, and the necessities of life were either not available or you had no funds to acquire them. So you made them.

In museums around Kentucky you can see black-and-white photos of women gathered around a quilting hoop, or groups of gals churning butter or clustering around a hot stove or canning food while little kids play around their feet. Any of these tasks could have been accomplished at home, alone. But they knew that work was made easier when accomplished with a friend. In fact, life was made easier when lived and shared with a friend. Woes were shared, emotions were mended, and prayers lifted up as traditions and values were passed around the quilting hoop.

Times haven't changed that much. Isolation is still a big factor with moms. We're a mobile society and move thousands of miles away from the support of our own mothers, grandmothers, and extended families. Moms need support from other moms. Don't go it alone.

Moms can feel isolated in their own four walls, and need support. I encourage you to get that support through a local church group or through an organization like MOPS (Mothers of Preschoolers). I recently came across a great ministry for moms called Hearts at Home, founded by Jill Savage. If you are online you can check them out on the Web at *www.hearts-at-home.org*. You'll find challenging articles, a bulletin board, secular and Christian networking opportunities for moms at home, and information on their regional conferences designed to encourage mothers at home (and those who want to be stay-at-home moms).

As you involve yourself in your Christian community of moms, you won't feel so alone. Sharing the common bond of motherhood will develop long-lasting friendships, renew hearts, convey truths, and lift up prayers. You'll return home refreshed and ready to meet the needs of your family.

How Others See It

Donna Partow

Young mothers today rarely have the ready-made support system offered by nearby family members, the kind of support that our mothers and grandmothers could take for granted. That's why it is so important for you to take the initiative to join an organization like MOPS (Mothers of Preschoolers) or similar mothers' group. Chances are the other mothers in the group struggle with the exact same issues you face. Don't wait for someone to reach out to you, take the initiative and set the pace.[7]

The Lasting Impressions of a Mother's Love

In the summer of 1997 a nation mourned the loss of their princess. The world grieved as Princess Diana, the most watched woman in the world, was buried.

I confess I'm a news junkie—and during that week, I wrestled the channel changer out of the King of the Remote's hands and watched countless news shows covering the story. Daily, I read local and national newspapers and magazines to keep up on breaking news. Through the tragedy, what impressed me most about this fairy-tale princess was a thread that reporters wove into all the coverage. From dignitaries to lowly ordinary citizens, the people spoke of the love Princess Diana had for her sons.

A Newsweek headline read, "A Mother Before All Else." The subtitle said, "Even Diana's critics praise the way she raised her boys. How will they cope in the years ahead?"

That same summer I attended the funerals of two mothers. The first was a thirty-eight-year-old wife and mother of two young sons. All who mourned with the family had concern for the children left behind and silently wondered how they would cope.

A few weeks later I attended the funeral of a sixty-two-year-old wife and mother of nine children. Even though these children were adults, their mother seemed to be the glue that held their extended family together. I had concern for the children left behind and silently wondered how they would cope.

If you asked the children left behind how they cope now, I'm sure they would say they cling to memories. Memories of a gentle touch. A loving gesture. An infectious smile. Memories of a loving mother.

Mary, the mother of Jesus, met in the Upper Room with the other believers after Jesus had ascended back to heaven (John 20:17). I imagine the women gathered around Mary, offering the encouragement and support she so desperately needed. She held memories in her heart not only of a smiling son, but of a sacrificial Savior pouring out his blood. Memories of a powerless mother watching in helpless agony as they crucified her son. An angel's message thirty-three years earlier made her spirit rejoice, yet a prophet warned her that a sword would pierce her heart. Scripture records three times that Mary "treasured all these things in her heart."

Whether we must watch the death of a child, as Mary did, or stand helplessly by and watch one dear to us destroy himself or herself with bad choices, we have a Savior who knows what suffering is. He can comfort us in our own suffering. One way he sends strength and encouragement is through other women who cross our paths, offering their friendship in our times of need.

Final Thoughts

- A mother has the blessing of loving and being loved by her children. She has the power to create, sustain, and shape another life and the responsibility to carry out her mission in God's way. Look to his Word for wisdom in fulfilling this role of mothering.

- Children are a gift from God. He delights in his children and provides mothers with a special gift—a heart transformed into a treasure box filled with an abundance of love. This loving heart pulls you to be with your children.

- Get a better understanding of your children by discovering their learning styles. As much as possible, accept who they are. Major in developing their strengths.

- Motherhood can be lonely and a time of isolation as you spend most of your waking hours with your children. Look to other moms for support. You will find encouragement from other women as you travel down this road together.

Questions to Deepen Your Understanding

1. Children are a gift from God. According to Deuteronomy 6:5–7, what are we to impress upon our children?

2. The apostle Paul instructed older women to teach younger women. What were they to teach them to do?

3. How did Hannah help her son, Samuel, grow to be one of the greatest Hebrew prophets?

4. Based on the example of King David giving instructions to his son Solomon, what instruction can we parents give our children that is key to their success in life?

5. As parents, what can we learn from Samson's mother?

6. What gift did God give believers that fills us with hope, confidence, and safety?

7. As Eunice raised her son Timothy alone, what did she do that had the most important influence on his life?

read on

Some of Georgia's favorite books for realizing the blessings, power, and responsibilities of a mother's love:

• *The Birth Order Book*, Dr. Kevin Leman, Revell

• *Bringing Out the Best in Your Child*, Cynthia Ulrich Tobias and Carol Funk, Gospel Light

• *Every Child Can Succeed*, Cynthia Ulrich Tobias, Tyndale House

• *Got Teens? Time-Tested Answers for Moms of Teens and Tweens*, Jill Savage and Pam Farrell, Zondervan

• *A Mom's Ordinary Day Bible Study Series*, Zondervan

• *Mothers and Sons: Raising Boys to Be Men*, Jean Lush and Pam Vrdeevelt, Baker Books

• *The Power of a Praying Parent*, Stormie Ormartian, Harvest House

• *The Power of Mother Love*, Dr. Brenda Hunter, WaterBrook Press

• *Professionalizing Motherhood*, Jill Savage, Zondervan

• *Trend-Savvy Parenting*, Dr. Mary Manz Simon, Tyndale

• *Your Girl: Raising a Godly Daughter in an Ungodly World*, Vicki Courtney, Broadman and Holman

Chapter 5: Home Front or Battlefront?

Developing Meaningful Relationships Within Your Family

What's in This Chapter

- God's Miracle of Love
- The Love Triangle
- God's Wedding Trousseau
- The Train Whistle
- Snapshot: Rebekah
- Her Role—His Role
- Tough Times in a Troubled Marriage
- The Middle Ground—Finding Solutions for Everyday, Ordinary Problems
- SOS!
- All the Queen's Horses . . .
- Decisions, Decisions: In or Out?
- Separation or Divorce?
- Separation

Here We Go

I've always said I could get along with my family if it just weren't for the people involved. Too many times the home front slowly turns into a battlefront where the family fights a daily war. The arsenal is filled with the ammunition of hurtful words fired back and forth at one another. Children get caught in the cross fire and suffer battle fatigue. The home becomes less of a collection of adjoining rooms and more like separate barracks in various occupied territories. Individuals don't unite and support one another; to survive, they hunker in their bunkers.

foundation
the fundamental principle on which something is founded

As Dr. Phil would ask, "How's that working for you?" Strong, loving families raise children who build strong, loving relationships inside and outside the fort called home.

We want to raise strong children because, among other reasons, they are the **foundation** for our future. In turn, God is the foundation we build our children upon, for "unless the Lord builds the house, its builders labor in vain" (Psalm 127:1).

How we get along with one another will determine if we live in a war zone or live in peace. The heartbeat of the family is the woman, who somehow holds it together. She may be a mom, wife, sister, or daughter, but she seems to most often be the peacekeeper. She's called to love her family—beginning with loving her husband.

united
Genesis 2:23–24

check this out

How Others See It

John C. Maxwell

The best thing you can do to strengthen your family is build your marriage relationship. It's certainly the best thing you can do for your spouse, but it also has an incredibly positive impact on your children. My friend Josh McDowell wisely stated, "The greatest thing a father can do for his children is to love their mother." And the greatest thing a mother can do for her children is to love their father.[1]

God's Miracle of Love

GENESIS 2:18 (NASB) *Then the Lord God said, "It is not good for the man to be alone; I will make him a helper suitable for him."*

I read it in a magazine, so I know it must be true. It's here! No longer do you have to go to your local witch doctor for a brew; you can drive to your nearest department store for your very own love potion. It will cost you sixty bucks for a tenth of an ounce, but the manufacturer maintains it will boost your attractiveness, and satisfied customers will prove it. They claim it has something to do with molecules and the science of love.

The article on the science of love was fascinating as it broke down the chemistry of love and began to explain why opposites attract and why couples stay together even in the worst of times. While that may be interesting, I have a much simpler explanation.

God designed this concept of love. God created Eve as a helpmate to Adam. Poor guy, he was lonely. That's why opposites attract—men need help. They need a balance, a different perspective, and as much as men hate to admit it, a woman completes a man. God completed Adam when he created Eve from his side. He was her flesh and bone. They were <u>united</u> as one—physically, sexually, spiritually, and emotionally. It was the miracle that completed creation. The same miracle completes a man and a woman's marriage today as a wife becomes one with her husband.

When I saw the article on the love potion, I almost ran out to snatch up a bottle, but then I realized a tenth of an ounce wouldn't last very long and changed my mind. Love may be a science, but it's also a gift from our Creator and a choice. Love isn't sprayed from a bottle; love is deep within our hearts and souls.

The Love Triangle

GENESIS 2:23–24 *The man said, "This is now bone of my bones and flesh of my flesh; she shall be called 'woman,' for she was taken out of man." For this reason a man will leave his father and mother and be united to his wife, and they will become one flesh.*

For every two couples who get married there is one divorce. Because of this, churches around the country are encouraging a form of marriage covenant called the Community Marriage Agreement. Some states offer this strict agreement as an alternative to a regular marriage license. In a nutshell, under this agreement divorce is no option—you commit to a covenant of faithfulness.

Covenants are standing contracts between two partners. This unique relationship called marriage is between a husband and a wife, where a man and a woman can live in a sexual relationship within the approval and laws of their social group. A Christian union takes it one step further. It is a covenant between a man, a woman, and God—a love triangle. If that triangle is kept intact, a lifelong commitment to faithfulness can stand the test of time as two become one. Love is not merely emotion. Love is primarily choice and action.

Bob Russell, minister of one of the largest churches in America, Southeast Christian Church in Louisville, Kentucky, has a wonderful book, *Marriage by the Book*. He writes that before performing a marriage ceremony he almost always counsels with a couple and will draw a triangle on a piece of paper and write at the top "God," and at the lower corners, "husband" and "wife." Then, tracing the ascending lines of the triangle, he points out how the closer you get to God, the closer you become to each other.[3]

God's Wedding Trousseau

COLOSSIANS 3:12–14 *Therefore, as God's chosen people, holy and dearly loved, clothe yourselves with compassion, kindness, humility, gentleness and patience. Bear with each other and forgive whatever grievances you may have against one another. Forgive as the Lord forgave you. And over all these virtues put on love, which binds them all together in perfect unity.*

Something old, something new, something borrowed, something blue. I'm sure those words have a ring of familiarity, especially in the month of June. Like many of you, I was a summer bride. We just celebrated our anniversary, and fun-filled memories flooded my mind.

I sat back and tried to remember what I had for the four traditional wardrobe items needed to wed. "Something old" was a Bible of my husband's grandmother I held with my bouquet. "Something new" was my beautiful Southern-belle wedding gown. "Something borrowed" was a hat and a veil that were perfect for my dress that I borrowed from my girlfriend Karen. And "something blue" was an antique hanky with blue embroidered flowers.

With all wedding items in place, as tradition says, we were destined for a wonderful marriage and new life.

The apostle Paul's letter to the church at Colossae underscores that in this new life in Christ, believers are starting anew—the old life is dead. Believers could toss out the old clothing; God laid out a new wardrobe for their brand-new life in Christ.

Likewise, when we unite in holy matrimony, we leave our old lives behind and start a brand-new life with a new wardrobe as a married couple—united together in Christ. He gives us ingredients not only for a successful walk in life, but also ingredients for our hearts and actions for a successful walk down the aisle and throughout the journey called marriage.

God's Wedding Trousseau

Spiritual Clothing	Scripture
Compassion (loving-kindness, mercy)	• "He has caused his wonders to be remembered; the Lord is gracious and compassionate" (Psalm 111:4). • "Jesus called his disciples to him and said, 'I have compassion for these people'" (Matthew 15:32). • "Finally, all of you, live in harmony with one another; be sympathetic, love as brothers, be compassionate and humble. Do not repay evil with evil or insult with insult, but with blessing, because to this you were called so that you may inherit a blessing" (1 Peter 3:8–9).
Kindness (goodness, loyalty)	• "As servants of God we commend ourselves in every way . . . in purity, understanding, patience and kindness" (2 Corinthians 6:4, 6). • "Be kind and compassionate to one another, forgiving each other, just as in Christ God forgave you" (Ephesians 4:32). • "She openeth her mouth with wisdom; and in her tongue is the law of kindness" (Proverbs 31:26 KJV).
Gentleness	• "A gentle answer turns away wrath, but a harsh word stirs up anger" (Proverbs 15:1). • "Be completely humble and gentle; be patient, bearing with one another in love" (Ephesians 4:2). • "[Your beauty] should be that of your inner self, the unfading beauty of a gentle and quiet spirit, which is of great worth in God's sight" (1 Peter 3:4).
Humility	• "The fear of the Lord teaches a man wisdom, and humility comes before honor" (Proverbs 15:33). • "Humility and the fear of the Lord bring wealth and honor and life" (Proverbs 22:4). • "Humble yourselves before the Lord, and he will lift you up" (James 4:10). • [Jesus spoke,] "Take my yoke upon you and learn from me, for I am gentle and humble in heart, and you will find rest for your souls" (Matthew 11:29).

God's Wedding Trousseau (cont'd)

Spiritual Clothing	Scripture
Humility (cont'd)	• "For whoever exalts himself will be humbled, and whoever humbles himself will be exalted" (Matthew 23:12). • "Humble yourselves, therefore, under God's mighty hand, that he may lift you up in due time. Cast all your anxiety on him because he cares for you" (1 Peter 5:6–7).
Patience	• "The end of a matter is better than its beginning, and patience is better than pride" (Ecclesiastes 7:8). • "Love is patient, love is kind" (1 Corinthians 13:4). • "Being strengthened with all power according to his glorious might so that you may have great endurance and patience" (Colossians 1:11).
Forgiveness	• "You are forgiving and good, O Lord, abounding in love to all who call to you. Hear my prayer, O Lord; listen to my cry for mercy" (Psalm 86:5–6). • "Forgive us our debts, as we also have forgiven our debtors" (Matthew 6:12). • "For if you forgive men when they sin against you, your heavenly Father will also forgive you" (Matthew 6:14). • "If you forgive anyone, I also forgive him. And what I have forgiven—if there was anything to forgive—I have forgiven in the sight of Christ for your sake" (2 Corinthians 2:10).
Love	• "Hatred stirs up dissension, but love covers all wrongs" (Proverbs 10:12). • "A new command I give you: Love one another. As I have loved you, so you must love one another. By this all men will know that you are my disciples, if you love one another" (John 13:34–35). • "Be imitators of God, therefore, as dearly loved children and live a life of love, just as Christ loved us and gave himself up for us as a fragrant offering and sacrifice to God" (Ephesians 5:1–2). • "Husbands, love your wives and do not be harsh with them" (Colossians 3:19).

God's Wedding Trousseau (cont'd)

Spiritual Clothing	Scripture
Love (cont'd)	• "Above all, love each other deeply, because love covers over a multitude of sins" (1 Peter 4:8). • "Then they [older women] can train the younger women to love their husbands and children" (Titus 2:4). • "Dear friends, let us love one another, for love comes from God" (1 John 4:7).
Unity	• "Teach me your way, O Lord, and I will walk in your truth; give me an undivided heart, that I may fear your name" (Psalm 86:11). • "Make every effort to keep the unity of the Spirit through the bond of peace" (Ephesians 4:3). • "If you have any encouragement from being united with Christ, if any comfort from his love, if any fellowship with the Spirit, if any tenderness and compassion, then make my joy complete by being like-minded, having the same love, being one in spirit and purpose. Do nothing out of selfish ambition or vain conceit, but in humility consider others better than yourselves. Each of you should look not only to your own interests, but also to the interests of others. Your attitude should be the same as that of Christ Jesus" (Philippians 2:1–5).

The Train Whistle

All was quiet in the house. I was up late, burning the midnight oil, getting caught up on some writing. A cool breeze blew through an open window, and I heard the faint sound of a train's whistle, as the train moved down the tracks.

The whistle took me on a journey as I remembered our first little apartment that was situated by a railroad track. I could almost feel the room shake as it did many years ago when that train rumbled down the tracks every night at midnight. You could set your clock by it.

Ah! Such sweet memories. Young newlyweds, fresh out of college and ready to conquer the world.

We set up housekeeping in an efficiency apartment. When I say efficiency, I mean efficiency. It was teensy-weensy. We had a little storage trailer parked right outside our door left over from my husband's traveling days with a gospel quartet. It was our spare closet. We used it to store our clothes and other items that wouldn't fit into the apartment. The bathroom was so small you could use the shower, brush your teeth, and weigh yourself all at the same time. The bed was so close to the stove you didn't have to leave the bed to cook. It gave a new meaning to breakfast in bed. But we were newlyweds, we were in love, and those things didn't seem to matter as long as we were together.

But before too long, the honeymoon wore off and all of a sudden that apartment was way too small. We needed our own space. Needless to say, we found a larger duplex and hence the search-and-find mission for something bigger and better began and continued for years to come.

Sometimes I long for those simpler days when all we needed to survive was love, dreams, and peanut-butter sandwiches. But I know if we'd stayed in that state of mind, we wouldn't have grown and matured in the relationship that has sustained us through the years.

We're still in love, but it's a deeper, more meaningful love. We've grown together and love each other more now than ever. We've shared the everyday walk of life and the emotions and conflicts that go along with it. We've fought, but we've made up. We've comforted each other in times of sorrow and death. We've packed and unpacked moving vans way too many times. We've experienced the pain of losing a baby and the jubilation of the birth of our son. We've raised him together and watched him mature into a godly young man. We've been on the brink of divorce but, by the grace and faithfulness of God, made it through. We've been broke, and we've prospered. I know we would not have made it on our own. I credit our marriage to the common love we share in Christ—a love not formed on romance alone, but on the unity of one in Christ with like goals, dreams, and purpose.

The train traveled on down the tracks and the whistle faded, but the memories of our life together will never fade from my heart. We will continue to build upon our past and look forward to our future, rumbling down the tracks of life, journeying together hand in hand.

What You Can Do

Five Little Things You Can Do to Strengthen Your Marriage:

1. Love your spouse as you wish to be loved.

2. Do an unexpected act of kindness. "Sweet nothings" can mean everything in the midst of a hurried and harried day.

3. Find something to praise your spouse for: a personal quality, a nice outfit, a recent accomplishment.

4. Make a date with your spouse. Husbands and wives need time alone together. Set a date and time tonight.

5. Forgive your spouse for anything he may have done to upset you. Let him know immediately that he is forgiven.[4]

Snapshots of Women in the Bible
Rebekah (Genesis 24:1–67)

She knew when they looked at her they envisioned beautiful grand-children to carry on their names. She heard them bartering with her father, trying to arrange for their sons to marry her, but her father always waited and never agreed to any price, no matter how high. Father told her he'd know when the situation was right. Until then, she would have to be patient.

Rebekah didn't know why he waited. She wondered how she could get him to change his mind and arrange her marriage. There were more than enough suitable men in her region. She should know—her beauty attracted them like bees to a beautiful flower. But she knew she must wait and trust her father.

With a pitcher on her shoulder in the cool of the evening, Rebekah made her way down the dusty path to the well. It was crowded with villagers gathering to water their animals. Near the well she noticed a weary stranger sitting among his camels. As with most men, when his eyes fell on her, they brightened. She glanced his way but went about her business drawing water—although she did wonder why he had not watered his thirsty camels. As she turned to make her way back up the path, the stranger asked her for a drink. He had kind eyes, and she gladly quenched his thirst. Seeing the man had no pitcher with which to draw water for his animals, Rebekah graciously asked if she could water his herd (see Illustration #8). She knew it would be a long, hard task; ten camels would lap up gallons of water, but she was willing. Rebekah was known for her enthusiastic spirit, her kindness to strangers, and always going the extra mile. Other village ladies shook their heads and went about their own business.

Rebekah expected nothing in return for watering the camels, but this man, Eliezer, not only gave her gifts of gold, but he stopped and praised the **Lord** for making their paths cross.

They arranged for Eliezer to lodge with her family. She ran ahead to tell her parents who was coming for dinner. Rebekah loved the rhythmic jingle her new bright gold bracelets made as she hurried home. Her pace grew with each clink of the metal.

Illustration #8
Well and Water Jug—Rebekah probably drew water from a well like this one and carried the heavy jugs by balancing them on her head. She would have had to draw approximately 250 gallons of water to satisfy Eliezer's camels, because each camel would drink up to 25 gallons of water.

check this out

covenant
Genesis 15:18
mother
Genesis 12:1–3

Lord
"Lord" in the Old Testament referred to the essence of God, his power over his people and the earth.

kinsmen
relatives or family members

covenant
a special binding promise, like a treaty

Eliezer praised the Lord as he rounded up his camels. The Lord had answered his prayer. He had been sent to his master Abraham's **kinsmen** on an important mission to find a wife for Abraham's son Isaac. God had made a <u>covenant</u> promise to Abraham that he would be the father of many nations. Abraham said the Lord would guide Eliezer, and so he had.

There was no negotiation regarding Rebekah. Her father, Bethuel, sat in awe of Eliezer's story. He knew the Lord led Eliezer to Rebekah and that God's hand would be on this marriage. Bethuel would not go against the Lord. He told Eliezer to take her and go. Knowing she may never return to her homeland, Rebekah's mother and brother wanted more time to say good-bye, but Eliezer insisted they must depart quickly. The family asked Rebekah if this was what she wanted. It was. She wanted to be married. This man promised her she would be a <u>mother</u> of nations. She, too, perceived the hand of God leading Eliezer. She said she would go.

Scripture says the servant told Isaac the whole story. Isaac was probably still breathless not only from her beauty, but from seeing the Lord's hand in his life. He took her to be his wife, and he loved her.

In a time of marriage negotiations, God made the final arrangement as he led his servant to Rebekah, a woman willing to see and believe the sign of God. This woman's faith was so strong that she was willing to commit to a man she had never seen.

Rebekah exhibited two qualities important in a strong marriage:

1. The willingness to leave all that is familiar behind. She left her family, friends, and homeland to follow God's lead.

2. She trusted God and made a lifelong commitment to her marriage. In a culture where love was not a prerequisite for marriage, God rewarded her with a man who truly loved her all of her days. The children of their union, Jacob's descendants, are called Israel, God's chosen people.

How Others See It

Les and Leslie Parrott

A good marriage is made up of . . . two people who take ownership for the good as well as the bad. They are a responsible couple.

A good marriage is made up of . . . two people believing good wins over bad. They are a hopeful couple.

A good marriage is made up of . . . two people walking in each other's shoes. They are an empathic couple.

A good marriage is made up of . . . two people healing the hurts they don't deserve. They are a forgiving couple.

A good marriage is made up of . . . two people living the love they promise. They are a committed couple.[5]

Her Role—His Role

EPHESIANS 5:21–33 (MSG) *Out of respect for Christ, be courteously reverent to one another. Wives, understand and support your husbands in ways that show your support for Christ. The husband provides leadership to his wife the way Christ does to his church, not by domineering but by cherishing. So just as the church submits to Christ as he exercises such leadership, wives should likewise submit to their husbands.*

Husbands, go all out in your love for your wives, exactly as Christ did for the church—a love marked by giving, not getting. Christ's love makes the church whole. His words evoke her beauty. Everything he does and says is designed to bring the best out of her, dressing her in dazzling white silk, radiant with holiness. And that is how husbands ought to love their wives. They're really doing themselves a favor—since they're already "one" in marriage.

No one abuses his own body, does he? No, he feeds and pampers it. That's how Christ treats us, the church, since we are part of his body. And this is why a man leaves father and mother and cherishes his wife. No longer two, they become "one flesh." This is a huge mystery, and I don't pretend to understand it all. What is clearest to me is the way Christ treats the church. And this provides a good picture of how each husband is to treat his wife, loving himself in loving her, and how each wife is to honor her husband.

In this long passage of Scripture, I used *The Message* because I couldn't say it any better. *The Message* is a contemporary rendering of the Bible from the original languages, crafted to present its tone, rhythm, events, and ideas in everyday language.

This is a tough passage for women, because in ancient times women were seen as property. Culture and customs from throughout the ages seem to trickle down to the modern day and declare something to be "gospel" when it was not God's intention. Jesus granted women dignity. (See chapter 10 for more on women in the church.)

The tough word we wives have to overcome is *submit*. Or should I say the tough passage we are quoted is this: "Wives, submit to your husbands." *The Message* explains the passage at the emotional level. At the heart level. "Wives, understand and support your husbands in ways that show your support for Christ."

Wives were never intended to be doormats for their husbands. Now, this is not a green light for placing yourself in situations that are ungodly or contrary to God's Word, or for allowing violence against you or your children. As husbands and wives maintain unity and relationship in Christ and are submissive to God's plan and structure for the family, we recognize value and purpose in our lives together—just as God intended.

Through this passage in Ephesians and other Scriptures noted, let's see how Paul taught the early Christians about their roles and responsibilities in marriage.

Roles and Responsibilities in Marriage

Wife's Role	Husband's Role
• Maintain unity and a personal relationship with Christ. (Matthew 16:33)	• Maintain unity and a personal relationship with Christ. (Philippians 4:8)
• Pray for your husband. (John 16:24)	• Pray for your wife. (Ephesians 6:13–18)
• Show respect and honor. (Proverbs 18:14)	• Be a Christ-centered leader of your family. (1 Corinthians 11:3)
• Support and share what you have with your husband. (1 Peter 3:3)	• Love your wife as Christ self-sacrificially loved the church. (Colossians 3:19)
• Be gentle in your inner beauty, use faith to follow and offer submission so Christ is seen in your actions. (1 Peter 3:1–2)	• Be considerate, tender, and gentle. (1 Peter 3:7)
• Be a "helpmate" and submissive to God's family plan and roles of each spouse. (Genesis 2:21–23)	• Forgive your wife. (Matthew 6:14–15)
• Forgive your husband. (Luke 6:37)	• Make a commitment to remain faithful to your wife. Honor your vows. (Hebrews 13:4; Proverbs 5:15–18)
• Make a commitment to remain faithful to your husband. Honor your vows. (Hebrews 13:4; 1 Corinthians 6:16)	• Maintain sexual intimacy with your wife. (1 Corinthians 7:3–5; Proverbs 5:15–18)
• Maintain sexual intimacy with your husband. (1 Corinthians 7:3–5)	• Provide for, care for, and protect your wife. (Genesis 3:16)
• Love your husband. (Titus 2:4; John 13:3–35)	• Raise godly children. (Psalm 119:11)
• Raise godly children. (Psalm 127:4, Deuteronomy 6)	

How Others See It

Gary Smalley

Honor is a way of accurately seeing the immense value of someone made in God's image. God created each one of us as a one-of-a-kind person, with unique gifts and personality. He sees us as precious and valuable. When we see others as God sees them, when we recognize and affirm their value, we help create a safe environment that encourages relationships to grow.[6]

Tough Times in a Troubled Marriage

I love weddings, and it's guaranteed I'll cry at every one I attend. I used to be a wedding photographer and I loved every moment of it. The only problem was, photographers aren't supposed to cry. Blurred vision while looking through a lens is not a good thing.

I loved snapping away and capturing on film the excitement of the day, the tenderness and love in the newlyweds' eyes, and the anticipation of living a life happily ever after. Never in a million years would newlyweds think that their dreamy romance would turn into a troubled marriage and nightmare. It breaks my heart when I hear of a happy couple I photographed years ago now broken by tough times and a troubled marriage.

Scripture offers encouragement and solutions to broken relationships. With God's help and the advice and wisdom from a professional Christian counselor, a marriage that may look like it's over can have a new beginning, a healing, and a true restoration.

If the reality of divorce or separation has landed on your doorstep, God has not abandoned you. When you turn to him in your loneliness and despair, he will walk beside you—or even carry you—each step of the way.

Let's see what the Bible says about tough times in a troubled marriage.

The Middle Ground—Finding Solutions for Everyday, Ordinary Problems

EPHESIANS 4:1–3 *As a prisoner for the Lord, then, I urge you to live a life worthy of the calling you have received. Be completely humble and gentle; be patient, bearing with one another in love. Make every effort to keep the unity of the Spirit through the bond of peace.*

Before we dive headfirst into the deeply troubled marriage, let's cover some middle ground. Every day we face problems we may have no control over or problems we may have a choice about—stress, disappointments, sibling rivalry, in-laws, sickness, death, grief, financial crisis, moves, choices, change. Life. Let's see what the Bible has to say about resolving differences in our everyday, ordinary married life.

Examples From the Bible

Bible couples facing ordinary and not-so-ordinary problems:

• **Adam and Eve** made the conscious decision to disobey God, and they suffered the consequence as they brought sin into the world. They also had to choose to keep on loving each other after they were banished from paradise. Their lives were forever changed. God did not abandon them. They did not abandon each other as they navigated unfamiliar territory—a change—a new beginning. (Genesis 3–4)

- **Abraham and Sarah** packed up and moved to lands unknown. Sarah handled the stress by remaining calm. The Bible says she was a "gentle and quiet spirit." They both put their trust in God and remained faithful to his leading and promises. (Genesis 12:4; 15:5–6)

- **Isaac and Rebekah** began their life together, as did most ancient couples, in an arranged marriage. This one also just happened to be arranged by God. They not only learned to love one another, but they also fell in love. Rebekah was a willing worker, easy to get along with, and eager to go the extra mile. Rebekah comforted Isaac after his mother's death. They faced obstacles and struggled with decisions over their children. We can learn from Rebekah's mistake of helping her son Jacob deceive Isaac. Deception and dishonesty in a marriage lead to distrust and destruction. (Genesis 24–49)

- **Jacob and Rachel** plunged into their marriage with in-law problems from the get-go. Jacob agreed to work seven years for Rachel's hand in marriage, but his future father-in-law tricked him into working seven more years. But he was willing to pay the price. Jacob and Rachel stayed committed to each other and endured with patience. (Genesis 29)

- **Amram and Jochebed** were faced with the potential death of their son. They worked together on a creative plan to protect their son and save his life. Their son Moses was saved, and he eventually led the Israelites out of captivity. (Exodus 1–2:11)

- **Boaz and Ruth** had to work through the legal issue of the kinsman-redeemer before Boaz could take Ruth as his wife. Ruth, a widow, moved beyond her grief and faced life with an optimistic attitude. Boaz didn't wait for the problem to solve itself. He was a problem solver, and he took action. Their son Obed became the father of Jesse and the grandfather of King David. (book of Ruth)

- **Elkanah and Hannah** faced deep disappointment when Hannah was unable to have children. Elkanah was gentle and kind as he showed her great compassion. He looked to God and prayed for Hannah and her sorrow. Their faith carried them through this struggle. (1 Samuel 1:8)

- **David and Michal** faced violence by the hand of her own deranged father. She was forced to choose between devotion to her father or love and trust for her husband. Michal chose to trust her husband David, and she saved his life. As time passed, Michal allowed circumstances to make her bitter toward her husband. She chose to dwell on negative circumstances beyond her control. (1 Samuel 18:20–21)

- **Joseph and Mary** shared a deep devotion to God. As they faced an unknown future and public humiliation, Joseph supported and remained loyal to God and Mary. They stepped out in faith and started their journey united. Mary gave birth to Jesus, the Savior of the world, God's Son. (Matthew 1:18; Luke 1)

gentle and quiet spirit
1 Peter 3:4

• **Aquilla and Priscilla** ran a tentmaking business together. They
faced financial and physical uncertainties when they were uproot-
ed from their home and business during a time of persecution.
They worked together in business and taught the Gospel together. They remained true to their faith and spread the Gospel in
their daily life. (Acts 18:2, 18, 26)

Instead of letting the everyday problems of life weaken and chip away at
your marriage, let problems build and strengthen the bond between you
and your husband.

How Others See It

Gary Chapman

Love is the most powerful weapon for good not only in the world but in
a troubled marriage. When we choose to reach out with a loving attitude
and loving actions toward our spouse in spite of past failures, we are creating a climate where conflicts can be resolved, wrongs can be confessed,
and a marriage can be reborn.[7]

SOS!

MATTHEW 7:24–25 *Therefore everyone who hears these words of mine
and puts them into practice is like a wise man who built his house on
the rock. The rain came down, the streams rose, and the winds blew and
beat against that house; yet it did not fall, because it had its foundation
on the rock.*

If you cling to the promise that a house built on a strong foundation (the
foundation of God) will withstand the storms of life, you can hold on and
stand firm for your marriage. The life of your family may depend on lonely
you, equipped with little more than your SOS distress call—and God's
transforming power.

Examples From the Bible

A mended relationship is shown in the story of Gomer, the unfaithful wife
of **Hosea** (Hosea 2–3). She became a slave in prostitution. It is believed
other men fathered two of her three children. To reconcile their marriage
relationship, Hosea sought out Gomer, bought her out of slavery, and forgave his straying wife. This also is an illustration of how God sought and
redeemed his nation Israel despite the unfaithfulness of his people.

Your ship is sinking and you're screaming for help. The fierce gale stings you with relentless wind and rain. You're sending out the SOS signal, but there is no response. You feel that if a few more waves crash in, your marriage will be lost in a sea of despair.

Don't give up. Don't lose hope. Your problem is you're sending the signal to the wrong person—your spouse. Chances are, he's lost that loving feeling and can't find the lifeline. Remember, most men won't stop and ask for directions after driving around lost for hours. Why do we then expect them to jump in headfirst and ask for help on deep personal issues? You need help first from God and his Word, then from a professional counselor.

Successful relationships are all about getting along and understanding people. If we try to understand the motives behind our own behavior and our spouse's behavior, we may be better armed to confront and resolve issues. I make no claims to being a counselor, but I have benefited from the advice and guidance of a counselor in hanging on to my commitment to marriage when the storm raged against us.

There are no quick fixes to mending marriages, but there are solutions. Making a commitment to God and your spouse to stay together and work toward resolving your differences is the first step to a successful marriage. Hang on to your beliefs, anchored to the truths found in the Bible. You may not know what the future holds, but you can find **peace** in knowing that God will not **forsake** you. He is with you every step of the way.

During a time of strife in my marriage, I found that when I looked inward, there were things I needed to change. I began to make those changes, but it was hard. I'm a "take charge" kind of gal, but I had to realize that I can only take charge of me. As much as I would like to be Queen of the World, I'm responsible for my actions, alone. I needed to leave the rest up to God.

Forgiveness is a stepping-stone to **reconciliation**. Forgiveness means letting go of **anger** and **bitterness**. It does not mean that you approve of the behavior you're forgiving. It means you give up the notion that you have the right to hurt someone back. On a daily basis I have to surrender everything over to God, allowing him to work in my life and marriage.

My sea of despair slowly calmed, but there are still occasional squalls that pop up out of nowhere. Even in these moments of discouragement, the Bible and help from my counselor have turned me back into a seafaring voyager.

think about it

check this out

peace
John 14:27
forsake
Joshua 1:5

peace
harmony or calm feelings
forsake
leave, abandon, or give up on
forgiveness
a decision not to punish or seek revenge for an offense against you
reconciliation
the making of peace between people, a settling of differences
anger
a desire to fight back
bitterness
feelings of hatred and resentment

walk on stormy water
Matthew 14:22–31

Peter was able to walk on stormy water as long as he kept his eyes fixed on Jesus. Similarly, take your eyes off the storm and look to the One who can calm the seas. This is the surest way to find days ahead that will be smooth sailing.

What You Can Do

Stepping-stones to reconciliation:

1. Forgive: "Be kind and compassionate to one another, forgiving each other, just as in Christ God forgave you" (Ephesians 4:32). "For if you forgive men when they sin against you, your heavenly Father will also forgive you. But if you do not forgive men their sins, your Father will not forgive your sins" (Matthew 6:14–15).

2. Let go of anger and bitterness: "Everyone should be quick to listen, slow to speak and slow to become angry, for man's anger does not bring about the righteous life that God desires" (James 1:19–20). "God has called us to live in peace" (1 Corinthians 7:15). "See to it that no one misses the grace of God and that no bitter root grows up to cause trouble and defile many" (Hebrews 12:15).

> ## How Others See It
>
> ### Gary Smalley
>
> Forgiveness involves two actions. The first one is pardon. Basically, that is like erasing their offenses toward us. We immediately wash their offenses away like a wave washing away a message in the sand. Second, forgiveness involves caring for the offending person because most people who offend us have something in their own heart that needs healing. When we forgive others, they are released and healed, but we are too.[8]

Steps you can take to begin rebuilding a healthy relationship:

- Choose to believe that God can work to heal your marriage.

- Commit to going for professional counseling, keeping appointments, and following the advice of your counselor.

- If your spouse is unwilling to go for counseling, go alone.

- Remove unhealthy outside relationships from your life. Cut ties from anyone who is destructive to your marriage.

- Be a conduit of God's love.

- In conversations, replace *you* with *I*. For example, instead of saying, "You make me feel . . . ," say, "I feel this way . . ."

- Throw out the words *you always* and *you never* from your vocabulary if used in an accusing way.

- Choose to be optimistic. Dwell on the positive. Work on things you can change in your own life. Pray for things you have no control over. Let God take control.

- Work as a team with your spouse to complete tasks (parenting, counseling, budgeting, and so forth).

- Take the time to *remember when*. If you can't visit where you first met, take a walk down memory lane with photo albums and scrapbooks to rekindle the love you first shared.

- Display wedding pictures, happy family vacation photos, and first-baby photos to jog memories of fun, memorable times.

- Keep an open, gentle line of communication. Refrain from yelling. Listen with your heart.

- Schedule alone-with-each-other time—a weekly date or an overnight getaway if possible. If your budget doesn't allow for trips, arrange for your children to stay overnight with family or friends and turn your home into a romantic hideaway.

- Buy or make thoughtful cards or little gifts and surprise your husband. It helps rekindle romance.

- Worship and pray together.

- Reach out and serve an individual or a ministry in need. Serving helps you think of others instead of your own problems.

All the Queen's Horses . . .

The buzzing alarm woke me from a sound sleep at 3:00 A.M. I jumped out of bed, headed downstairs, and switched on the TV to join millions of worldwide viewers gazing starry-eyed at the wedding of the century. That was years ago, and my newlywed husband thought I was nuts for getting up in the middle of the night to watch Princess Diana and Prince Charles say "I do." But of course he couldn't understand. Cinderella hadn't been his childhood idol; she had been mine, and this

was definitely a twentieth-century Cinderella Wedding, with horse-drawn carriage and all. I wasn't about to miss it.

The years since then have flown by for me, but judging by all the news stories, I'm sure those same years seemed like eternity to the royal couple. Di was supposed to be like Cinderella: move to the palace, marry the prince, and live happily ever after. But as the world watched, the magic ended. Di's sparkling eyes turned dark and empty when she glanced at Charles. Her heart-melting, shy smile was reserved only for the camera, and her shattered emotions became tabloid gossip.

I never wanted this fairy-tale romance to end. I always hoped Charles and Di would come to their senses, renew their commitment, give in to the queen's persistence, and give their marriage another try. But it was official in September 1996 when the clerk's red rubber stamp stained the divorce papers. The marriage was over. Another romance ended. All the queen's horses and all the queen's men couldn't put Charles and Di back together again.

Wouldn't it be nice if Cinderella's fairy godmother could say "Bibbidi-Bobbidi-Boo" and instantly make your marriage perfect? We all know it takes a lot more than that to turn romance into a lifelong marriage. What is needed is not a fairy godmother but having God as the central focus of the union.

Over the past twenty-seven years of marriage, I have to admit my husband and I have not had a fairy-tale romance. But with Christ as the head of our home, my house is my castle, my husband is my prince, and God is our King.

Though all the queen's horses and all the queen's men could not put life back together for Di and Charles, I know the King of kings could have put all the shattered pieces back together.

Your marriage has hope if you choose to pick up the pieces of your shattered lives and place them in God's hands, for "he healeth the broken in heart, and bindeth up their wounds" (Psalm 147:3 KJV).

How Others See It

John Trent

Whatever it is that you need to overcome the curse and break the cycle of divorce in your life, I encourage you to choose life. To call on God for His help. And to look expectantly for Him to show up, empowering you to do your part and to do for you those things that are beyond your grasp. He's a big God. A miracle-working God. And He loves you.[9]

Decisions, Decisions: In or Out?

JAMES 1:5 *If any of you lacks wisdom, he should ask God, who gives generously to all without finding fault, and it will be given to him.*

James, the brother of Jesus, is writing to the new believers who were scattered about the Roman world when they fled from persecution. James knows that godly wisdom is a great gift. He gives a simple plan to get it: If you need wisdom, ask for it. God will give it to you.

Up 'til now we've concentrated on finding the wind for the sails of your drifting marriage and overcoming marital problems. But you may be the reader who is shaking her head, thinking that I just don't understand what you're going through. Maybe you are in a physically abusive relationship; you've forgiven the **infidelity** time after time; and in order for you and your children to survive, you see no alternative but divorce.

So let me make this clear: In no way am I saying to allow your husband to abuse you or your children. Get to safety and seek professional help immediately. Do not keep the abuse secret. Physical abuse is not only damaging to you; it is also harmful to your children's physical and emotional state.

If you are being emotionally abused, turn to God and ask him for wisdom in your situation. Repeated, prolonged attacks on your worth as a person hurt deeply. Seek help from a professional counselor or your pastor. Then follow James's advice, and ask God what he wants you to do.

Leaving a physically abusive marriage is an important decision. It is more difficult to decide if you should leave an emotionally abusive marriage. In extreme cases, divorce or separation may be your only options. These should be your last resort.

When you feel you've depleted all of your options, continue to ask God for wisdom in order to have the knowledge to make the <u>right</u> <u>decisions</u>. Wise women seek God. God is the <u>source</u> of wisdom, and wisdom is found in <u>Christ</u> and the Word.

right decisions
Colossians 1:9–12
source
Psalm 111:10
Christ
Colossians 2:2–5

infidelity
sexual unfaithfulness of a spouse
right
correct action

How Others See It

Gary Chapman

Is there hope for women who suffer physical abuse from their husbands? Does reality living offer any genuine hope? I believe the answer to those questions is yes. An abused wife can become a positive change agent in the marriage, but I do not believe that she can do it alone. She will need

divorce
Malachi 2:16

divorce
legal and formal disso-
lution of a marriage
impacted
affected, influenced

the help of a trained counselor, the support of family or friends, and she will need to draw upon her spiritual resources. I urge you if you are in an abusive marriage to seek counseling immediately. It will be worth the time, effort, and money you spend, and it offers the greatest potential for a positive outcome in what has become a destructive marriage.[10]

Separation or Divorce?

MATTHEW 19:8–9 *Jesus replied, "Moses permitted you to divorce your wives because your hearts were hard. But it was not this way from the beginning. I tell you that anyone who divorces his wife, except for marital unfaithfulness, and marries another woman commits adultery."*

Separation or **divorce** was not part of God's original plan. But when sin entered the Garden of Eden, human hearts hardened and Adam and Eve turned their backs on God's original design.

In Old Testament times, the family was structured with the husband as the head of the household. Wives and children were sometimes treated like property. But God gave laws for the people of Israel to live by. God's Law described what types of marriages were forbidden, and gave other guidelines for marriage so that God's people could have clean, healthy, blessed relationships.

No-No's for Marriage

Scripture Reference	What You're *Not* Supposed to Do
Leviticus 18:1–29 (unlawful sexual relations)	• no sexual relations with close relatives • no sexual relations with your neighbor's wife • no sexual relations with the same sex • no sexual relations with an animal
Exodus 20:14 (one of the Ten Commandments)	• You shall not commit adultery.
Deuteronomy 22 (laws and guidelines for marriage violations)	• no cross-dressing • no falsely trashing a woman's reputation • no sleeping around • no marrying your stepparent

How Others See It

Gary Chapman

There are no "and they lived happily ever after" divorces. The effects of divorce linger for a lifetime. This is not to say that there is no life after divorce. It is to say that life after divorce is always **impacted** by life before the divorce. Because the marriage relationship is unique among human relationships and involves deep emotional ties on the part of the husband and wife, there is no walking away without pain."

Seek counsel before you make the final decision on divorce. Know that while God hates divorce, he loves you and will never turn his back on you.

Examples From the Bible

The Bible speaks of men whose hearts were **hardened** as they turned away from God's commands. Tough consequences always resulted from their actions:

- In the days of Noah, humanity's heart turned from God. The earth was corrupt and full of violence and God destroyed the earth with a flood. Noah, a righteous man who walked with God, preached the impending destruction, but only he and his family were saved. (Genesis 6:9–22)
- At Sodom and Gomorrah, humanity's heart turned from God. The wickedness and sin of these cities was so great that God destroyed the cities with brimstone and fire from heaven. (Genesis 18:20; 19:24)
- King Saul's heart turned from God as he disobeyed God's commands. Saul was replaced by David, a man after God's own heart. (1 Samuel 15:11; 13:14)
- Pharaoh's heart was hardened so that he would not listen to Moses in order that God could do many more signs and wonders. The children of Israel would see that God's hand was against Egypt. (Exodus 7:3–5)
- The children of Israel's hearts were hardened as they grumbled and complained and tested God because of their thirst for water in the wilderness at the place called Meribah. (Psalm 95:8; Exodus 17:7)
- The writer of Hebrews encouraged believers to keep from allowing their hearts to be hardened by sin's deceitfulness. (Hebrews 3:13)

Separation

1 CORINTHIANS 7:10–11 *To the married I give this command (not I, but the Lord): A wife must not separate from her husband. But if she does, she must remain unmarried or else be reconciled to her husband.*

Paul wrote to the church at Corinth (see Illustration #13) to bring help to their relationships. Early Christians apparently wondered if they could serve Christ better by being single. They wanted to know if marriage was a stumbling block to their service. Paul encouraged them to stay in their marriages, but if for any reason they separated, they should work toward reconciliation.

separation
agreement by which a
husband and wife live
apart temporarily

So even if infidelity is not involved, but you cannot withstand the physical abuse or extreme emotional battering from your spouse, Scripture implies you are permitted to separate. This is not intended as a trial run for divorce, but as a **separation** with the intent to reconcile. It is a time to get relief, a time to seek counsel, a time for prayer, and a time for positive behavior change.

Reconciliation is the making of peace between people. Christ gave us the supreme example of reconciliation as he brought reconciliation between God and humanity:

- "We also rejoice in God through our Lord Jesus Christ, through whom we have now received reconciliation" (Romans 5:11).

- "All this is from God, who reconciled us to himself through Christ and gave us the ministry of reconciliation: that God was reconciling the world to himself in Christ, not counting men's sins against them. And he has committed to us the message of reconciliation" (2 Corinthians 5:18–19).

- "God was pleased to have all his fullness dwell in him, and through him to reconcile to himself all things, whether things on earth or things in heaven, by making peace through his blood, shed on the cross" (Colossians 1:19–20).

Examples From the Bible

The Bible mentions at least two marriage separations, neither of which were because of mistreatment:

- Moses and his wife, Zipporah, separated for a time. Moses left Midian for Egypt with Zipporah and their two sons as God commanded. Zipporah eventually returned to Midian with their children. There is no mention of her until after Moses led the Israelites out of Egypt. Then his father-in-law brought Zipporah and their sons to reunite and reconcile with Moses. (Exodus 4:18–19; 18:5)

- David and Michal were separated due to the attempts of King Saul, Michal's father, upon David's life. Michal heard of her father's plan to kill her husband, and she helped David escape. Years passed as David hid in the hills. King Saul gave Michal in marriage to another man, named Paltiel. Seven years later, after Saul was dead and David became king, he sent for Michal and they reunited. Yet Michal's love and adoration for David turned to bitterness. True reconciliation did not occur in their marriage, for Michal chose bitterness over love and forgiveness. (1 Samuel 18; 2 Samuel 3–6)

If you choose separation, the Bible clearly states that you must remain unmarried. During this time, your spouse may decide that he doesn't want to reconcile. He may end up divorcing you, but I encourage you to stay true to God's Word and trust that God will not abandon you.

caveat
a notice; warning
detachment
withdrawal

How Others See It

Jan Silvious

This final **caveat**, "remain unmarried," is a good test for you personally. Are you willing to face the fact that your mate may not reconcile, may never marry anyone else, and may not die for a long time? Are you willing to live without a mate and still be content? I have found that this is a good personal litmus test for an individual bound to a fool through marriage when things are stressful and strife is at a high pitch. Ask yourself, *Am I willing to separate, remain unmarried, or be reconciled?* If not, then "**detachment**" is the option that will allow you to remain married, to hope in God, and to maintain a sense of peace in the midst of your circumstances.[12]

Final Thoughts

- Strong families are the foundation of our next generation. Strive to build your family on God's principles—the only firm foundation that will last.

- A love that lasts is a love built like a triangle with God as the head of the family, joining husband and wife.

- Love is not merely emotion. Love is primarily choice and action.

- A Christ-centered love overcomes anger, bitterness, and resentment.

- Everyday problems in your lives can be used as a catalyst for growth and tools to strengthen your marriage.

Questions to Deepen Your Understanding

1. What foundation must our families and marriages be built upon?

2. What does Scripture want us to include in our spiritual trousseau?

3. What important elements did Rebekah exhibit in her marriage? How did God reward Rebekah when she followed his lead?

4. When is divorce permissible according to the Bible? What is the intended goal of separation?

read on

Some of Georgia's favorite books for developing meaningful relationships within your family:

• *The Blended Family,* Focus on the Family Marriage Study Series, Gospel Light

• *Breaking the Cycle of Divorce,* John Trent, Tyndale

• *The DNA of Relationships,* Gary Smalley, Tyndale

• *For Women Only,* Shaunti Feldhahn, Multnomah

• *Healing the Scars of Emotional Abuse,* Greg Jantz, Revell

• *I Love You More,* Les and Leslie Parrott, Zondervan

• *Life in a Blender,* Sandi Patti, Word

• *Love Must Be Tough: New Hope for Marriages in Crisis,* James Dobson, Multnomah

• *Loving Solutions,* Gary Chapman, Northfield Publishers

Chapter 6: Relationships in the Family Tree

Striving for a Balanced and Healthy Relationship With Your Extended Family

What's in This Chapter

- My Mama Didn't Raise No Fool
- Word of Caution
- Personality Puzzle
- Snapshot: Abigail
- In-Laws or Outlaws?
- Honor His Father and Mother
- The Legacy of Family Peace
- I Wish My Mama Lived in My Village
- Heritage Drives
- Your Turn to Care for Your Caregiver
- Snapshot: Ruth and Naomi
- Facing Our Parents' Deaths

Here We Go

PROVERBS 3:13–18 *Blessed is the man who finds wisdom, the man who gains understanding, for she is more profitable than silver and yields better returns than gold. She is more precious than rubies; nothing you desire can compare with her. Long life is in her right hand; in her left hand are riches and honor. Her ways are pleasant ways, and all her paths are peace. She is a tree of life to those who embrace her; those who lay hold of her will be blessed.*

The book of Proverbs is like a guidebook for finding wisdom. There is no treasure or jewel greater than wisdom. Wisdom is knowledge and understanding applied to life. Solomon, author of Proverbs, compares wisdom to a life-giving tree, and those who are nourished by this tree and the ways of God will live a blessed and happier life. In the next few pages, we'll consider how we can apply wisdom (the tree of life) to our relations (the family tree).

There are times you wonder about your family tree. You may even be tempted to just chop it down and feed it into the chipper. But we all know we need to resolve problems and not destroy, deny, or run from them. Especially if family is your problem.

One of the most difficult battles in developing meaningful connections with relatives is handling troublesome relationships within your extended

fruit
the result, product, or
consequences of
something

family. Your family problem may be with a sibling, a parent, or an in-law, but like it or not you are related, and you will have to deal with your family sooner or later. You may want to go into the Witness Protection Program, but the Feds don't make that available just for the asking.

The key to unlocking these intertwined and sometimes difficult relationships in your family tree is understanding. Understanding just who they are. Understanding what makes them tick. Understanding what pushes their buttons (and how to avoid pushing). Understanding what makes them feel valued.

In this chapter I hope I help you find your key to understanding. Let's see what the Bible has to say about being your best with your extended family.

> ## How Others See It
>
> ### Gary Smalley
>
> Life is relationships; the rest is just details. God made you for relationships. You can't change that. You can work either with or against this DNA, but you can't choose whether it exists. The only choice you have is whether you will work to make those relationships great or allow them to cause you—and others—great pain. So choose wisely. Choose life. And be prepared to take personal responsibility to make the decisions—even the hard ones—that can keep joy, peace, and satisfaction flowing into your relationships.[1]

My Mama Didn't Raise No Fool

PSALM 1:1–3 *Blessed is the man who does not walk in the counsel of the wicked or stand in the way of sinners or sit in the seat of mockers. But his delight is in the law of the Lord, and on his law he meditates day and night. He is like a tree planted by streams of water, which yields its fruit in season and whose leaf does not wither. Whatever he does prospers.*

If we are to be like a "tree planted by streams of water, which yields its fruit in season and whose leaf does not wither" (Psalm 1:3), we will be constantly watered and nourished by the Word and bear **fruit** as we live in Jesus. By using the fruit of the Spirit we can deal with our most difficult relationships. "But the fruit of the Spirit is love, joy, peace, patience, kindness, goodness, faithfulness, gentleness and self-control. Against such things there is no law" (Galatians 5:22–23).

It should come as no surprise that love heads the list, because "God is Love" (1 John 4:8), and the greatest of Christian qualities is love (1 Corinthians 13:13).

The fruit of the Spirit is the outward expression of Christ's love in us. Below is a table of the fruit of the Spirit with descriptions of each aspect.

provocation
to bring something about

- *Love:* the love of Christ that unites man with God and man to man. (John 15:12–13)

- *Joy:* the celebration of God's love. (John 15:11)

- *Peace:* the ability to live in harmony with God and man. (John 14:27)

- *Patience:* calmness under **provocation** or strain. Applies both to God's patience toward us and our patience toward others. (1 Corinthians 13:4)

- *Kindness:* the outward expressions of godly affection as we grow in Christ. (Colossians 3:12)

- *Goodness:* love in action, as in "acts of goodness." (2 Thessalonians 1:11)

- *Faithfulness:* enduring, reliable loyalty. (Hebrews 10:23)

- *Gentleness:* free of harshness, like the kind spirit of Christ. (1 Corinthians 4:20–21)

- *Self-control:* discipline in heart and actions as we follow God's teachings. (Acts 24:25)

Let's take a look at the relationships among Miriam, Aaron, and Moses, whose story is found in the book of Exodus. The Bible gives us a glimpse of these siblings' family photo album.

- *Miriam.* Scripture shows us a snapshot of the important role that Miriam had in protecting and saving Moses from being killed as a baby. As a young child, Miriam helped her mother hide Moses in a basket in the Nile River. Pharaoh's daughter took Moses as her own and raised him in the palace. The second snapshot is shown when Miriam celebrated her brother's leadership and the Hebrews' deliverance from captivity. As the celebration wears off, hardships follow in the desert, and wrinkles crease her face, we see a snapshot of discontentment, disloyalty, and jealously as she and her brother Aaron question Moses' leadership. The Scripture tells us that God became angry with Miriam and struck her with leprosy. Instead of seeking revenge for their prideful attitudes, Moses begs God to heal his sister, and Miriam is healed.

- *Moses* was saved from Pharaoh's edict of death and raised by Pharaoh's daughter. As a young man, Moses fled Egypt and the luxury of palace living after he killed an Egyptian. Pharaoh, once again, wanted him dead. While Moses was in the wilderness, God called upon him to take the task of leading the nation of Israel out of slavery. Insecure in his communication skills, Moses asked God to send someone else. It angered God that Moses would question him, and he told Moses his brother would speak for him. God reunited Moses with his family and sent Aaron to be his voice. After suffering from many plagues, Pharaoh released the children of Israel, and Moses led the great Exodus from Egypt.

- *Aaron*, the oldest sibling, is introduced when God tells him to go to Moses in the desert. Right off the bat that tells us that Aaron already knew God and had a personal relationship with him. Even though in captivity, the Hebrews carried on their traditions of faith. I'm sure Aaron has heard about Moses over the years; after all, Moses lived with royalty. But this may be the first time Aaron saw his little brother since Moses was a baby. Instead of being jealous that he worked as a slave while Moses lived in a palace, Aaron was happy to see his brother and greeted him with a kiss. Aaron isn't bashful. He's a great speaker, and he is willing to follow God's lead. Even though he's the oldest and probably had the leadership skills, he serves as a spokesperson for Moses, and they work side by side as a team from that day forward. Through his obedience, Aaron experiences freedom from slavery, he has the holy experience of being in God's presence, and he and his sons became the first priests in the tabernacle.

As siblings, Miriam, Aaron, and Moses definitely faced major conflicts, not only in their walk of life but in their family relationships. But they continued to work as a team with the same goal—to obey, worship, and glorify God.

God's original plan was for families to live in harmony. Wouldn't it be paradise if we all grew up in Christian homes and shared the same belief system? Reality is, sin entered the Garden, and all family members don't love or follow God. That's where it starts to get a little sticky with our family relationships. We don't have the same goal.

I'm no different from Miriam and her siblings; our extended family has had our fair share of difficulties over the years. I have to remind myself of my life's purpose—to obey, worship, and glorify God. As believers, when we focus on our purpose in this life, difficult and broken relationships in our family tree always have the potential for being mended.

personality types
one's customary frame of mind or natural disposition

Word of Caution

Tamar, one of David's daughters, was raped by her half brother Amnon (2 Samuel 12:1–13:30). When her full brother, Absalom, found out about the rape, he told her to remain quiet. It took two years, but Absalom took his own revenge and had Amnon murdered. The devastating part of this family's story is that during the time Tamar stayed in Absalom's home, even though she was innocent, she lived in shame and disgrace because of her hidden secret. The Scripture describes her as "a desolate woman." Tamar could not move beyond her circumstance.

If you encounter sexual abuse or violence by a relative or anyone else, do not remain quiet. Seek professional help. Your life does not have to be defined by a tragic event of violence. You can recover and move forward. God will provide hope and a healing for your future.

How Others See It

Paula White

Too many people today are predicting their endings based on their beginnings. In life the most important thing is not where you start, but where you finish. I am so thankful that God can interrupt a person's life and change the course of history for that person for His good. God does not use your past to determine your future . . . so why should you? It's a tragedy to plan your future comparing it to your past. Stop using what was to determine what will be![2]

Personality Puzzle

Several years ago, while attending a conference on **personality types** and behavior, I sat in amazement as Florence Littauer took attributes of each personality and connected all the strengths and weaknesses piece by piece, like a puzzle. Before my very ears she described members of my family. A light went off in my head and I suddenly understood not only my family better, but just about everyone else too.

The four basic personality types that Florence describes are listed in the following chart.

The Four Personality Types[3]

Personality	Characteristics
Popular Sanguine	Outgoing Desires fun Emotional Outspoken Relationship-oriented
Perfect Melancholy	Introverted Desires perfection Organized Pessimistic Task-oriented
Peaceful Phlegmatic	Introverted Desires peace Unemotional Pessimistic Relationship-oriented
Powerful Choleric	Outgoing Desires power or control Outspoken Strong-willed Optimistic

think about it

In all of our personality profiles, we have major weaknesses. To live in harmony with others, we can't just say, "Well, that's me; take it or leave it." We each have certain specific traits that usually are the cause of difficulties in our relationships. Since my mama didn't raise no fool, I knew I had to take a good look in the mirror and face whatever foolish behavior I found before I could jump headfirst into understanding those around me.

Examples From the Bible

From character traits of individuals described in the Bible, listed below are examples of personality types:

- **Popular Sanguine:** Jezebel, the wicked queen who persecuted the prophets and worshiped the false god Baal, was a materialistic woman who loved living in the lap of luxury. She loved being the center of attention and partying with her sensuous cult. Jezebel displayed traits of the Popular Sanguine, who is outgoing, desires fun, and is outspoken and emotional (1 Kings 16:31—2 Kings 9:37). And don't worry—just because a person has a Popular Sanguine personality, that doesn't necessarily mean they're as evil as Jezebel!

- **Perfect Melancholy:** Martha, the sister of Lazarus and Mary, was very task-oriented and had to have everything perfect as she prepared and served a meal for Jesus and his followers. Martha displayed traits of the

Perfect Melancholy as she desired organized perfection and was pessimistic. (John 11:1–12:2)

- **Peaceful Phlegmatic:** Thomas, a disciple of Christ, was pessimistic and doubtful. When the other disciples told him that they had seen the risen Jesus, he doubted and would not believe unless he saw for himself. Thomas displayed traits of the Peaceful Phlegmatic. (John 20:24–29)
- **Powerful Choleric:** Simon Peter, an apostle of Christ, was ready to fight and go to prison or death with Jesus. He drew his sword and cut off the ear of a servant when men came to arrest Jesus. He displayed traits of a Powerful Choleric with his strong will, impulsive outspokenness, and optimism. (Luke 22:33, 50)

personality puzzle
the whole picture of your personality and how it fits with other personality types

How Others See It

Florence and Marita Littauer

While we cannot force others to change—although we may try—and we can't make them adore us, we can learn to get along with them. . . . When you understand the emotional needs of the **personality puzzle**, you can give others what they need instead of what you need. When we can change our perspective and do unto others as they would like and not as we wish to do according to our own personality, we can transform relationships.[4]

Snapshots of Women in the Bible
Abigail (1 Samuel 25:2–44)

Abigail's heart raced when she saw a servant running toward her. Chest heaving breathlessly, he collapsed at her feet. His garment was drenched with sweat. Fearing bad news, she grabbed a pitcher of water to quench his thirst so she could hear his urgent message. She knew her foolish husband, Nabal, must have done something terrible again.

The servant described how David and his warriors had protected Nabal's flocks both day and night during sheepshearing. When David sent his men to ask for gifts of food, Nabal insulted David and refused him. Upon hearing the insults, David armed four hundred of his men and swore to kill Nabal's household. The warriors were on their way, and the servant rushed to Abigail because Nabal would listen to no man.

Abigail had no time to pity her foolish husband. She had been the recipient of Nabal's mean spirit. The servant was right; she knew what Nabal was capable of and knew he would not listen to reason. But this time he had

Goliath
I Samuel 17:1–51

gone too far. His folly could bring immediate death upon her entire household. She paced anxiously, concocting a plan she hoped would save them.

She instructed her faithful servant to gather gifts of loaves, wine, sheep, corn, raisins, and figs. She ordered him to go ahead of her, meet David and his warriors, and present her gifts. Abigail then quickly dressed in her most beautiful clothes to meet the man who held her life in his hands.

She mounted her donkey and prodded it to the path David and his men were traveling on. Her hands trembled as she saw the dust cloud of four hundred warriors drawing closer. At last they came into view ahead, marching around a bend. Asking God for courage, she ran and fell at David's feet in a gesture of honor and humility. In her wisdom she took full responsibility for not knowing that his men guarded their workers.

If she could deflect David's heart of revenge away from Nabal and toward her, perhaps he would see a beautiful woman and stop long enough to listen. She knew of this David who as a boy stood against the giant Philistine, Goliath, with only a sling. She begged him to let God have revenge, assuring him that "the lives of your enemies [God] will hurl away, as from the pocket of a sling" (1 Samuel 25:29). She begged him not to let a vengeful act haunt him later, when he would be king.

The beauty, wisdom, and courage of this woman took David by surprise. He blessed her, blessed God, and changed his attack plans. Their lives were spared.

Abigail returned home to a drunken husband and decided to wait until morning to tell him of her actions. Upon hearing of his narrow escape, Nabal immediately suffered a heart failure and ten days later died at the hand of God.

Upon hearing the news of this newly widowed woman, David sent a messenger to ask Abigail to marry him. Abigail accepted. David gained political status in the area, as well as a beautiful, intelligent, and wealthy wife who took care of his financial needs. Abigail married the man who would be the second king of Israel.

In this snapshot of Abigail, we see that she lived in a less than ideal circumstance with her mean-spirited, foolish husband. But she did not stand idly by and watch when his behavior nearly destroyed the household. She looked to God for wisdom, she accepted the reality and truth of the situation, and she took immediate action, mustering up the courage and the plan that saved her family.

In-Laws or Outlaws?

PROVERBS 23:24–25 *The father of a righteous man has great joy; he who has a wise son delights in him. May your father and mother be glad; may she who gave you birth rejoice!*

Proverbs calls our attention to the wisdom of our parents. We are to honor, respect, and appreciate them for giving us life, and treasure their teachings. If we grow to live righteous lives, we bring great joy to our parents.

Sometimes when you reflect on your marriage vows, "for better, for worse," you feel the "worse" part is dealing with in-laws. Getting along with difficult personalities can be stressful, but it is not impossible. You can have meaningful relationships with the ones who raised your husband. If we heed their advice, there are some instances where we gain wisdom from our outlaws. I mean, in-laws. Let's see what the Bible says about in-laws.

Examples From the Bible

- Isaac and Rebekah grieved over their new daughters-in-law, Judith and Basemath. Their son Esau had married these foreign women who worshiped foreign idols. (Genesis 26:34–35)

- King Saul, David's father-in-law, became jealous and feared his countrymen would want David as king. Saul attempted to kill David and became his persistent enemy. (1 Samuel 18:6–29)

- Peter was so concerned about his sick mother-in-law, he immediately spoke to Jesus about her illness. Jesus came and healed her. After she was healed she got up and fixed them a meal. (Mark 1:30–31)

- Laban was Jacob's father-in-law. He tricked Jacob into marrying his daughter Leah, when he originally agreed to let Jacob marry Rachel. Jacob worked seven more years to marry Rachel because of his love for her. (Genesis 29:10–30)

- Ruth, a widow, was so devoted to her grieving mother-in-law, Naomi, that she left her country to follow Naomi and adopt Naomi's God. (Ruth 1:16)

Honor His Father and Mother

EXODUS 18:7–9 *So Moses went out to meet his father-in-law and bowed down and kissed him. They greeted each other and then went into the*

bush
Exodus 3:2
Egypt
Exodus 12:31–13:22

calling
God's direction or
purpose for your life
burnt sacrifice
ritual of burning a
sacrifice to honor
and thank God

tent. Moses told his father-in-law about everything the Lord had done to Pharaoh and the Egyptians for Israel's sake and about all the hardships they had met along the way and how the Lord had saved them. Jethro was delighted to hear about all the good things the Lord had done for Israel in rescuing them from the hand of the Egyptians.

As a young man, when Moses fled Egypt to Midian, he married Zipporah. There he tended sheep for his father-in-law, Jethro, for forty years. It was while Moses was out in the fields with the sheep, doing an ordinary day's work, that he encountered God in the burning <u>bush</u> and realized the **calling** upon his life.

Moses knew that God's call required him to return to Egypt. He wanted to bring his wife and sons with him. Out of respect for his father-in-law, and probably wanting his approval, Moses requested Jethro's permission to leave. Jethro gave Moses his blessing and Moses embarked upon one of the greatest journeys recorded in history as he led the Jews out of <u>Egypt</u>.

Somewhere along the way, Zipporah and Moses' sons were sent back to Jethro. Exodus 18 describes when the family reunited. Jethro was overjoyed with the deliverance, brought Moses' family to him, and declared a new belief that the Lord was greater than any other gods. Jethro then offered a **burnt sacrifice** to God.

The next day, Moses sat as judge, trying to resolve everyone's problems. It took all day and dragged on into the night. Jethro saw that Moses had a micromanaging problem. Others were capable of dealing with most of these problems, so Jethro suggested that Moses handle only the hardest cases and reminded his son-in-law that Moses needed to be pursuing his real calling: "Teach them the decrees and laws, and show them the way to live and the duties they are to perform" (Exodus 18:20). Moses immediately turned Jethro's idea into policy, more evidence of Moses' special respect for his father-in-law.

Moses' workday became easier, allowing him to focus less on the urgent and more on the important, because he listened to his father-in-law. Jethro found an enthusiastic faith in the true God, because he listened to his son-in-law. This is how family is meant to work.

The Legacy of Family Peace

The infamous Hatfields and McCoys are known through the nation for the longest and bloodiest family feud in American history. No one

really knows how this feud ever began. But one theory attributes it to a forbidden marriage between sweethearts in the families. It became in-laws against in-laws, and eventually when the in-laws broke the local law, it became outlaws against outlaws. My husband can trace his ancestors back to the feud's stomping grounds in Matewan, West Virginia, and that's where we headed one sweltering summer day. Now, my husband's families weren't descendants of the Hatfields or McCoys, but his great-grandfather Moses Alley had a farm that joined the Hatfield farm. They were neighbors.

The terrain is considered the roughest in the eastern United States. Road improvements were in process, but the only way in was a two-lane road that wound round and round to the highest peak, only to realize at the top that you had to descend down and down again into a valley. With mountain after mountain, Dramamine became my closest friend.

We finally found Matewan, population 600. We strolled the deserted downtown streets on an early Sunday afternoon, somewhat disappointed that we hadn't found the old home place and, chances were, wouldn't. We dined at the only restaurant in town and came across a treasure: Mrs. Aileen Phillips. She came over to introduce herself to these strangers in her town. After we explained our quest, she was overjoyed and filled with information about our family. She gave us directions to the old home place, cemetery, and even a key to the Historical Museum.

We headed back up the mountains, and about a mile out of town we found the house and cemetery. Most of the family farm had since been sold, except for one section that sat high on a mountain overlooking the creek and valley below. Overgrown trees, vines, and buses covered up the dilapidated old house and fenced-in cemetery. In ninety-degree heat and with monster mosquitoes on the attack, we attempted to scale the fence to read the headstones. But after a feeble attempt and fear of major injuries and rattlesnakes, we gave up and settled for a photo session with our son and his dad standing where his pioneer ancestors once stood. It was amazing to think that even though shut off from the rest of the world in that rugged mountain country and surrounded by hardship and turmoil, the families had made a good life for themselves and their loved ones.

Heritage is part of who we are. Moses Alley was born the year after the first shot rang out and started the famous feud. Yet over the next

check this out

Ten Commandments
Exodus 20:1–17

Ten Commandments
God's laws given to
Moses for the
Israelites

honor
to show great respect
or high regard for

thirty years of this bloody war, and even having been a neighbor, he was never listed among those who sided with them. He was a peaceful farmer, a carpenter, and like his father before him, a circuit-riding preacher. His children remembered his building coffins for victims of the feud but never taking part. The woman at the diner said that as a small girl, when she heard Moses preach she "experienced a touch of heaven."

Even though Moses Alley never met his great-grandson, my husband, he touched his life as he passed down that spiritual heritage from generation to generation. Thousands upon thousands of people across the world have been influenced by this mountaineer. Unlike his rowdy neighbors, Moses enjoyed a peaceful relationship with his family, including his in-laws, on the very same mountaintop known for a family feud. Family peace can be your legacy too.

We are instructed in the **Ten Commandments** to **honor** our fathers and mothers. In marriage, husband and wife become one. If you are one with your husband, then his parents are your parents. That means you are to honor them. Our relationships don't have to be family feuds.

> ## How Others See It
> ### Susan Alexander Yates
> God has called us to serve our mates and to honor our parents. These two foundational principles are vital in building friendships within the family. It will not always be easy. It may be inconvenient and costly to honor your parents. And you will not be able to please everyone. Your ultimate job is not to keep everyone happy, but to be faithful to God's calling, which is to love your spouse, to nurture your children, and to care for your parents.[5]

What You Can Do

How do we honor our in-laws? Five little tips:

1. When you talk about them, accentuate the positive, not the negative.

2. Listen with an open mind and heart. Be open to their wisdom and advice.

3. Keep close contact with them, unless the relationship is causing problems. If so, defuse the possible explosion by detaching physically until you and your husband can confront and handle the problem together.

4. Care for them when they are sick.

5. Encourage your children to call or write. (If we want our children to honor us, they must see how we respect and honor our own parents.)

Lois
2 Timothy 1:5

I Wish My Mama Lived in My Village

PROVERBS 17:6 *Children's children are a crown to the aged, and parents are the pride of their children.*

In Bible times, headdresses and garlands were worn to show honor and respect. They were given by those who loved and admired the one who was crowned. Likewise, grandchildren are the crown of grandparents' lives, their pride and joy. Grandparents love to admire the new generation of life from their own children.

Unlike today, in Bible times the whole extended family lived together, worked side by side, and shared daily in each other's lives. Sometimes one "household" could constitute an entire village of family and relatives, a true clan.

As we raised our son, living three thousand miles from my mom and dad was a heartbreak for me. I reflect on growing up with my grandmother and the wonderful impact she had on my life. Granny Curtis was a quiet wallflower, yet spirited and fun. She could have been Sophia's twin on the TV series *The Golden Girls*. She was small in stature, but a giant in faith; uneducated, yet filled with godly wisdom. Her life was long and every life she touched was blessed. She will live in our hearts forever. Yet my children won't know their grandparents, as I knew mine.

Make every effort to include the rest of your clan in your life. Your children will experience confidence and stability if they have a deep sense of who and where they spring from.

We as adults need the support, wisdom, and love of our parents and grandparents. But it is also a privilege to be a grandparent—and a great responsibility.

Lois, a grandmother, is mentioned in the Bible as playing a vital role in planting seeds of faithfulness in her grandson, Timothy. Those tiny seeds of faithfulness grew into full bloom, because Timothy played a vital role in establishing the first church.

Examples From the Bible

Scriptures where we can find grandparents and the blessing of grand-children:

- Blessing to Rebekah of thousands of grandchildren. (Genesis 24:60)
- A grateful grandfather is joyful when he sees his grandchildren before he dies. (Genesis 48:11)
- God blessed Job with grandchildren and great-grandchildren. (Job 42:16)
- "A good man leaves an inheritance for his children's children." (Proverbs 13:22)
- Grandchildren are a blessing. (Proverbs 17:6)
- It is a blessing to see your grandchildren. (Psalm 128:5–6)
- Passing the spiritual legacy down from one generation to the next. (Psalm 145:4–7; Joel 1:3)
- Grandchildren were blessed because they obeyed their parents' and grandparents' commands. (Jeremiah 35:1–16)
- Children and grandchildren are taught to provide for their grandparents in need. (1 Timothy 5:3–4)
- Timothy was influenced by his grandmother (2 Timothy 1:5–6).

What You Can Do

Five little things that grandparents can do to help plant the seeds of faith in their grandchildren:

1. Pray for them daily.

2. If you don't live close, send cards, call, write, or e-mail. Let them know that you love them.

3. Tell them stories. Make it an adventure. They'll be amazed how well you got along without color TV and computers. Let them get to know how God walked with you during your struggles, joys, and successes.

4. Take an interest in your grandchildren's special gifts and hobbies. Work alongside them and encourage their giftedness.

5. When the opportunity arises, share your faith. Grandparents have a way of accepting and loving grandchildren that sometimes gets them to listen when they turn a deaf ear to their parents.

If your grandmother doesn't live in your village, you can still be close even though many rivers and woods separate you. Take time to go through photo albums and tell your children about the images captured on film. My father-in-law, Papa Ling, died before our son Philip was born, yet Philip is well acquainted with Papa Ling. He even knows the traits and habits he inherited from Papa Ling because we keep Grandfather's memory alive in our hearts. Grandparents are a blessing . . . tap into their resource.

ancestors
Matthew 1:5

patriarchs
the founders of the Hebrew families in the Bible

How Others See It

Charles R. Swindoll

God's **patriarchs** have always been among his choicest possessions. Abraham was far more effective once he grew old and mellow. Moses wasn't used with any measure of success until he turned eighty. Samuel was old when the God of Israel led him to establish the "school of the prophets," an institution that had a lasting influence for spirituality and godliness in the centuries to come.[6]

Heritage Drives

coffee break

There were four of us siblings: Sherry, Connie, David, and me. Add one station wagon (naturally . . . this was way before minivans), Mom, Dad, and even the family dog, and you've got the cast of characters. On Sunday afternoons Dad would pile four grumbling, reluctant kids into the wagon to go for a drive. None of us kids were thrilled about the journey, but we knew that at the end we would pull into the ice-cream shop. So the hour or so spent driving had a pretty good payoff. Besides, that way we had plenty of time to reflect and decide which ice-cream flavor we wanted: vanilla or chocolate. (This was also before anybody had conceived of thirty-one flavors.)

My dad cruised the countryside, pointing out to us the one-room schoolhouse he had attended, or the swimming hole where he had spent countless hours playing with his buddies, or the cemeteries that held our <u>ancestors</u>. All these years later, I now realize I've had a longer-lasting payoff than merely ice cream. Because all those places are etched in my mind, I have heritage. Little did I know as we peered out the windows of that station wagon we were actually looking into the windows of our past.

Dad's Sunday afternoon "heritage drives" helped me understand my dad, his way of thinking, his vision and dreams for his children.

honoring their parents by providing for their needs
Matthew 15:1–9

Pharisees
teachers of the law

Through those places I saw his undying love for God and his family of the past, present, and future. To my surprise, the blessings were well worth the trip.

Your Turn to Care for Your Caregiver

1 TIMOTHY 5:3–4 *Give proper recognition to those widows who are really in need. But if a widow has children or grandchildren, these should learn first of all to put their religion into practice by caring for their own family and so repaying their parents and grandparents, for this is pleasing to God.*

The apostle Paul writes to young Timothy with instructions on how to lead, encourage, and serve his ministry. It's a letter from one old pastor to one young pastor.

He gives guidelines for the leaders of the church to provide for widows of the church and for others who may be in need. However, he makes it clear that it is first the responsibility of the widow's family to care for her and to provide for her needs. The church is there for her as a backup if she has no other means of support.

Paul echoes the words of Jesus—"put their religion into practice"—when Jesus rebuked the **Pharisees** on a similar subject and called them hypocrites for not <u>honoring their parents by providing for their needs</u>.

My paraphrase is, "Practice what you preach!"

According to a survey by the National Alliance for Caregiving and the American Association of Retired Persons, an estimated 22.4 million households in the United States—nearly one in four—are now providing care to a relative or friend age fifty or older, or have provided care during the previous twelve months. Other surveys suggest that today's baby boomers—adults born between the mid-1940s and the mid-1960s—likely will spend more years caring for a dependent parent (an average of eighteen years) than for their own children (seventeen years).[7]

Now that my husband and I are forty-something and our parents are in their seventies, we are in that life transition and role reversal where it's our turn to be caregivers. We're putting our religion into practice.

My dad is a big planner, so he already has special insurance in case the need arises for long-term care. But what if his plans don't come off as intended, or what if I don't think the care facility is adequate? What if he and Mom are treated like just another number, unloved, or wanted just for the income they bring?

I was privileged to see love in action when both of my grandmothers needed special long-term care. My parents sacrificed time, energy, and finances to be with their mothers when needed most. My parents were there to help bathe them, feed them nibbles of food, read favorite passages of Scripture, and pray with them. My grandmothers knew they were loved.

A person's greatest need is to know that he or she is loved. Our expression of love and gratitude to our parents needs to surface when the caregiver role changes. The ones who gave us life and provided for our every need, now need to be cared for. As their children, and as people of faith, we must do right by them.

The ingredients needed in our hearts to be loving caregivers include:

- Compassion—with a tenderness of heart that draws you to your parents' side, to feel their suffering and pain—is needed foremost. Once your heart and eyes are opened to their pain, you willingly will walk alongside them.

- Simple acts of kindness will overflow as you put yourself to use.

- Humility will surface as you humble yourself to clean up the ugly and smelly side of illness. You humble yourself as a servant to your parents and to God as you gain strength to carry on.

- Your meekness, gentleness, and patience will smooth away the fears and calm the spirit of your ailing parent.

- You will need to carry their burden and forgive past failures so you can continue to give graciously and love unconditionally as Christ loved us.

How Others See It

Joni Eareckson Tada

The attitude of reverence and acknowledgment of God's authority and power must be present with you in every circumstance: at the deathbed, in the waiting room, and in the nursing home. At every point of decision and every expression of hope, we must acknowledge his sovereign will.

God is the giver and sustainer of life, and he is holy. Our dependence upon him for wisdom must be accompanied by the knowledge that we are accountable to him for how we apply that wisdom. When he shows us something through wisdom and his word, we have to agree not to second-guess, manipulate, or misconstrue.[8]

What You Can Do

Here are some guidelines to help you think through the needs of your aging parents:

- People do not age identically. Each situation should be assessed independently. Look at your loved one as an individual rather than as a stereotypical old person.

- When symptoms of deterioration are recognized and a more structured environment is needed, assist aging parents with making decisions while they still are competent. The adult child may need to clarify issues and give advice. But the privilege of deciding for oneself is important. Your parents have a right to be consulted about their future.

- Take time to listen to what your aging parents have to say. Observe the entire situation by listening and learning about their hopes, fears, anxieties, and plans for the future.

- The goal is for your parents to remain in their own home and be as independent as possible for as long as possible.

- What is right for one family may not be possible or even right for another. Don't base your decisions on someone else's circumstances.

- If time is needed to make a decision and adequately prepare, arrange temporary admission to a convalescent or nursing home.

- Circumstances change, and caregiving may not be possible indefinitely. A backup plan is a good idea and should include respite care for extended weekends or evenings out.[9]

Examples From the Bible

- Joseph, the ruler of Egypt under Pharaoh, showed compassion when he sent for his family to save them from the famine. His aged father came to Egypt with all of his sons, their wives and children, their livestock and

Moabites
descendants of Moab, the son of Lot by incestuous union with his daughter

property (Genesis 46:1–48:10). Joseph provided for his father until his death. Scripture records his loving relationship and acts of kindness. "Now Israel's eyes were failing because of old age, and he could hardly see. So Joseph brought his sons close to him, and his father kissed them and embraced them" (Genesis 48:10).

- Ruth, a young widow, left her homeland to accompany her widowed mother-in-law Naomi. She provided for both of them by gleaning from the barley fields (see illustration, page 154). Ruth's commitment to Naomi is a famous quote from the Bible: "Where you go I will go, and where you stay I will stay. Your people will be my people and your God my God" (Ruth 1:16).

- Peter's mother-in-law lay in bed with a fever. Out of love for her, Peter asked Jesus to help her. Jesus healed her and she got up and waited on them. (Luke 4:38–39)

Snapshots of Women in the Bible
Ruth and Naomi (Ruth 1–4)

When famine hit the area surrounding Bethlehem, Naomi and Elimelech tried to escape its results by moving from Judah to Moab. The **Moabites** were enemies of the Jews, and God had warned the Jews not to have anything to do with them. While in Moab, Elimelech died, leaving Naomi a widow. Then, contrary to God's command, her two sons married Moabite women. The sons died too, leaving Naomi in a foreign land with no relations except two "forbidden" daughters-in-law.

Eventually the famine in Judah ended. Since Naomi had few ties in Moab, she decided to move back to her homeland and her own extended family. In a selfless gesture, she released her daughters-in-law from any commitment to her. She encouraged them to remain with their own people and find new husbands. One daughter-in-law, Orpah, took Naomi's advice. But the other, Ruth, could not be dissuaded. In one of the most stirring speeches of commitment in the Bible, she told her mother-in-law, "Don't urge me to leave you or to turn back from you. Where you go I will go, and where you stay I will stay. Your people will be my people and your God my God. Where you die I will die, and there I will be buried. May the Lord deal with me, be it ever so severely, if anything but death separates you and me" (Ruth 1:16–17).

Naomi and Ruth made it back to Bethlehem. Naomi had left there relatively wealthy, only to return empty, poor, and bitter. But she didn't stay

gleaning
Leviticus 19:9–10
kinsman-redeemer
Deuteronomy 25:5–10;
Ruth 4:14

gleaning
gathering leftover grain
after harvest
kinsman-redeemer
a person who takes
responsibility for a
deceased relative's
property and family

that way for long, because God had an extraordinary plan of deliverance for Naomi and her "forbidden" daughter-in-law.

Ruth did the only thing she could and began **gleaning** in the grain fields so the two women would have food (see Illustration #9). It was hard physical labor in the hot sun, but each morning she went back to the fields.

One day, she unwittingly began gleaning in fields belonging to Boaz, a relative of Elimelech, Naomi's dead husband. Through the family grapevine, Boaz had heard about Ruth's kindness and loyalty to Elimelech's widow. Apparently Ruth was beautiful enough for Boaz to notice her in the field. After making inquiries and finding out who she was, Boaz offered her his protection and told her not to go into any other fields. He even made sure she had extra grain. When Ruth came home and told Naomi about Boaz, Naomi praised God. Because Boaz was a relative, in Jewish law he could potentially be a **kinsman-redeemer**, take Ruth as his wife, and redeem Naomi's property.

In the end, Boaz married Ruth. (I'm leaving out a few plot twists, so you might want to read the story yourself.) God had provided for both the old widow and the young widow. But the story was larger than their lives. Boaz and Ruth produced a son, Obed, who was the grandfather of King David; and ultimately, David's lineage produced the Messiah.

Illustration #9
Man Using Sickle—
Harvesters would use
sickles to cut the
wheat stalks.
Man Gathering Wheat
Into Sheaves—After
the stalks were cut,
they were gathered
into "sheaves."
Gleaning—Old
Testament Law
allowed the poor to
follow the harvesters
and gather the grain
that fell to the ground
during harvesting. This
is what Ruth did.

In this snapshot of in-laws, we see love in action. Naomi and Ruth clung to each other and first did everything they could to survive, then surrendered and let God do the rest while they patiently waited on him. God turned a funeral filled with grief and sorrow into a wedding celebration complete with joy and new life.

God's plans are often far better and grander in scope than we can imagine. Who would have guessed that God wanted the Messiah to have a Moabite woman as his ancestor? But there she is (Matthew 1:5–6). After Naomi lost all the men in her life, and before God's redemption came, she must have had days of despair. Just as God surprised her with blessing upon blessing, he may have similar surprises in store for you. God truly redeems those he loves, and he still works through those who love him and "walk by faith, not by sight" (2 Corinthians 5:7 NASB).

In Naomi's time, a childless widow became the responsibility of her dead husband's brother, who would marry her, buy back the property of the deceased, and provide for the widow. Naomi gained redemption of her property through the marriage of Ruth and Boaz. Then Boaz gave her lineage through Obed. God offers us redemption through our "kinsman-redeemer," Jesus Christ. Through his death on the cross, Christ paid the price for man's redemption and salvation. In effect, he bought us back. And he has made us part of an eternal lineage. "In him we have redemption through his blood, the forgiveness of sins, in accordance with the riches of God's grace that he lavished on us with all wisdom and understanding" (Ephesians 1:7–8).

Facing Our Parents' Deaths

2 CORINTHIANS 5:1 *Now we know that if the earthly tent we live in is destroyed, we have a building from God, an eternal house in heaven, not built by human hands.*

My sweet little granny Curtis not only showed me how to live, but she also showed me how to die.

Her life was long, and everyone that knew Granny was blessed. She was a wonderful mother and grandmother. All of the grandkids could count on a safe, loving haven at her home.

A few months before she died, she could not recuperate from the flu. She normally was very healthy. She walked three miles a day, had a great diet, and remained very active. She was a survivor. She beat cancer at a young age and a severe heart attack just fifteen years earlier. But after several visits with her physician and no improvement, he admitted her to the hospital for tests. A few days later we learned she had terminal cancer.

Granny didn't waste any time making a decision. That day she decided she wanted to die at home surrounded by family and friends.

accept Christ
John 1:12; 3:16–18;
Matthew 7:21–23;
1 John 1:9

Hospice home care assisted with her medical needs. In just a matter of days, her health deteriorated, she grew weaker, and she became confined to bed, enduring an agonizing, painful, horrifying death.

At times her house—filled with flowers, cards, and friends—looked more like a funeral home. It was a blessing for her. Before she died she knew how many people loved her, and, previously unbeknownst to her, how many lives she had touched. She gained comfort from prayers, having the Bible read to her, and knowing everyone was close by and loved her. After a few short weeks she died in her family room, surrounded by her loving family.

Facing death is facing solitude and separation from all we know. Yet as believers we know it is the end of one life and the beginning of another. Granny prepared for that time. Many times when I was a little girl we would stop by her house and find her alone in the family room reading her Bible, seeking God. The Christmas before she died, while saying good-bye to my sister's family who lived out of state, Granny said, "This will probably be the last time I'll see you." She looked up and pointed to the sky with a grin. My brother-in-law laughed and gave her a big hug and tried to reassure her that "she was as healthy as a horse" and would outlive us all.

I've always wondered if Granny went back into her living room with a big smile on her face, for as time would tell, she knew her travel plans. She was in touch with her Maker. Six months later she was gone, and she is not forgotten. She spent her life here on earth preparing to spend eternity in heaven.

Granny will live in the hearts of every life she touched. I'll cling to her memories until I see her once more in heaven as she awaits my arrival.

Examples From the Bible

There is hope in life after death. You can <u>accept Christ</u> and claim heaven as your eternal home. Offer comfort by reading these Scriptures to your loved one facing death:

- Heaven is a holy dwelling place (Deuteronomy 26:15; 1 Kings 8:30; John 14:2).
- Heaven is more desirable than earth (Psalm 73:25).
- David yearned for heaven (Psalm 84:2).
- Eternal pleasures await us (Psalm 16:11).

- Heaven is God's throne (Isaiah 66:1).

- Jesus awaits those who believe in him (Luke 23:43).

- Jesus was taken up into heaven (Luke 24:50–52).

- Jesus describes heaven (John 14:1–6).

- Stephen saw the heavens as he was being stoned to death (Acts 7:55–56).

- We have hope in eternal life with God (1 Thessalonians 4:13–17).

- A "great cloud of witnesses" await us in heaven (Hebrews 12:1).

- Our inheritance is waiting in heaven (1 Peter 1:4).

- We will be made pure and whole in heaven (1 John 4:1–3).

- John describes heaven (Revelation 4:1–11).

- There is no pain, suffering, or death in heaven (Revelation 21:4).

- Heaven is a beautiful place (Revelation 21:19).

"Do not let your hearts be troubled. Trust in God; trust also in me. In my Father's house are many rooms; if it were not so, I would have told you. I am going there to prepare a place for you" (John 14:1–2).

How Others See It

Anne Graham Lotz

There will be no painful comparisons and no sibling rivalry in heaven. Every relationship will be reconciled and restored. Can you imagine? There will be humility and harmony, love and laughter, peace and joy, silence and singing, kindness and thoughtfulness, unity and purity, contentment and consideration. One day our heavenly home will be ready. With loving eagerness and anticipation of our joy, the Father will open the door to His House and gather His children home.[10]

Final Thoughts

- Contrary to the naysayers, you can get along with almost anybody—it just takes tons of effort, research, wisdom, and understanding on your part. Family will always be a part of our lives. They may bless us or haunt us, but it is up to you to decide how you will respond. Be willing to forgive.

- Maintain healthy communication with the ones you call family. Discovering your own personality and temperament will help you understand yourself and others as you strive to live in harmony.

- You can cultivate rewarding relationships with your in-laws. You have the power and wisdom from the Bible to transform the feud into friendship, and gain perspective and wisdom from your in-laws.

- Grandparents can play a vital role in nurturing, supporting, and building faith in our families. Grandchildren are their pride and joy. Take the effort to build upon their foundations and include them in your lives.

- Open your heart and eyes to the physical needs of your parents. As you become the caregiver of your aged parents, love them with your whole heart during this last passage of their lives.

Questions to Deepen Your Understanding

1. According to Proverbs 3:13–18, what do we need to acquire to live a blessed and happy life?

2. What spiritual nourishment do we need to handle difficult relationships?

3. What was the main ingredient in Miriam, Moses, and Aaron's relationship that saw them through conflict?

4. What personality type did Martha display?

5. What were Abigail's husband's negative attributes?

6. What suggestion did Moses' father-in-law give to Moses?

7. According to Scripture, who is responsible for taking care of the needs of widows?

read on

Some of Georgia's favorite books for striving for a balanced and healthy relationship with your extended family:

- *Changing Places: A Christian's Guide to Caring for Aging Parents*, Betty Benson Robertson, Beacon Hill Press

- *Deal with It!* Paula White, Nelson Ignite

- *The DNA of Relationships*, Gary Smalley, Tyndale

- *Foolproofing Your Life*, Jan Silvious, WaterBrook Press

- *Getting Along With Almost Anybody*, Florence Littauer, Revell

- *Heaven, My Father's House*, Anne Graham Lotz, W Publishing

- *Personality Plus*, Florence Littauer, Baker

- Web sites for information on caring for the elderly: Administration on Aging, *www.aoa.dhhs.gov;* National Association of Home Care, *www.nahc.org;* National Association of Professional Geriatric Care Managers, *www.caremanager.org;* State Health Insurance Assistance, *www.medicare.gov.*

- *Who's Pushing Your Buttons*, John Townsend, Integrity Publishers

- *The World's Greatest Guide to Family Relationships*, Gary Chapman and Randy Southern, Moody Publishers

Part Three

Bread, Breadwinners, and Bread Bakers

Chapter 7: Money, Money, Money

Discovering Smart Ways to Handle Money and Overcome Financial Failures

What's in This Chapter

- The Platinum Path to the Poorhouse
- Snapshot: The Prophet's Widow
- I Want It, and I Want It Now!
- The Big Question
- For Richer, for Poorer
- Snapshot: Lot's Wife
- Daddy Warbucks or Mommy Warbucks?
- Balance More Than Your Budget
- Stop, Thief!
- Give It Away
- Kids and Money
- Money-Back Guarantee

Here We Go

"It's my money and I'll do with it what I want!" Whoa! How many times have you either heard that statement or proclaimed it yourself? Well, contrary to popular belief, it's not your money. Actually, it's God's money. He has graciously loaned it to us. How we view and use his money will not only affect the quality of our lives in the physical realm, but also in the spiritual.

God created the universe and owns everything in it. He doesn't need our money. If he wants money, he can whip up a solid-gold planet. But he uses money as a meter. God can monitor our hearts' condition when he watches how we manage, spend, save, and let go of our money. He can look deep into our hearts and see the motivation that lies behind our actions, "for where your treasure is, there your heart will be also" (Matthew 6:21).

I don't know why or where people get the notion that women don't "do" money well. Maybe it's the same place they get the mother-in-law and dumb-blonde jokes. When it comes to money, I don't think there is a gender difference. The truth is, men and women can both be financially irresponsible and have issues on how to spend, how to save, or how to give away money. That's probably why money was a big topic of discussion for Jesus.

"How-to" money books have always been on the top of the *New York Times* bestseller list. The topics range from quick and dirty ways to make money, to how to safeguard your finances, how to invest, how to buy insurance, and how to plan for college, retirement, and death.

The Bible itself is a fantastic how-to book and has a great deal to say about money. Rest assured you're not the only financially challenged woman on the planet. With a little encouragement and guidance from the Word, you can discover smart ways to handle money and overcome financial failures. Money: It's not yours. It's God's!

Examples From the Bible

Jesus spent a great deal of time teaching on money:

- Give to the needy (Matthew 6:1–4).
- Your treasure in heaven (Matthew 6:19–20).
- Use your money to help spread the Gospel (Matthew 10:9–10, 41).
- Pay taxes (Matthew 17:24–27).
- God is generous (Matthew 20:1–16).
- Tithe plus more (Matthew 23:23).
- Use your resources to care for your family (Mark 7:11–13).
- Place God before money (Mark 10:17–31).
- Paying taxes to Caesar (Mark 12:13–17).
- The widow's blessed offering (Mark 12:41–44).
- Spend money on worship (Mark 14:4–5).
- Good Samaritan pays for a stranger's care (Luke 10:35–37).
- Be rich toward God (Luke 12:13–21).
- Be trustworthy (Luke 16:1–13).
- Be generous to the poor (Luke 16:19–31).
- Be humble in giving (Luke 18:9–14).
- Be honest in business (Luke 19:1–9).
- Do not waste (John 6:12).

The Platinum Path to the Poorhouse

PROVERBS 22:7 *The borrower is servant to the lender.*

The book of Proverbs has a lot to say about wealth. Scholars believe the sayings in Proverbs were compiled as a collection of instructions for the young men and future leaders of Israel, so we presume most of these guys came from wealthy families. And as we all know, just because Papa knew how to handle and accumulate wealth doesn't mean that little Hilkiah got the wealth gene. So in order to lead, Israel's finest young men were taught how to handle money.

In Bible times, if you were unable to pay back a loan, you could be forced to be the lender's slave until the loan was paid in full. Likewise, today, through our bad spending habits and the mentality of "buy now, pay later," we can easily become slaves to the lender as we work ourselves to death trying to pay off our debts.

I just received another one in the mail. The letter read, "Congratulations, Georgia Curtis Ling, you've been preapproved for a Platinum Card with a credit line up to $100,000. Platinum is more than a status symbol. . . ."

You know the rest of the story. You feel flattered until you find out credit card companies issue cards to just about anybody, including the dead and occasionally man's best friend. Due to living on credit, our nation now has more individuals filing for bankruptcy than ever. We live from paycheck to paycheck as our financial lives spin out of control. You start out with the regular old credit card, move on up to flashing that Gold Card, and after the Gold has lost its luster, you covet the shine and prestige of the Platinum. Before you know it, you've gone from Platinum to the poorhouse in no time. If the next letter from the credit company were honest, it would read, "Congratulations! You are a slave to your lender!" Wise up. Get out of debt and stay out.

Two of the best Bible-based books I've read on wising up financially are the bestseller *Financial Peace* and *The Total Money Makeover* by Dave Ramsey, a financial consultant and popular radio talk-show host. He experienced devastating financial ruin after getting too far into debt and nearly losing everything he owned.

Elijah
I Kings 17:1
Elisha
I Kings 19:19–21
Law
Leviticus 25:39–42
slaves
Nehemiah 5:1–5

prophet
a holy man with a spe-
cific, personal mission
from God

Tips from Dave Ramsey on credit card debt and payoff:

1. Throw a "plastic surgery party" with your family. That's right, cut the credit cards up.

2. Quit borrowing more money.

3. Start your debt reduction immediately.

4. Prioritize your debts in ascending order with the smallest remaining balance first and the largest last. Do this regardless of interest rate or payment.

5. Pay the debts off in this new order.

6. As you pay off the first debt, take the amount you used on that payment and add it to the next payment on the list.[2]

How Others See It

Dave Ramsey

I know that suggesting you stay out of debt is radical and may seem utterly ridiculous, but I am tired of seeing grown adults on the brink of suicide, widows left with a legacy of debt, and children who are taught by example that if I want it I get it now. Dump debt. If you don't, remember you are instantly the servant to the lender.[3]

Snapshots of Women in the Bible
The Prophet's Widow (2 Kings 4:1–7)

The widow sat alone on the dusty floor in her little empty house and wept bitterly. She rocked back and forth, clutching her own arms for comfort. The one who once held her in his arms was dead. She grieved for the loss of the man she loved, but now she faced a greater threat: the loss of her sons.

Her husband died and left them with nothing. She could have coped with that loss, for her husband was a man of God, a junior **prophet** in training under Elijah and Elisha. They lived in a small community of loving, caring, and godly people. She knew she could rely on them in her time of need. But her husband had left them in debt, and under the Law, her creditors had the right to take her children as slaves to repay the debt. She couldn't bear to lose her sons. Even with her mind paralyzed with fear, she knew she must go to the only man she could turn to.

She drew her scarf of mourning over her face, and in her black <u>sackcloth</u> she ran to Elisha, the prophet. She hoped this man of miracles had one for her. The widow fell at his feet and told her story. Elisha, too, mourned for the loss of one of his students and listened to her with compassion and wisdom.

Elisha asked what she had in her home. Did she have nothing of value? The widow said she only had a jar of oil (see Illustration #10) her husband had used for <u>anointing</u>. Elisha nodded his head in contemplation. Finally, he instructed her to go to her neighbors and to borrow as many empty vessels as she could find. Then she was to take her sons into the house, shut the door, and pour the jar of oil into the vessels.

It made no sense. The contents of one little jar would only moisten the bottom of one empty vessel; why assemble a house full of them? But instead of questioning the illogical instructions, she quickly obeyed. A glimmer of hope lit in her heart as she ran home, called her sons, and went from house to house gathering vessels.

When they had done as Elisha instructed, they closed the door and huddled around the first vessel. She held the tiny bottle of oil and looked into the questioning eyes of her sons. Then she began carefully pouring the oil.

Her heart beat faster as she saw the oil well up in the first jar. The boys smiled in puzzlement. A new light danced in their hollow eyes as they grabbed another container and watched it fill. Then another, and another, and another until all were filled! Their miracle had come! Sunbeams shone through the cracks in the roof onto the full containers, and the oil glistened like gold as the widow wrapped her arms around her sons and wept tears of joy.

The widow told the boys to stay inside the house with the door shut, as she had to go learn what to do next.

She ran through the community to Elisha and excitedly told him what happened. She requested his further <u>guidance</u>. Elisha told her to go, sell the oil, pay her debts, and live on the rest. The prophet's widow trusted this man of God, received a miracle, and her mourning was turned to joy. Now her sons would not be taken as slaves to repay her husband's debt.

This widow's snapshot reveals a woman who knew she must take action even though life had taken a horrific turn for the worse. She turned to a wise, trustworthy man. She followed his advice by using what little she

sackcloth
Genesis 37:34
anointing
Luke 7:44–50
guidance
Proverbs 12:15

sackcloth
a coarse black cloth, usually made of goat's hair, worn as a sign of mourning
anointing
Persons and things were anointed with oil to signify separation unto God.

had to get out of debt. In his wisdom, Elisha knew she and her family needed to experience this miracle together. Facing adversity, then experiencing God's grace and deliverance together as a family, would bond them as one.

If you've become a slave to your debtor, first pray for wisdom, then seek advice from a godly person you can trust. Take action and use what you have before going to others for help. Involve your family in this challenge. Empty your heart of pride, anger, and resentment and let God pour himself into you, for he is able to do immeasurably more than all we ask or imagine, according to his power that is at work within us" (Ephesians 3:20).

I Want It, and I Want It Now!

1 TIMOTHY 6:6–10 *But godliness with contentment is great gain. For we brought nothing into the world, and we can take nothing out of it. But if we have food and clothing, we will be content with that. People who want to get rich fall into temptation and a trap and into many foolish and harmful desires that plunge men into ruin and destruction. For the love of money is a root of all kinds of evil. Some people, eager for money, have wandered from the faith and pierced themselves with many griefs.*

The apostle Paul hit the nail on the head. Godliness with contentment is the key to life. It is the key that unlocks the door of the plastic prison of credit card debt and the key that opens the heart to a new way of life.

When we focus on wanting more things, we are saying that God has not given us enough. His gifts to us are endless—the ability to see new buds on the trees, smell garden roses, feel crisp fall air against our skin, taste fresh apple cider, hear snow crunch beneath our boots. The love of money gets our eyes off God's greatness and makes us dissatisfied with what we have.

There is nothing inherently wrong with wealth. Wealth and poverty are both litmus tests of our character. Contrary to misquoted Scripture, money is not the root of all evil. The love of money, also known as greed, is the root of all evil. Greed can become an all-consuming drive that can throw you off balance and even lead you into physical and spiritual bankruptcy.

Examples From the Bible

If greed had a face, it would look like one of these:

- **Delilah** is known throughout history as the one who betrayed her lover Samson. The Philistines were enemies of **Samson** and they wanted him dead. They approached Delilah and offered her a huge sum of money to find the secret of Samson's strength. Her greed motivated her acts of betrayal. (Judges 16:5)

- **Judas Iscariot**, one of the twelve disciples of Jesus, was not content with the direction of Jesus' ministry. Judas betrayed Jesus for thirty pieces of silver and turned him over to Jesus' enemies to be crucified. (Mark 14:10, 43)

- **Simon the Sorcerer** amazed the people of Samaria with his sorcerous power. Philip, an evangelist, came to town and preached about Jesus. Simon became one of his converts. When Simon saw the miracles the apostles were able to do, he offered them money to purchase the secrets of their special gifts. Peter rebuked him, saying his heart was not right— Simon only wanted special powers to continue manipulating people. (Acts 8:9–24)

Advertising works! That's why companies spend millions and millions of dollars to make you believe that you will be the happiest woman on earth, your children will love you, your significant other will shower you with affection, and you'll have fun-loving friends if you live in a mini-mansion, drive the coolest car on the block, buy the latest techno gadget, shop for the latest sexiest shoes and lingerie, and take exotic vacations, all purchased on your low-interest credit card and redeemed with spending points.

Delilah
means "dainty one"
Samson
twelfth judge of Israel; known for his strength
Judas Iscariot
disciple who betrayed Jesus

Month after month Americans fall prey to advertising gurus and fail to pay off credit-card debts. And installment debt keeps creeping higher and higher.

Does that sound familiar? We're just like the little kid in the toy store pitching a fit because we want it and we want it now, and we'll maneuver our finances around until we get what we want . . . now!

As much as I would like to blame plastic for our financial crises, I can't. We need to take a look inside, put away childish behavior, and start anew, following the apostle Paul's example: "When I was a child, I talked like a child, I thought like a child, I reasoned like a child. When I became a man, I put childish ways behind me" (1 Corinthians 13:11). We can find true contentment in Christ if we honor God with our finances and material possessions.

What You Can Do

Words of a wise woman shopper:

- "Honey, what about this?" (Make joint decisions on purchases over $100.)

- "Where's your sales rack?" (Never pay full price.)

- "Gucci? Gucci who?" (Buy quality, but without the designer label attached.)

- "Put it down, walk away, and nobody gets hurt." (Never buy on impulse.)

- "May I read the fine print, please?" (Investigate. Never believe what advertisers say. "No money down" translated is "Pay big interest later!")

- "It'll be cash." (Cash only! On average, you'll spend 38 percent more if you charge it.)

- "I would like a refund, please." (Take it back if the product is faulty.)

- "Where's the scissors?" (Use coupons. Shop around and find a grocer that discounts, then buy in bulk.)

- "On the thirteenth day of Christmas my true love said to me, 'Let's go shopping!'" (Buy during after-Christmas sales for your kid's next winter coat and other big-cost items.)

When we search for contentment in the wrong place we remain unfulfilled even when we reach our goals. A wealthy businessman visited a psychiatrist because of deep depression. "I have everything I ever wanted," the businessman said. "If I manage to find something to buy that I don't have, I don't even have to go get it myself. I have so much money I can pay someone to buy it for me. I have no reason for living."

The Big Question

My dining room table looked as if a tornado had swept up a mail truck and dumped all its contents on my table. Copies of the newspaper I write for were stacked up high in one corner, a tall pile of paid bills teetered in the middle, and a shorter stack of unpaid bills hunkered patiently beside them. There were outdated magazines, statements, documents, business materials waiting to be filed, and a lone calculator. The table was proof I was a member of the Messies' Club of America.

Summer had been a whirlwind of out-of-town trips. While away, I had neighbors feed Alice the cat, and pick up our mail and drop it off on the dining room table. I intended to go through the mail and relocate it to my office, but I didn't follow through, so the mail piled up.

As I looked at the award-winning Messies Unite table, several words popped into my head: Priorities. Reorganization. Time management. Those bills were a telltale sign of where my financial priorities lay. The unfiled bank statements and documents screamed "Organize us!" and the unread magazines and business materials sent a message that flashed like a yellow neon sign: Time Management! Time Management!

That still, small voice whispered these questions to my heart: What are your priorities? Where are you wasting time? What can you delegate? What can you say no to? Is this a good role model for your child?

advice
Philippians 2:1–4

What changes can you make in reorganizing your time and life? Are you glorifying God in whatever you do?

As those questions whirled around in my head, I knew I had some major planning to do. I still don't have all the answers, but I have one big question that is a great starting point: What is my purpose for living?

Actually, I already know that answer. It just has to be reaffirmed daily with these words: "Whether, then, you eat or drink or whatever you do, do all to the glory of God" (1 Corinthians 10:31 NASB).

Sorry, I've got to cut this a little short. I have to go reorganize and manage my time.

For Richer, for Poorer

PHILIPPIANS 2:14–15 *Do everything without complaining or arguing, so that you may become blameless and pure, children of God without fault in a crooked and depraved generation, in which you shine like stars in the universe.*

In Philippians, the apostle Paul encourages the believers at Philippi (see Illustration #13 on page 180) to mend relationships. He wants them to work it out not only for their own sakes, but as a testimony to those watching. For realistic solutions to the money time bomb, as women of the Word, we need to heed Paul's advice and stop arguing, grumbling, and complaining. We need to get along with our better half when it comes to finances. Our lives are to be a beacon of Christ and his power in our community, not fodder for gossip in divorce court.

Money problems can, at times, cause explosive marriage problems. Whether rich or poor, too many happy couples end up in divorce court because they allowed their financial behaviors to destroy their marriage. Make an effort to resolve the money issue not only for your marriage, but for your witness.

When it comes to marriage and money we can learn from Paul's <u>advice</u> to the Philippians. No matter what your temperament and spending behavior, in marriage you must work together on a budget, come to an agreement, and commit to a financial plan you can both live with. (You may also have to add an extra dose of patience, forgiveness, and apologies along the way.) Stop arguing and find a solution to your financial problems before it's too late.

The book of Proverbs points out, "All hard work brings a profit, but mere talk leads only to poverty" (14:23). We need to take action and quit just talking about getting finances in order. Actually sit down together, remember your love for one another, and unite in your purpose, vision, and spirit. Don't let money pull you apart. It's not worth it.

I recently heard a friend of ours preach a series on money. It was based on a 10–10–80 plan (see Illustration #11). He entitled the sermons "Give God Your Best, Put a Few in Your Nest, and Live Wisely on the Rest." His simple plan: tithe 10 percent of your income, save 10 percent, and on the 80 percent left, choose to live wisely.

In marriage it seems most of us get stuck on the "live wisely" part. Since opposites seem to attract, it's inevitable that you'll have differences of opinion on how to live on the 80 percent. As a wise counselor once told me, "If you have a budget when conflicts arise, then you can blame the budget instead of attacking and blaming each other. Then make adjustments, either in your budget or your behavior."

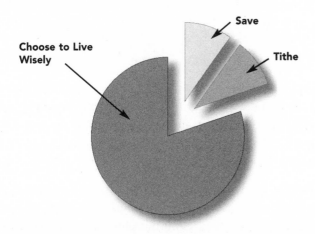

Choose to Live Wisely

Save

Tithe

Illustration #11
Pie Chart for Your Money—This chart gives you a picture of the 10–10–80 approach to financial planning. As you can see, after tithing and saving, you will still have plenty left over.

How Others See It

Dave Ramsey

Successfully married couples learn that the "you" in "unity" is a silent syllable. You win at marriage by losing your selfish need to get your way in every battle. I am not saying that you must be a doormat, but I am saying most of the turf that couples battle over isn't nearly as important as the damage the battle brings to a relationship. You get happy marriages by giving up selfish desires in order to win together—winning at creating your visions and goals that flow out of your shared values.[5]

separated
Genesis 13:1–18
warned
Genesis 18:16–33

gate
the inside entrance of
the city, where judges
sat to witness legal
transactions

Snapshots of Women in the Bible
Lot's Wife (Genesis 13 and 18)

Lot and his family <u>separated</u> from his uncle Abraham. The land could not support the wealthy possession of livestock and herdsmen they both owned, so Lot chose the plain of Jordan, a beautiful oasis outside the cities of Sodom and Gomorrah. There, Lot's clan pitched their tents and set up camp.

Was it Lot's wife who wasn't content? Maybe the plains were too boring and she longed for the festivities and excitement of the city housekeeping (see Illustration #12). Or was she tired of living in a tent and wanted a big stone house of luxury inside the city gates? For whatever reason, eventually Lot and his family moved from living near this wicked, sinful city, to living in the middle of it. When next we see Lot, he is sitting daily at the city **gate**, the ancient equivalent of city hall.

The Lord <u>warned</u> Abraham of the forthcoming destruction of Sodom and Gomorrah. Abraham begged God to spare Lot, so the Lord sent angels to warn Lot and lead him to safety. Upon their arrival at the gate, Lot greeted the angels (unaware of their real identity) and quickly led them to his home, for fear the townsmen would harm them.

Lot's fears became reality as men, young and old, surrounded his house and demanded sex with the strangers. As these sinful townsmen shouted at Lot, he feared they would break in and wipe out not only the strangers, but also his family. In desperation, he stepped outside and offered the mob his daughters for their sexual gratification in place of the angels.

The angels pulled Lot inside the house and blinded the men who were trying to break down the door. Eventually the angels led Lot's family out of the city, warned them of the cataclysmic punishment about to descend from heaven, and told them to flee without looking back. But Lot's wife couldn't let go. As she fled, she cast one glance back at the lifestyle she loved, and God turned her into a pillar of salt.

In Lot's wife's reaction we see an example of how she and her husband were not like-minded. Lot followed God's instructions and ran for his life, while Lot's wife loved the things of the world more than God.

Your own personal relationship with God should be your top priority. He will direct you to put your family next in priority. Wealth and riches may or may not come, but we have to cherish and be content with God and let go of what holds us back from surrendering all to him. Are we pitching our tents ever closer to wickedness, putting our families a distant second, all in the name of money and career? My prayer is found in Proverbs 30:7–9: "Two things I ask of you, O Lord; do not refuse me before I die: Keep falsehood and lies far from me; give me neither poverty nor riches, but give me only my daily bread. Otherwise, I may have too much and disown you and say, 'Who is the Lord?' Or I may become poor and steal, and so dishonor the name of my God."

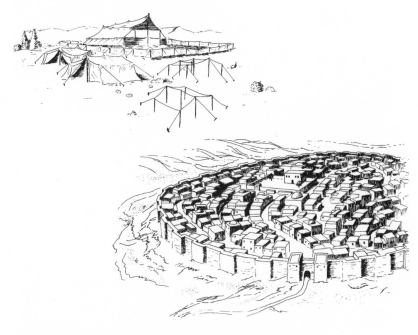

Illustration #12
Tent Living vs. City Living—The lure of the city, even with its wickedness, moved Lot's wife from the outskirts of town into the center of sin.

Daddy Warbucks or Mommy Warbucks?

PROVERBS 23:12 *Apply your heart to instruction and your ears to words of knowledge.*

As Scripture encourages, "apply your heart to instruction and your ears to words of knowledge" (Proverbs 23:12), we can improve our financial portfolio if we understand and face our traits, and learn how to tame the negative side of our temperaments and build on the strengths.

Who's the "Big Spender" in your family? You or your husband? It is unusual to find a couple with the same temperament. If you do, you usually read about them in the paper, like Bonnie and Clyde.

We talked about different temperaments in chapter 3 when dealing with getting along with family. When it comes to finances and spending behaviors, you've got to know the personality traits, temperaments, strengths, and weaknesses of you and your spouse. This will give you more insight on the "whys" of your spending behavior and will help make a positive change.

Our temperaments affect everything we do. Temperament can determine how big or small our house will be, how much we spend or save, and even what type of car we cruise around in or limp along with. You and your husband are not financially challenged; you just have different personality challenges. You can change your behavior.

Examples From the Bible

Couples' temperaments and differences:

1. **Isaac and Rebekah** (Genesis 24)
   - Isaac: loner, peace-loving, trusting
   - Rebekah: high-spirited, helpful, scheming
   - Compatibility: probably good; they shared a heritage of faith and family

2. **Jacob and Rachel** (Genesis 29)
   - Jacob: resourceful and hardworking with a deeply spiritual and emotionally vulnerable side
   - Rachel: bright, determined, competitive
   - Compatibility: assumed to be good; Jacob adored Rachel

3. **Boaz and Ruth** (Book of Ruth)
   - Boaz: loyal, hardworking, sincere, brave
   - Ruth: loyal, fair, generous, honorable, optimistic
   - Compatibility: apparently excellent; both partners were honorable, kind, and loyal

4. **Samson and Delilah** (Judges 16)
   - Samson: charming, brave, rebellious, vengeful, a womanizer
   - Delilah: greedy, self-centered, manipulative
   - Compatibility: low; neither partner seemed to truly value the other

5. **Elkanah and Hannah** (1 Samuel 1–2)
   - Elkanah: patient, gentle, kind, devout
   - Hannah: passionate, intensely devout, true to her word
   - Compatibility: excellent; mutually devoted to God

Balance More Than Your Budget

PROVERBS 21:5 *The plans of the diligent lead to profit as surely as haste leads to poverty.*

We all have weaknesses in our behaviors, but we can't use that for an excuse. God wants us to honor him with everything, including our finances. Are you a fun-loving sanguine who buys on impulse and somehow you've gotten yourself in way over your head with debt? Get control and plan ahead. Are you a controlling choleric who manages money pretty well, but you come across like a drill sergeant demanding to know down to the penny how much was spent? Lighten up, show a little love and tenderness, put family feelings over money. What about those budget-minded melancholies (that's me!) out there who are afraid to let go of the money, and if you do it takes you forever to plan the release? Don't be afraid; take a little risk. And last but not least, what about Mrs. Easygoing Phlegmatic, who never has a say and lets everyone do what they want, just to keep peace? Speak up, be heard; you are a valued member of your family. Follow God's guidelines. Honor him with tithes and offerings.

Examples From the Bible

How spending time with Jesus transformed others:

- **Simon Peter**—impulsive, passionate, fearful—moved from fear to boldness. (Luke 22:31–34; Matthew 14:22–31; 16:13–19; Acts 2:14)

- **James**—ambitious, short-tempered, judgmental, self-righteous—became committed enough to die for the sake of Christ. (Matthew 4:18–21; Mark 3:17; 10:35–40; Luke 9:52–56; Acts 12:1–2)

- **John**—ambitious, self-righteous—moved from judgmental to loving. (Luke 9:52–56; John 19:26–27; 21:20–24)

- **Andrew**—eager to please—became someone who told others about Christ. (Matthew 3:18; John 6:8–9; 12:22)

check this out

Law
Leviticus 27:30–34;
Genesis 14:20

tithes
contribution to God of
one-tenth of the pro-
duce of one's land or
income

• **Nathanael**—doubtful, honest, straightforward—turned from doubt to belief. (John 1:45–51; 21:1–13)

• **Thomas**—doubtful—turned from doubt to belief and courage. (John 14:5–6; 20:24–29; 21:1–13)[7]

How Others See It

Ellie Kay

As a military family who moved twelve times in thirteen years, we learned that home is where our family is—not the physical dwelling that we live in. Sure, we want a nice, big, spacious place to call our own, but we can learn to be content in a smaller one if our family is together. Your kids will always remember your home as bigger than what it was. But even more than that, they'll remember what happened between the walls that you called home.[8]

Stop, Thief!

MALACHI 3:8–10 *"Will a man rob God? Yet you rob me. But you ask, 'How do we rob you?' In tithes and offerings. You are under a curse— the whole nation of you—because you are robbing me. Bring the whole tithe into the storehouse, that there may be food in my house. Test me in this," says the Lord Almighty, "and see if I will not throw open the flood-gates of heaven and pour out so much blessing that you will not have room enough for it."*

We find in the book of Malachi that God had been faithful to his people, yet Israel kept turning away from him. One glaring wrongdoing was their refusal to follow the <u>Law</u> in giving **tithes** and offerings. God required the Israelites to give a standard amount (one-tenth of their income) back to him. The Israelites were required to give their tithes to the priests, Levites, aliens, widows, and orphans.

Because they refused to tithe, everyone suffered. The widows and orphans suffered because they went hungry. The priests suffered because they were supposed to benefit from the offerings of animals and food, but these were lacking. Those who refused to give their tithes suffered as God held back his blessing on the people. God suffered heartache and disappointment as he watched his people rob him of love and honor. Though they started out robbing God, they ended up robbing themselves.

I think by nature we are takers, not givers. From day one as cute little babies we enjoy receiving every need or want we might have. I think God

     WHAT'S IN THE BIBLE FOR WOMEN

set up the principle of giving because he knew that if we didn't have guidelines, it would be easy for us to slip back into that selfish-baby mode, just receive with a smile, and forget to pay honor to whom honor is due.

Jesus praised the widow who gave her offering of two <u>mites</u>, hardly enough to buy a loaf of bread. When compared to the gifts of the wealthy, the cash value of her gift was hardly enough to notice. But the devotion behind it was another matter. That devotion, beginning there and spreading throughout the world, has built hospitals and helped the needy, fed the hungry, and encouraged the imprisoned. Today the world knows more about that poor widow than about the richest Jew of her day.[9] Failing to tithe is like robbing God and robbing ourselves.

check this out

mites
Luke 21:3–4

Examples From the Bible

"Mary (called Magdalene) . . . ; Joanna the wife of Cuza, the manager of Herod's household; Susanna; and many others. These women were helping to support them [Jesus and the disciples] out of their own means" (Luke 8:2–3). These women accompanied Jesus and his disciples proclaiming the Good News of the kingdom of God. The Bible's listing them and their contributions shows how valuable and meaningful their financial support was to Jesus' ministry as they freely gave from their own wealth.

How Others See It

Joel Osteen

You can't rob God and expect Him to bless you at the same time. You must realize, God doesn't need your money or your time or your talent. When God asks us to give, it's not because He's trying to get something from us. No, it's because He's trying to get us to put some seed in the ground so we can reap a harvest. God abides by the laws He has established, and if you don't sow, you will not reap.[10]

Give It Away

2 CORINTHIANS 9:6–7 *Remember this: Whoever sows sparingly will also reap sparingly, and whoever sows generously will also reap generously. Each man should give what he has decided in his heart to give, not reluctantly or under compulsion, for God loves a cheerful giver.*

You don't have to be a farmer to understand what the apostle Paul wrote to the Corinthian church (see Illustration #13). A picture is worth a thousand words, and Paul is painting a masterpiece. He reminds us of what any smart farmer knows: in order to produce a bountiful harvest, he has to plan for it, plow it, plant it, and then pick a peck of produce. He also knows what to expect from what he sows. A few seeds will not produce a bumper crop.

Some Christians respond to this teaching by saying, "I don't have to tithe! That system was the Old Testament law. I live in the New Testament era of grace!" While you are technically correct, the teaching of the New Testament regarding money calls for far more generosity than the Old Testament.

Illustration #13
The Roman Empire—Within thirty years of Jesus' resurrection, the Gospel had spread through the Roman Empire. There were Christian groups in most of its major cities. The well-known apostles Peter and Paul were influential in sharing the Gospel throughout the empire.

Jesus said, "Give to the one who asks you, and do not turn away from the one who wants to borrow from you" (Matthew 5:42). "Give to everyone who asks you, and if anyone takes what belongs to you, do not demand it back" (Luke 6:30). Would you rather give a tithe, or give to every single charitable cause who makes a request of you? Hello? If you get as many fund-raising solicitations as I do, 10 percent is a bargain!

helping others
Luke 6:38

Jesus taught, "When you give to the needy, do not let your left hand know what your right hand is doing" (Matthew 6:3). So genuine New Testament giving would be to close your eyes, plunge your hand into your wallet or purse, blindly clutch at a bunch of bills, and give away whatever you grabbed!

Okay, maybe that's not the most accurate explanation of Matthew 6:3. But don't miss my point. The New Testament indicates that our priority list should have money on the low end and <u>helping others</u> on the high end. We should not only tithe, but give from our hearts with additional expressions of love and honor as we watch God work through our gifts.

When I write out a check to my church in a tithe or a love gift to a ministry in need, it's like I'm sending a thank-you note to God, honoring him for his many blessings on my life.

Kids and Money

> **DEUTERONOMY 6:6–7** *These commandments that I give you today are to be upon your hearts. Impress them on your children. Talk about them when you sit at home and when you walk along the road, when you lie down and when you get up.*

As parents we have the responsibility to teach our children all the commandments, laws, and principles found in Scripture. As we go about living life, we are to constantly impress these principles in our children's hearts and minds.

You have to admit it, an ATM has to be one of the coolest and most convenient inventions in banking. Money on demand! However, it can be a negative teaching tool for our children. To them, it's a magic money machine.

When our son was a toddler, we were out running errands, and he asked to stop for a snack at a drive-through window. When I told him I didn't have any extra cash, he suggested we just go to the money machine to get some more! Just like the old Dorito's commercial—eat them, we'll make more. Ouch!

We must teach our children at an early age the basics of economy. We don't want them to grow up and be the poster children for the sequel to *Dumb and Dumber*. They must know how to manage their income. Who better to teach them than their parents?

Remember the 10–10–80 rule? "Give God your best, put a few eggs in the nest, and live wisely on the rest." That's a great way to start with your children. When it comes to kids and what they learn, more is caught than taught. That means the best way to teach them is by example. Then follow up on your example with short instructive lessons. One of the greatest investments for your children's future is to teach them about money.

Money-Back Guarantee

I learned my first lesson on giving at an early age. When I was eight, my parents became Christians and were baptized. They were trying to raise a young family with four kids, build a family business, put shoes on our little feet, and set food on our table. They barely scraped by. But from studying the Scriptures my dad became convinced that he needed to begin tithing. He didn't know how the family would manage it, but he felt it had to be done.

So he began praying about his decision. Then his best friend came to him with a business opportunity. A national specialty advertising company was looking for a representative in that area. They had initially approached Dad's friend, but he had too many irons in the fire. He suggested Dad's name. So along with his family business, Dad added a moonlighting job and began selling immediately. Within several weeks the income from his moonlighting covered his initial tithe, plus the tithe from his advertising sales.

That was more than thirty years ago. In retirement Dad still sells advertising part time and continues to increase his earnings year after year. Needless to say, he is an advocate of tithing and giving above one's tithe. And he always practiced what he preached. Dad has used his sales techniques to encourage other Christians to tithe, offering a money-back guarantee. To this day, he's never had a dissatisfied customer.

So that's how I grew up in a tithing family. My parents taught me first to tithe from my allowance, then from cash gifts, and eventually, as I joined the workforce, from my paycheck. As a kid, I was merely practicing the letter of the Law. But as I grew and began my own personal relationship with Jesus, I discovered the fulfillment of the Law and the love of God. That's when I began giving above my tithe. I just followed my heart.

When you study Old Testament history, you will see that the people of Israel did not regard the laws of God as burdens, but as a joy. The Law was God's expression to Israel that they were his holy people. Their gratitude and obedience motivated God's continued generosity and set them free from slavery. They strayed from the Law, but whenever they repented, God always blessed them. (For one example, read about Josiah in 2 Kings 22:17–20.)

If we're really children of God, we won't consider giving a burden, but a joy. Let's willingly give our gifts to God, for his glory.

Final Thoughts

- The road to debt-free living requires taking a good look at the woman in the rearview mirror, then reading these road signs: STOP using credit cards. GO seek wise financial advice. YIELD to sound counsel. CAUTION, don't give in to the entrapments of materialism. If you can't afford it, don't buy it. Replace compulsion and consumption with contentment.

- If you allow, money problems can destroy your marriage. If you can't come to an agreement on your own, seek counsel in working together and devising a plan you both can live with.

- Our temperaments play a vital role in our financial behaviors, good or bad. Discover your and your husband's temperaments. God made us unique; don't let those differences tear you apart. If we learn from one another, we can both benefit from those very things that drive us nuts.

- We honor God with our giving through our tithes and offerings of love. Everyone benefits from giving it away . . . especially the giver.

- The future of our world economy lies in the hands of our children. It is our responsibility to teach our children godly principles of finances, for what they do or don't know about money will either hurt or help them and generations to come.

Questions to Deepen Your Understanding

1. What does the Scripture say about being in debt?

2. The prophet's widow overcame financial ruin. What was the first step she took in solving her problem?

3. What is the key that unlocks the door to a plastic prison? According to 1 Timothy 6:6–10, where do you find that key?

4. Why is it so important to get along with your spouse when it comes to finances?

5. What kept Lot's wife from being like-minded with her husband?

6. Why did Jesus praise the widow who gave a small offering that was barely enough to buy a loaf of bread when others gave large amounts of offering?

7. According to the apostle Paul in 2 Corinthians 9:6–8, how are we to give?

read on

Some of Georgia's favorite books for discovering smart ways to handle money and overcome financial failures:

- *Debt-Proof Living*, Mary M. Hunt, Faithworks

- *Discovering God's Way of Handling Money*, Crown Financial Ministries

- *Financial Peace*, Dave Ramsey, Viking Press

- *How to Save Money Every Day*, Ellie Kay, Baker

- *In Pursuit of Peace*, Joyce Meyer, WarnerFaith

- *Living Well as a Single Mom*, Cynthia Yates, Harvest House

- *A Mom's Guide to Family Finances*, Ellie Kay, Spire

- *Money Doesn't Grow on Trees: Teaching Your Kids the Value of a Buck*, Ellie Kay, Baker

- *The Total Money Makeover*, Dave Ramsey, Thomas Nelson

- *Trend Savvy Parenting*, Dr. May Manz Simon, Tyndale

- *Your Best Life Now*, Joel Osteen, WarnerFaith

- *Your Kids Can Master Their Money: Fun Ways to Help Them Learn How*, Ron Blue, Judy Blue, and Jeremy White, Tyndale

Chapter 8: All I Do Is Work, Work, Work

Enjoying Work Inside or Outside the Home

What's in This Chapter

- Daylight 'Til Dark, or Nine to Five
- Working Women
- Take This Job and Love It!
- A Tale of Two Modern Women
- Catfight!
- Lunch Is on Me
- Snapshot: Lydia
- Office Romance: The Good, the Bad, and the Ugly
- The Good Office Romance
- The Bad Office Romance
- The Ugly Office Romance
- Bringing Work Home
- This Is God's Company
- Snapshot: Priscilla
- If I Learned Everything I Need to Know in Kindergarten, Why Am I Still in School at Forty?
- Sister Heads Back to School

Here We Go

Believe it or not, work is not a dirty "four-letter word." Our Creator experienced great fulfillment and pride in his creation of the universe. As a matter of fact, Scripture tells us that God saw his handiwork and said it was good. He liked his work!

He even had a job in mind for Adam: God placed him in the Garden of Eden to tend and care for it. Work was <u>good</u> . . . that is, until sin entered the Garden and man turned away from God's original plan. The privilege and pleasure of gardening turned to dread and drudgery as God <u>cursed</u> the land. Man would forevermore struggle to make a living.

Not only did Adam work, but God's Son worked too. Jesus spent all but the last three years of his life as a <u>carpenter</u>, either helping his earthly father or working on his own.

The Bible is filled with stories of women who worked and worked and worked. As a matter of fact, those who were <u>idle</u> were told to get busy.

check this out

good
Genesis 1:26
cursed
Genesis 3:16–19
carpenter
Mark 6:3
idle
I Timothy 5:13

cursed
to say a thing is worthy of evil or trouble

If work for you seems like a "four-letter word," let's take a look at what the Bible has to say about women and their toil. With God's help, maybe you can recover your whistle while you work!

Daylight Till Dark, or Nine to Five

COLOSSIANS 3:23–24 *Whatever you do, work at it with all your heart, as working for the Lord, not for men, since you know that you will receive an inheritance from the Lord as a reward. It is the Lord Christ you are serving.*

Whatever you call work, or whether or not you have a boss you consider a hard taskmaster, you can learn from the apostle Paul addressing the slave/master relationship. Millions of slaves kept the Roman Empire functioning. As slaves such as <u>Onesimus</u> became believers in Christ, Paul admonished them to do their work as if they were doing it for the Lord. They were to work having the attitude of a sincere, obedient servant. But Paul knew slaves were not compensated according to the difficulty or quantity of their work, so he reminded them that ultimately our eternal inheritance and relationship with Christ are our reward.

His instructions parallel with our employee/employer relationships. As with the Roman slaves, in everything we do, the first step in making work . . . um, work, is: strive to please Christ. Put him first, and then everything else will fall into place.

Women have always worked. The ancient Bible woman worked from dawn until dark. Her tasks included:

- providing food and clothing for her family
  (Genesis 27:9; 1 Samuel 2:19)

- educating the younger children (Proverbs 1:8)

- baking bread (1 Samuel 28:24)

- sewing each garment by hand (Exodus 35:25)

- gathering water every night at the local well for her family
  (Genesis 24:11)

She worked! She didn't have the conveniences of a local 7-Eleven or a department store. And we think we have it hard with only one microwave and limited grocery delivery!

Working Women

In early America, the Native American woman worked just to survive. The black slave woman worked at backbreaking labor for no wage. The white woman worked on farms and raised food to help make a way for her family. Women have always worked. And worked and worked. It wasn't until the late eighteenth century, when textile mills in New England needed women's sewing skills, that women began to "go" to work and punch a time clock.

The face of the work clock is forever changing. For sheer quantity, America now has the highest number of women in the workforce ever. We're seeing a nontraditional time clock tick toward a more flexible schedule as women attempt to structure work in new ways so they can spend more time with their families at home. It's always a struggle to juggle career fulfillment, finances, and a balanced family life.

How Others See It

Elizabeth George

As wise women, you and I are to dedicate our lives to knowing and doing God's will. Then, as we seek to do His will, the management of the minutes, the hours, and the days of our lives will come much easier. Why? Because we will be traveling in God's direction, toward God's will. Instead of struggling against God and His plans and purposes for us, we'll be seeking to do God's work God's way. That's the key to life management, my dear sister—doing God's work God's way![1]

Take This Job and Love It!

ECCLESIASTES 3:11–13 *He has made everything beautiful in its time. He has also set **eternity** in the hearts of men; yet they cannot fathom what God has done from beginning to end. I know that there is nothing better for men than to be happy and do good while they live. That everyone may eat and drink, and find satisfaction in all his toil—this is the gift of God.*

Solomon, the author of Ecclesiastes, was known for his wisdom and for the enjoyment of the pleasures of a rich lifestyle. The theme of the book centers around the question "Is life really worth living?" The answer is— yes! Life is a gift from God. Be happy and do good while you live. Enjoy your family, enjoy your work, and enjoy the simple pleasures of food and drink. But Solomon also reminds us that we only find true satisfaction in

Life is a gift from God.
Genesis 2:7

eternity
the desire or yearning of a forever home with God

seeking and doing the will of God in our lives, as God placed "eternity" in our hearts.

think about it

Worldly pleasures never satisfy—only God can satisfy your soul. Only God gives meaning to work . . . meaning to life . . . meaning to death. Solomon wraps the book up with one last thought: "Fear God and keep his commandments" (Ecclesiastes 12:13). What a salutation!

God Gives Meaning

Meaning	Scripture
. . . to Life	• "You have made known to me the path of life; you will fill me with joy in your presence, with eternal pleasures at your right hand" (Psalm 16:11). • "I have been crucified with Christ and I no longer live, but Christ lives in me. The life I live in the body, I live by faith in the Son of God, who loved me and gave himself for me" (Galatians 2:20). • "Do not conform any longer to the pattern of this world, but be transformed by the renewing of your mind. Then you will be able to test and approve what God's will is—his good, pleasing and perfect will" (Romans 12:2).
. . . to Work	• "Commit to the Lord whatever you do, and your plans will succeed" (Proverbs 16:3). • [Jesus said,] "As long as it is day, we must do the work of him who sent me. Night is coming, when no one can work. While I am in the world, I am the light of the world" (John 9:4–5). • "We worked night and day, laboring and toiling so that we would not be a burden to any of you. We did this, not because we do not have the right to such help, but in order to make ourselves a model for you to follow. For even when we were with you, we gave you this rule: 'If a man will not work, he shall not eat'" (2 Thessalonians 3:8–10).
. . . to Death	• "Jesus said to her, 'I am the resurrection and the life. He who believes in me will live, even though he dies; and whoever lives and believes in me will never die'" (John 11:25–26). • "For the wages of sin is death, but the gift of God is eternal life in Christ Jesus our Lord" (Romans 6:23). • "Remember this: Whoever turns a sinner from the error of his way will save him from death and cover a multitude of sins" (James 5:20).

An ongoing battle has caused division among women not only in the secular community but in the Christian community. It's the to-work-or-not-to-work-outside-the-home debate. We've already seen that work is a necessity ordained by God. How and where God wants you to work is between you and him. Personally, I know without a shadow of a doubt that during the mom season of my life, God's will for my life is to be a mom, wife, and writer who works from my home office. As I wrote in chapter 3, it took eleven long years for our son to arrive. When he did, we lived three thousand miles away from my extended family, and I made the commitment that I would stay at home with Philip. But that choice was up to God and me—just like the choice you make is between you and God. "The mind of man plans his way, but the Lord directs his steps" (Proverbs 16:9 NASB).

There are many reasons why we work: fulfillment, creativity, survival, and God's calling placed in our hearts. No matter what our reasons, we are challenged to make a difference in whatever field we call work.

A Tale of Two Modern Women

Does the product Sister Schubert's Rolls ring a bell? Women like Patricia Schubert Barnes, a successful Christian businesswoman and CEO of her company, Sister Schubert's Homemade Rolls, can inspire us. They produce more than one million rolls a day. In an interview with *Clarity* magazine, they reported this caring woman has an open-door policy with her surrogate "family" and listens and prays with them. She was quoted as saying, "The Lord wants me to take care of these people (employees). Sometimes you think this is a business and you're not supposed to be so caring about these people, but these people are my responsibility. I feel strongly that I have to maintain this business so they can have a place to come to work and buy food for their families."[2]

Patricia Schubert Barnes not only bakes and sells what I think are the best-tasting rolls on the market, she's a great example of living and working to the best of her ability, realizing that work and life are a gift from God.

If you have a baby, then you've probably heard of the Baby Einstein Company. When Julie Aigner-Clark's daughter was born in 1994, she knew she wanted to stay home with her. "She became my world. I wanted to play with her and read to her and do the things I knew intuitively were good for my child," she explained. "At the same time, I realized I missed what I had focused on so much—literature and art—and I thought it would be so great if my child loved this as much as I do." She launched the Baby Einstein Company in 1997 and shot the first video in the basement of her Atlanta home, using her daughter's most prized stuffed animals and toys as props.[3]

The company was phenomenally successful. When the company grossed over $20 million in the fifth year, they became overwhelmed. Clark explained, "Baby Einstein started out as a fun way to have a professional life outside of my mommy life. Bill [husband] and I looked at each other and said, 'The people who were supposed to benefit the most—our children—are benefiting the least.'" The Clarks sold Baby Einstein to Disney in 2001.

Clark now has the money to finance a new venture: the Safe Side, a collaboration with John Walsh, host of *America's Most Wanted*, that presents safety information for parents and children.[4]

Clark's story is all about individual choices that were best for her home life and business life. It's all about knowing when the timing is right, evaluating priorities, accepting change, and making life work for you and your family.

How Others See It

Luci Swindoll

As Christian working women, our greatest calling is to love people, to line up our causes with the overall cause of Christ, and to allow Him to use us to effect meaningful changes in the lives of those around us. The journey to our desired destination is one of the most exciting spiritual adventures life has to offer.[5]

We've already seen that work is a necessity and ordained by God. How and where God wants you to work is between you and him. "The mind of man plans his way, but the Lord directs his steps" (Proverbs 16:9 NASB).

Catfight!

1 PETER 3:8–9 *Finally, all of you, live in harmony with one another; be sympathetic, love as brothers, be compassionate and humble. Do not repay evil with evil or insult with insult, but with blessing, because to this you were called so that you may inherit a blessing.*

Peter wrote to the Jewish believers in the churches of Asia Minor during a time of major persecution. Christians were being put to death by the Roman government, and Peter anticipated that the persecution would soon move into the lives of the believers he was writing to.

In a hostile world, what Peter wanted most was for his fellow believers to live in harmony. As never before, they needed one another to accomplish their work of spreading God's word.

Though we don't usually experience life-or-death persecution at work (thank you, Lord!), struggles and occasional conflicts seem unavoidable. We can be encouraged by Peter's words and overcome on-the-job friction by implementing his advice into our actions.

If there's something more chilling than being awakened in the middle of the night by the savage screams and hisses of a catfight, I don't want to know about it. Those wild screeches make you visualize paws and claws flying, fangs and teeth shining, backs arched and hair standing on end as the cats battle. With sunrise, you may see the reality of what you envisioned. Your cat may limp in sporting caked blood and swollen eyes, looking for a safe haven in which to curl up and sleep off the trauma.

Does that description remind you of anyone at your job? Most of us have seen women at work turn into Catwoman. We're so territorial, I'm surprised I haven't seen someone take SCAT animal repellent from her purse and spray it around her desk. Women are notorious for gossiping, backstabbing, undermining, and sabotaging each other. Meeow! We can be dangerous.

Examples From the Bible

The Scriptures speak against such mean and dangerous actions:

Gossiping

- "Do not go about spreading slander among your people" (Leviticus 19:16).
- "The words of a gossip are like choice morsels; they go down to a man's inmost parts" (Proverbs 18:8).
- "A gossip betrays a confidence; so avoid a man who talks too much" (Proverbs 20:19).

Backstabbing

- "Therefore, rid yourselves of all malice and all deceit, hypocrisy, envy, and slander of every kind" (I Peter 2:1).

- "The acts of the sinful nature are obvious: sexual immorality, impurity and debauchery; idolatry and witchcraft; hatred, discord, jealousy, fits of rage, selfish ambition, dissensions, factions and envy; drunkenness, orgies, and the like. I warn you, as I did before, that those who live like this will not inherit the kingdom of God" (Galatians 5:19–21).

Undermining/Criticizing

- "You, therefore, have no excuse, you who pass judgment on someone else, for at whatever point you judge the other you are condemning yourself, because you who pass judgment do the same things" (Romans 2:1).

- "So when you, a mere man, pass judgment on them and yet do the same things, do you think you will escape God's judgment?" (Romans 2:3).

- "Don't grumble against each other, brothers, or you will be judged. The Judge is standing at the door!" (James 5:9).

Sabotage by Lying

- "Whoever of you loves life and desires to see many good days, keep your tongue from evil and your lips from speaking lies. Turn from evil and do good; seek peace and pursue it" (Psalm 34:12–14).

- "He who conceals his hatred has lying lips, and whoever spreads slander is a fool" (Proverbs 10:18).

- "Do not testify against your neighbor without cause, or use your lips to deceive" (Proverbs 24:28).

- "Like a club or a sword or a sharp arrow is the man who gives false testimony against his neighbor" (Proverbs 25:18).

Revenge

- "It is mine to avenge; I will repay. In due time their foot will slip; their day of disaster is near and their doom rushes upon them" (Deuteronomy 32:35).

- "This is what the Lord Almighty says: 'Administer true justice; show mercy and compassion to one another. Do not oppress the widow or the fatherless, the alien or the poor. In your hearts do not think evil of each other'" (Zechariah 7:9–10).

- "Do not take revenge, my friends, but leave room for God's wrath, for it is written: 'It is mine to avenge; I will repay,' says the Lord" (Romans 12:19).

- "Do not be overcome by evil, but overcome evil with good" (Romans 12:21).

- "Finally, all of you, live in harmony with one another; be sympathetic, love as brothers, be compassionate and humble. Do not repay evil with evil or insult with insult, but with blessing, because to this you were called so that you may inherit a blessing" (I Peter 3:8–9).

responsible
Romans 12:18

Examples From the Bible

Catfights were not unknown in Bible times:

• **Peninnah** was one of the two wives of Elkanah. She is known for taunting Elkanah's other wife, Hannah. It is not known why Elkanah had two wives, but some commentators presume that Hannah was his first wife, and because she was unable to have children, Peninnah came into the picture. Peninnah may have felt that the only reason she was included was for her ability to have children. She may have feared that when her work was done, Elkanah would have no more use for her. This bitterness and jealousy led Peninnah to mistreat Hannah with taunting remarks. (1 Samuel 1:2–6; 11:2–4, paraphrased)

• **Syntyche and Euodias** were co-laborers with Paul as he built the early church. But in Paul's letter to the Philippians he told these two women to get along and even asked others to intervene and help them patch up their differences. (Philippians 4:2–3; 14:2, paraphrased)

As women of faith, we can't join in the catfight. (To get declawed, some of us may need to think of Jesus not as the Great Physician, but as the Great Veterinarian!) We are not responsible for, nor can we control, Catwoman's behavior, but we are <u>responsible</u> for our own actions. Our actions should follow the apostle Paul's encouragement to live in harmony, be sympathetic, love, be compassionate, and be humble. These actions reflect the love of Christ.

How Others See It

Hayley DiMarco

Do you think God smiles when you are mean, or when you are humble? If you want to live by his Word, then you have no choice but to drop the mean scene and pick up the good vibe. My cry to you, my dear ones, right now, is to decide to be mean-free. Choose to be godly and good over mean. Be a new, anti-mean woman.[6]

What You Can Do

In her book *Mean Girls All Grown Up*, Hayley DiMarco gives us great tips on surviving the mean girl:

Surviving a Quarantine Queen

Often the easiest and most subtle weapon of mean is exclusion.

1. Don't whine about being quarantined.

2. Don't figure out ways to get her back.

3. Do ask her if there is anything you've done to hurt her.

4. Do all you can to show her God's love through your actions.[7]

Surviving a Gossip Girl

I. Don't expect everyone to believe you when you attempt to correct her.

2. Don't go after her in retaliation.

3. Do overlook the insult.

4. Do attempt to make amends with her.[8]

Surviving the Slander Sister

I. Don't use slander as a weapon to get her back. You have your own soul to guard.

2. Don't allow yourself to become offended.

3. Do trust God to be true to his Word and to deal with a slanderer.

4. Do use this as an opportunity to practice humility.[9]

Lunch Is on Me

> **MATTHEW 5:13–16** *You are the salt of the earth. But if the salt loses its saltiness, how can it be made salty again? It is no longer good for anything, except to be thrown out and trampled by men. You are the light of the world. A city on a hill cannot be hidden. Neither do people light a lamp and put it under a bowl. Instead they put it on its stand, and it gives light to everyone in the house. In the same way, let your light shine before men, that they may see your good deeds and praise your Father in heaven.*

Jesus used salt and light as **metaphors** when he taught the famous Sermon on the Mount. We know that salt preserves, flavors, and creates thirst. Jesus' disciples were to become the "salt of the earth," and the "light of the world." As Christ's followers, we are as salt in the workplace. Our friendships can stop the decaying morals that surround us, flavor lives with the love of Christ, and create a thirst for God in our friends when they see something different about us and want to know more. As light, we can illuminate the path, give direction, and introduce others to Jesus, our closest friend.

Friendships and women go hand in hand. I think it's the nurturing trait that makes us enjoy friendships so much. I have several levels of friendships:

- school-mom friends

- church friends

- work friends

- best friends

Now, my small circle of best friends are my "forever friends," while the others seem to be "situational friends" that go in and out of the doorway of my life. Sometimes "situational" friends are people God places right smack on my doormat.

Work always has situational friendships. You can look at it two ways: either it was just the situation that brought you together, or God made your paths cross. You may have taken the job to fulfill your own purpose, but God has his own purpose in placing you there. Look for God's purpose. Develop friendships with women at work. Spring for lunch (or, depending on your budget, brown-bag it) from time to time.

How Others See It

John C. Maxwell

You cannot sustain a deep friendship with everyone, nor should you try. But you should cultivate genuine, deep friendships with a few people. And you can be a friendly, kind, supportive person to everyone you meet. You can treat every person as an individual, not simply a business "contact." If you put others first as people and then worry about business second, you're on your way to practicing the Friendship Principle.[10]

What You Can Do

Simple ways to express friendship to your fellow workers:

1. Sow seeds of encouragement when your co-workers are down, by giving a listening ear and directing their path to the Word. "Perfume and incense bring joy to the heart, and the pleasantness of one's friend springs from his earnest counsel" (Proverbs 27:9).

2. Celebrate co-workers' accomplishments and express how God has blessed them with their special gift or talent. Give a small gift. (Women love gifts. But you already knew that.) Inspirational gifts

are a great way to celebrate and deliver a message of God at the same time. "Rejoice with those who rejoice" (Romans 12:15).

3. Offer sympathy when your fellow workers grieve. Inspirational cards and books are a wonderful comfort when a seeker is trying to understand a loss. She can turn to the books in the privacy of her own grief and seek answers. "Blessed are those who mourn, for they will be comforted" (Matthew 5:4).

4. Shed light when days are dark. A smiling face and an encouraging word can brighten a co-worker's soul. They look to you for strength as you reflect the light of Christ. "Let your light shine before men, that they may see your good deeds and praise your Father in heaven" (Matthew 5:16).

Examples From the Bible

The Bible gives us examples of forever and situational friends:

• David and Jonathan were forever friends. Jonathan, the eldest son of King Saul, was David's closest friend. Their friendship began the day the two first met after David killed the giant Philistine, Goliath. David's friendship with Saul remained intact even though Saul's animosity toward David grew to the point of attempting to kill him. Jonathan was willing to surrender all claims to the throne rather than go against his beloved friend. (1 Samuel 18:1–4)

• A good example of situational friends were Joseph and his cell mate, the king's cupbearer. Their unusual situation brought them together along with the king's baker. The cupbearer and the baker each had a dream that made them worry. With God's help Joseph interpreted the dreams. He asked the appreciative cupbearer a favor. If the cupbearer were restored to his office, as Joseph predicted, he asked only that the cupbearer remember him. The cupbearer was restored to his position in the king's palace but forgot about Joseph until another situation occurred where remembering their friendship would benefit the cupbearer. (Genesis 40:1–41:40)

How Others See It

Dee Brestin and Kathy Troccoli

How often we've thanked God for our friendship, for helping us to see so much more together than either of us could have alone. We know that is the beauty of the body of Christ, helping one another see, helping one another to draw nearer to the Great I AM.[11]

Snapshots of Women in the Bible

Lydia (Acts 16:13–15)

check this out

seller
Acts 16:14
Messiah
John 4:25–42

Lydia's long purple tunic seemed to float in the breeze as she hurried through the streets to escape the city crowds. She looked forward to the peaceful countryside as a **reprieve** from the sounds of the prancing horses, the footsteps of the Roman legions, and the cries of the local merchants selling their goods.

Lydia was known all over the region as the <u>seller</u> of **purple**. Her customers were the Roman imperial family and Babylonian buyers who adorned their temples with her purple cloths. She was on a first-name basis with the rich and built her business as one of the best **dyers** in the region.

She hoped all the women she invited to the riverbank would be waiting for her, under the shade of the trees. This **Gentile** worshiped the God of the Jews, but there was no **synagogue** in Philippi, so she and others gathered at the riverbank on the **Sabbath** to pray and worship. She felt safe in the familiar surroundings, since they always met near the vats where her workers boiled the dye from the sea **snails** they harvested—a dye so beautiful, yet so foul in odor, that they had to process it away from the city.

Lydia greeted the women, pleased at today's turnout. After exchanging pleasantries, each woman removed her sandals, pulled her prayer shawl over her head, and began to pray that God would guide her to better understanding. They wanted to know God.

The voices of men drawing near interrupted their prayers. Lydia greeted the strangers. They introduced themselves as Paul, Silas, Luke, and Timothy, followers of the <u>**Messiah**</u>.

Lydia invited the newcomers to join them, for she was anxious to hear more about the Savior they spoke of.

Paul, the apparent leader of the men, explained he had not planned to visit Philippi, but just days before his travels he dreamed of a man who pleaded with him to come to Macedonia. Sensing the dream was from God, Paul changed his plans accordingly.

Having explained why he was in Philippi, Paul then began preaching about Jesus. Lydia's heart filled with an unspeakable joy. Her prayers had been answered. Her faithful God had sent these men to help them better understand. She asked Paul to tell her what she must do to become a

reprieve
rest; break
purple
royal purple was the most expensive and most coveted dye in the ancient world
dyers
people who colored clothing
Gentile
a non-Jew
synagogue
house of worship where Jews gathered
Sabbath
seventh day of the week; day of rest
snails
Purple dye is produced from a liquid secreted by snails' hypobranchial gland.
Messiah
expected and promised Savior, Jesus Christ

follower of Christ. Lydia and her household were baptized in the name of Jesus that very day at the river.

Lydia opened her spacious home to Paul and his companions, a rare treat for first-century Christians used to meeting in catacombs and the equivalent of government project slums. In Lydia's house, the first church in Europe was established. The woman who knew kings and merchants now carried along with her expensive purple dye an even more valuable treasure: a personal relationship with Jesus. The purple she sold was made for earthly kings, but now everything she owned, every decision she made, was for the true King of kings. Lydia's influence as a businesswoman helped her effectively witness to other businesspeople.

Lydia was open to the full knowledge of Jesus Christ because she had prepared her heart through worship and prayer. Because of her openness, Christianity spread to Europe. This businesswoman of God witnessed to friends and co-workers while she worked.

Office Romance: The Good, the Bad, and the Ugly

PROVERBS 4:23 *Above all else, guard your heart, for it is the wellspring of life.*

Years ago I read a handbook for marriage. The author had some good thoughts, but when he came to writing about the workplace, we parted company. He suggested that a woman should never be in the workplace, under any circumstances, because she was too weak. She would be tempted and would give in to an office affair. I couldn't believe my eyes. Now, that's the solution—build a fortress around your house so temptation can't get through your door! Did he forget about the mailman, the UPS man, and the pool man? Just lock her up and throw away the key.

We live in a world filled with **temptations**, but we are promised in 1 Corinthians 10:13, "God is faithful; he will not let you be tempted beyond what you can bear. But when you are tempted, he will also provide a way out so that you can stand up under it."

As we encounter romance at the office, we must always be on guard and protect our hearts.

What does the Bible say about the heart?

I. *From it springs personality, inner life, and character* (mentioned 257 times in the Scripture): "Yet Pharaoh's heart became hard and he would not listen to them, just as the Lord had said. Then the Lord said to Moses, 'Pharaoh's heart is unyielding; he refuses to let the people go'" (Exodus 7:13–14). "But the Lord said to Samuel, 'Do not consider his [Eliab's] appearance or his height, for I have rejected him. The Lord does not look at the things man looks at. Man looks at the outward appearance, but the Lord looks at the heart'" (1 Samuel 16:7).

2. *Emotional states* (found 166 times in the Scripture):

   • Intoxication: Nabal was merry in his heart and drunk (1 Samuel 25:36).

   • Joy: The priest's heart was glad (Judges 18:20).

   • Sorrow: Hannah's heart was sad (1 Samuel 1:8).

   • Anxiety: Eli's heart trembled in fear because the ark of God was taken (1 Samuel 4:13).

   • Love: The king's heart longed for his son Absalom (2 Samuel 14:1).

3. *Purpose of the heart:* to follow God (found 195 times in the Scripture). The right attitude of the heart begins with the heart being broken or crushed. Brokenness is necessary because a hard, stony heart does not submit to the will of God. But if you desire a clean heart, God will make your heart clean. "I will give them an undivided heart and put a new spirit in them; I will remove from them their heart of stone and give them a heart of flesh. Then they will follow my decrees and be careful to keep my laws. They will be my people, and I will be their God" (Ezekiel 11:19–20).

4. *Prayer for a clean heart:* "Search me, O God, and know my heart; test me and know my anxious thoughts. See if there is any offensive way in me, and lead me in the way everlasting" (Psalm 139:23–24). "Create in me a pure heart, O God, and renew a steadfast spirit within me" (Psalm 51:10).

5. *Benefits of a pure heart:* "Blessed are the pure in heart, for they will see God" (Matthew 5:8). "I pray that out of his glorious riches he may strengthen you with power through his Spirit in your inner being, so that Christ may dwell in your hearts through faith" (Ephesians 3:16–17).[12]

aloof
distant; unaware

Shannon Ethridge

Men and women struggle in different ways when it comes to sexual integrity. While a man's battle begins with what he takes in through his eyes, a woman's begins with her heart and her thoughts. A man must guard his eyes to maintain sexual integrity, but because God made women to be emotionally and mentally stimulated, we must closely guard our hearts and minds as well as our bodies if we want to experience God's plan for sexual and emotional fulfillment. A woman's battle is for sexual and emotional integrity.[13]

The Good Office Romance

RUTH 2:4–5 *Just then Boaz arrived from Bethlehem and greeted the harvesters, "The Lord be with you!" "The Lord bless you!" they called back. Boaz asked the foreman of his harvesters, "Whose young woman is that?"*

Ruth and Boaz's relationship started on a field during harvest—the workplace. Old Testament law allowed the poor to follow harvesters and gather the grain that fell to the ground during harvesting. This is what Ruth did on Boaz's field. Boaz took notice of her, asked his foreman about her, and offered her special protection and care. Following the appropriate customs, Ruth asked for Boaz to extend his protection to the point of matrimony. Boaz was deeply moved at her request because he was an older man and Ruth could have run after the younger fellas. Eventually they did get married and lived happily ever after. (For the whole story, see chapter 5, "Home Front or Battlefront?")

Bill Gates met his wife, Melinda, at Microsoft. They seem to be living a fairy-tale romance. Robin and Shaun are friends of mine who met at the office. You didn't read about their wedding on the cover of Newsweek, but they too are living happily ever after.

*The office can be a great place for a single woman to observe her possible future mate from a safe distance. You can be a fly on the wall and learn all kinds of things about a man. Robin sized Shaun up the first day. She thought he was pretty cute but was a little too **aloof**. But after further observation, she found she had mistaken self-confidence for arrogance. She watched how others responded to him—everybody liked him! He always managed to calm a crisis, and if emergency help was* *needed, he was always there. No one had anything bad to say about Shaun, and he never said anything bad about anyone else. He even talked about his church unashamedly. Robin fell in love with a man of integrity, character, and faith.*

Does Mr. Romance at the office have the character traits Scripture lists for a husband's role in a marriage? He should be willing to:

1. provide (Genesis 3:17–19)

2. protect (Ephesians 5:23)

3. serve and lead (Ephesians 5:23)

4. love sacrificially (Ephesians 5:25, 28–29)

5. nourish and cherish (Ephesians 5:28–29)

6. be understanding (1 Peter 3:7)

7. wash his wife with the water of the Word (Ephesians 5:26)

8. grant his wife honor as a co-heir of the grace of God (1 Peter 3:7)

How Others See It

Shaunti Feldhahn

If a man isn't convinced that his woman thinks he's the greatest, he will tend to seek affirmation elsewhere. He may spend more hours at work, where he feels alive and on top of his game, or he may spend too much time talking to the admiring female associate. . . . If affirmation is indeed everything, why should a man have to look for it in other places when he has a wife who loves and respects him? There's nothing wrong with work, sports, or hobbies—it's wonderful for him to feel alive and encouraged in those pursuits—but they shouldn't have to be a retreat from an unaffirming home life.[14]

The Bad Office Romance

EPHESIANS 4:31–32 *Get rid of all bitterness, rage and anger, brawling and slander, along with every form of **malice**. Be kind and compassionate to one another, forgiving each other, just as in Christ God forgave you.*

In the apostle Paul's time, the Ephesians needed a little instruction on how to live the new life they had in Christ. I think we can add Paul's guidelines to our Get Over the Bad Romance Survival Kit.

After a breakup, a hurting heart can turn to anger and bitterness. We are encouraged to tame our anger, work through our issues, be kind, and give up the right to get even. You may not want to patch things up with your ex. You may even need to distance yourself from all contact. But whatever you do, instead of anger, try kindness.

Down through time, Dear John letters have seemed the easiest way to end a romance. You write the letter, bid farewell, and never have to see the person's sad little face again.

Too bad that's not reality in the office. If you choose to date co-workers, you risk the consequences of an office romance gone bad. You may zip him a Dear John e-mail, a Dear John alphanumeric pager message, or a Dear John video conference call, but chances are, he's not out of your life. Unless you transfer out of the office, you'll probably see him in the elevator, at management meetings, at office parties, in the parking lot, and so on. That's where it gets tough.

It's awfully hard to practice what we preach when our hearts are wounded. But remember—the whole office is watching, and our actions speak louder than our words. Let your actions reflect kindness, compassion, and forgiveness, as you are a reflection of Christ.

The best advice to avoid this bad situation from the get-go: Don't date co-workers.

Items to help you get over the bad romance:

1. *Kindness*—"Be kind and compassionate to one another, forgiving each other, just as in Christ God forgave you" (Ephesians 4:32).

2. *Compassion*—"Therefore, as God's chosen people, holy and dearly loved, clothe yourselves with compassion, kindness, humility, gentleness and patience" (Colossians 3:12).

3. *Forgiveness*—"Forgive us our debts, as we also have forgiven our debtors" (Matthew 6:12).

of bitterness is to make the choice to forgive....You may find that it is still not possible to be at peace, but you will have provided the atmosphere for peace to reign on your side of the street.[15]

escape
1 Corinthians 10:13

infidelity
lack of sexual or emotional faithfulness

The Ugly Office Romance

GENESIS 39:9–10 *[Joseph said to Potiphar's wife,] "My master has withheld nothing from me except you, because you are his wife. How then could I do such a wicked thing and sin against God?" And though she spoke to Joseph day after day, he refused to go to bed with her or even be with her.*

Joseph was a handsome man, and the boss's wife took notice. She made no bones about it—she wanted to sleep with Joseph. We can learn from Joseph's reaction, for he was the forerunner of the Just Say No campaign. He didn't look in the mirror and think he still had it, returning to her the next day so she could stroke his ego. He stayed as far away from her as he possibly could. He didn't say, "Let's do lunch," and keep it a secret from the boss. He didn't feel sorry for this lonely woman and try to be her savior or counselor and say, "I'll call you later to help you out with your problem." He didn't fan the flame. Instead he hosed her down with the fire extinguisher called NO and then ran away.

Joseph was single. He didn't have a wife and family to betray, but he had a God he could not turn his back on. He knew that even unseen sins have consequences.

Guard your heart. Say no to an office affair and run, girl, run.

Most soap operas and TV melodramas deal with "who's sleeping with whom" at work. Some offices could provide the script word for word, because every day in the land of "equal opportunity," what started out as an innocent friendship with a married man at the office turns into either an emotional or physical affair. Marital **infidelity** leaves a path of deadly destruction: destruction of self-worth, destruction of the spouse and marriage, destruction of the innocent bystanders called children, and, in many cases, destruction of a career.

An affair is the ugliest of all office romances. Guard your heart and say NO. Honor yourself, your spouse, and God. There is no temptation so great that we cannot resist, for God will provide an escape. Look for the escape route and do like Mr. Gump: "Run, Forrest, run!"

Bringing Work Home

PROVERBS 16:3 *Commit to the Lord whatever you do, and your plans will succeed.*

If you think working from home is for you, the first thing you must do is seek God's guidance. We have peace of mind when our thoughts and plans are established in him and our works are entrusted to him.

Thousands of women want the flexibility and freedom to be at home with their kids. Each one wants to be her own boss and use her own unique creativity to turn her passion into profit.

I've seen women use unique abilities and turn fun into profit. Here's a list of a few businesses I know of personally that are run out of the home:

Ideas for Home-Based Businesses

Business Focus	Service or Product
Services	• home decorating • floral designs • wedding consultant • wedding photographer • clothing alterations • day care center
Sales	• kitchen accessories • cosmetic sales • children's books • photo album memory maker sales • long-distance provider • sales representative • online auctions
Specialty Items (sold at specialty stores but made at home)	• lotions • candles • jewelry • noodles (yes, noodles) • candy

If there is a market and you have talent and determination, you have a great combination for a winning business. Make your decision and build your business on prayer.

This Is God's Company

Disheartened and worried by recent events, my friend Helen lay in bed next to her husband, Martin, and admitted things had to change. She had to get out of her work situation so she could spend more time with their eight-year-old daughter, Stephanie.

A few weeks before, Stephanie had broken her arm and dearly wanted her mom to be a temperature taker and sickbed sitter. Helen's job in sales drew her away from home 50 percent of the time, and her inflexible boss hadn't let Helen stay home with Stephanie. Martin was wonderful about picking up the slack, but she knew her priorities had shifted away from home to work. Her heart told her she needed to turn her priorities around and be home with Stephanie.

That night Helen and Martin talked about starting a sales company Helen could own. Helen says that was a turning point when she surrendered everything to God. They prayed, seeking wisdom and guidance. Helen finished her prayer with, "If you want this to happen, let it; if not, close the door."

That was four years ago, and God flung the door wide open. Helen quit her position, set up a home office, and started Sales Pointe, a business that contracts with manufacturers and provides a service for retailers by demonstrating products to customers. (Sales Pointe people are the smiling faces you see in retail stores offering you samples of the latest product.)

Helen didn't have a paycheck for five months, but she trusted God to make a way, and he did. Somehow all the bills were paid. Each year the business has grown and is now a national company. Helen will tell

speaking
Acts 18:26

Aphrodite
the goddess of love
consecrated prostitutes
religious prostitutes of pagan temples

you the income is great, but the freedom of spending more time with her daughter is the greatest blessing of all. Helen uses her success story as a testimony about the power of prayer. With a contagious smile she says, "This isn't my company. This is God's company, based on prayer."

Helen and Martin took to heart Christ's teachings on prayer when he taught the Sermon on the Mount. We are to

- ask

- seek

- knock.

In other words, pray, pray, and pray.

Snapshots of Women in the Bible
Priscilla (Acts 18:1–3)

Fear filled the air as news of persecution spread from house to house like wildfire. The emperor Claudius was expelling all Jews from Rome. There was no time to gather all of their possessions. Priscilla and Aquila collected only their tent-making tools, wrapped them in the cloth used for their tents, tied them to their camel, and headed for Corinth. They left their home, friends, and family behind and clung to each other as they fled for their lives.

Priscilla knew God would provide for all their needs and was thankful that their tent-making craft seemed well suited for Corinth. The metropolitan city was the world's seaport, with an international marketplace of merchants selling everything from Babylonian ivory to Phrygian slaves. But Priscilla also knew they would meet opposition as they entered a city that embraced the temple of **Aphrodite**, which had over one thousand **consecrated prostitutes**. Priscilla had the reputation for speaking out for her Lord. She knew she had to continue speaking out about Jesus and leave her life open to God's lead in business and life.

Priscilla and her husband, Aquila, had begun their business in Corinth by the time Paul, a missionary and an apostle of Christ, visited. God had prepared a place for Paul to renew his energies and spirit as Priscilla and Aquila opened not only their home to him, but also included him in their tent-making trade.

Weak, fearful, and trembling, Paul had arrived in Corinth from Athens. He had been driven out of Macedonia by angry Jews. The people of Athens barely put up with him, and now in Corinth he met the familiar hostility he had experienced from other Jews in his travels.

As Paul worked away his stress with his trade, Priscilla and Aquila had the opportunity to learn firsthand from this apostle. Day after day they produced goods that provided for their daily needs and also provided funds for the new church to continue to grow. They surrendered all to God, ministering to Paul and endangering their lives to speak out, but God protected them in their work. They touched the lives of others, and, as a result, the Gospel continued to spread.

Everything Priscilla and Aquila did and everything they owned was God's, no matter where they went. God blessed the work of a wife and husband who together made a living from self-employment, and together lived their lives for God.

If I Learned Everything I Need to Know in Kindergarten, Why Am I Still in School at Forty?

PROVERBS 1:5 *Let the wise listen and add to their learning.*

Sometimes we find ourselves forced into learning a new skill. Something changed, and like it or not, you have to respond. You may have never planned to work full-time, but now you're a single mom and you need to go back to school to get a higher education to earn higher pay. Maybe your spouse is unable to work, or the pink slip just landed on his desk. Or maybe your children have flown from the nest and now you have the time to do and learn something you've always wanted to learn. One way or another, you find it necessary to retrain and enter the workforce.

Whatever the circumstances may be, consider learning a pleasure. God will give you strength and stretch your brain as you walk this new path. Remember, just by wanting to learn you're a step ahead. The writer of Proverbs says, "the wise listen and add to their learning" (1:5).

weak
I Corinthians 2:1–5
trade
Acts 18:3
endangering
Romans 16:3–4
others
Acts 18:18–28
strength
Psalm 28:7;
Isaiah 40:29
walk
Isaiah 2:3–5

> ## Examples From the Bible
>
> Major changes required these men and women of the Bible to learn something new:
>
> - **Adam and Eve** learned a new occupation in agriculture. Their status changed from overseers of the Garden of Eden to tillers of the soil. (Genesis 3:17)

- **Miriam** was probably in her eighties when her brother Moses led the children of Israel out of Egypt. Her occupation changed from "slave" to "freedom fighter" as she helped Moses and Aaron in leadership. (Micah 6:4; Exodus 15:21)
- **Esther** was an orphan Jewess who was chosen to be the new queen. She rose to the occasion and kept the Jews from being massacred by the wicked leader Haman. (Book of Esther)
- **Deborah** was a homemaker who counseled those who sought her advice. This led her to a position as one of the judges of Israel. Her wisdom was needed in time of war and Deborah learned to lead an army to victory. (Judges 4:9; 5:2)

A study has shown that if we continue to learn, our brains stay in good shape into old age. I guess, in other words, we need to give the old gray matter a jump-start from time to time to keep the juices flowing. Commit to learning one new activity or subject every year!

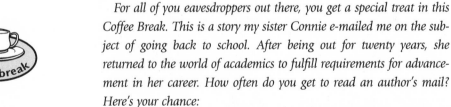

How Others See It

Lynda Hunter

Don't let fear paralyze you. Sometimes we ignore or avoid change, but it doesn't go away. You make the choice. Take charge. Look for opportunities to make change work for you.[18]

Sister Heads Back to School

coffee break

For all of you eavesdroppers out there, you get a special treat in this Coffee Break. This is a story my sister Connie e-mailed me on the subject of going back to school. After being out for twenty years, she returned to the world of academics to fulfill requirements for advancement in her career. How often do you get to read an author's mail? Here's your chance:

I left extremely early for my first class back in school. As you know, early is not my M.O. [modus operandi], but it was part of The Plan. The Plan was a simple one: attend and blend. Don't stand out in any way, try not to draw attention, just listen and learn.

I wasn't sure I wanted to leave my current position, but I felt that the continuing classes certainly couldn't hurt. You know I love learning, and I honestly enjoy studying, especially history. I hurt inside every time we pass one of those historical markers on the highway and Bruce [Connie's husband] won't stop to read it. Something happened there, something important enough to erect a marker, and I want to know what it was! I couldn't believe I was adding all this extra work in my already full schedule. I asked myself, Am I nuts?

In formulating The Plan, I went to campus a week early to register, map out my route to the classrooms, and scout out a perfect parking place. The parking was stressful, mainly because there isn't any! But I was able to find a lot close to my building, so that first morning I felt confident as I left for classes. I was ready. I had my campus essential, the ten-pound backpack. I dressed to match the students I had checked out the week before, and I made myself leave early.

Well, you know what they say about the best-laid plans. My plans crumbled as I turned onto Campus Drive. All lots were blocked because of a special event. I managed to find metered parking, but I had no change. I ran to a nearby convenience store for a pocketful of quarters, fed the meter, and looked around to get my bearings. I had no earthly idea where I was, and time was wasting. I found the YOU ARE HERE map and then rushed to class.

I opened the door and stood gasping for breath. My backpack felt like it weighed a ton, and my shoes were untied. It was like I had a neon sign flashing "I'm late!" over my head as I made my way into the classroom. After parading down a couple of aisles (nearly injuring several kids with the deadly, oversized backpack), I sat at the front of the class, close enough to read the instructor's notes. So much for blending in. This was not what I had planned. I only hoped it would get better.

It didn't. The real blow came to this forty-something student during our lunch break when the young man behind the register in the food court asked for my Faculty ID, so he could give me the faculty discount. I must have looked dumbfounded because before I could get a word out, the girls in my class gave him my student status. He mumbled an apology and I mumbled, "Thanks anyway."

I ate with the girls and they asked why I was taking these classes. I couldn't formulate a cool explanation, so I just told them I love to learn. They were totally confused. I already had a degree and a career. Why would anyone in their right mind put themselves through all this? (That was something I began to question myself at that point.) They said that once they got out of there, they didn't want to go back to school.

I suddenly remembered how I felt when I was their age. The year Bruce and I graduated from college, I was married, Curtis [their son] was five months old, and I was more than ready to get out there in the world and make a place for myself. I was struck with a revelation as I *thought about those girls. They were just beginning to learn. They had not lived their learning. There were experiences yet to come, lessons to be learned, and a life to be lived. It was all ahead of them. But I had already lived and learned. My experiences were broader, my understanding deeper, and my life richer because of it, but I never want to quit learning. There are things out there I still don't know, and places with markers erected that I have not yet seen. I did not learn in kindergarten all that I need to know.*

So I have a new plan. It's no longer "attend and blend." It's not even "listen and learn." Instead, my new plan is "live to learn, and learn to live." I like my new plan. What do you think?

Love ya. Connie.

How Others See It

Luci Swindoll

True professionalism is contrary to the steps that the world orders. It's not by might or power, but by tranquility mixed with grace. It's not by intimidation, but by courage mixed with vulnerability. It's not by workaholism, but by constancy mixed with balance. And it's not by a system of hierarchy, but by democracy mixed with servanthood. In every case it is contrary to the world. But it works.[19]

Final Thoughts

- Work is not a "four-letter word." You can find significance and fulfillment and make a difference in the lives of others at work. But you must place Christ first in your life and do everything as if you were working for him. When he is the center of our lives, we can balance the rest.

- Some workers will try to drag you into catfights. Turn the other cheek. Don't stoop to their level; instead, reflect Christ's love.

- The fragrance of romance will permeate the office from time to time. Be aware of the good, the bad, and the ugly of romance. Guard your heart, for it will determine the condition of the rest of your life.

- Working from home is not only a trend—it can be a wonderful way to get back in touch with your family. If this is for you, build the foundation of your business on prayer and God's guidance.

- Welcome continued learning as a challenge and a gift. "Live to learn, and learn to live" in this new adventure of your life.

Questions to Deepen Your Understanding

1. According to Scripture, how does God feel about work?

2. The apostle Paul gave us a simple plan for work. What did he encourage the Colossians to do?

3. Lydia spent time in prayer. How was her prayer answered? What was the result of her open heart, open home, and willingness to follow the message of Jesus?

4. How should we handle catfights at work?

5. How are we the "salt of the earth" at work?

6. What was the secret of the Proverbs 31 woman?

7. How did Joseph have the strength to withstand temptation?

8. Priscilla worked with her husband in their tent-making business. How did their trade help spread the Gospel?

9. What type of woman continues to learn?

read on

Some of Georgia's favorite books for enjoying work inside or outside the home:

- *Chicken Soup for the Working Woman's Soul,* Jack Canfield, Health Communications

- *Climbing the Ladder in Stilettos: 10 Strategies for Stepping Up Success* and *Satisfaction at Work,* Lynette Lewis, Thomas Nelson

- *The Difference Maker: Making Your Attitude Your Greatest Asset,* John C. Maxwell, Thomas Nelson

- *Discovering God's Will for Your Life,* Women of Faith Bible Study Series, Nelson Reference and Electronic

- *Every Woman's Battle,* Shannon Ethridge, WaterBrook Press

- *For Women Only,* Shaunti Feldhahn, Multnomah

- *High-Wire Mom: Balancing Your Family and a Business @ Home,* Kendra Smiley, Moody Publishers

- *I Married Adventure,* Luci Swindoll, Thomas Nelson

- *If Mama Ain't Happy, Ain't Nobody Happy: Making the Choice to Rejoice,* Lindsey O'Connor, Harvest House

- *Life Management for Busy Women,* Elizabeth George, Harvest House

- *Look at It This Way,* Jan Silvious, WaterBrook Press

- *Mean Girls All Grown Up,* Hayley DiMarco, Baker Publishing Group

- *Notes to a Working Woman,* Luci Swindoll, W Publishing Group

- *Winning with People,* John C. Maxwell, Nelson Business

Chapter 9: I Have a Glue Gun and I'm Not Afraid to Use It

Rediscovering the Lost Art and Joy of Homemaking

What's in This Chapter

Here We Go

Moms trade in briefcases and BMWs for diaper bags and minivans in order to come home. Kids step off of big yellow buses to come home. Dads click off their computers, check out of the office, and hit rush-hour traffic to come home. Runaways face the reality of the real world and call to see if they can come home. Every day men, women, boys, and girls turn their hearts toward home looking for a rest stop, a bite to eat, and a safe haven.

I truly believe that a woman is the heartbeat of the home. She is usually the one whose open arms call everyone else home.

One of the top-rated TV shows over the past few years has been *Extreme Makeover: Home Edition*. I admit it—I'm addicted. It's right up my alley. I've personally completely remodeled two homes and served as general contractor on our latest building project, a log cabin. I love that show!

If you're not familiar with it, I'll give you a brief description. There's a team of about six designers and more than one hundred construction workers who come in and completely remodel a home in seven days! It's sponsored by Sears. Pure brilliance on the part of their marketing department. They choose families with an extreme need, and surprisingly, nine out of ten shows have a Christian testimony included. It's amazing. Viewers witness not only the unbelievable transformation of the house, but during the final and emotional revel, they see how the home makeover has impacted the lives of the deserving and grateful family.

That's what I want to accomplish in this chapter—a "heart for home extreme makeover."

Proverbs 14:1 says, "The wise woman builds her house, but with her own hands the foolish one tears hers down." The writer is not referring to a woman as a carpenter who constructs the structure of the house, but as a woman who cares for her household, loves the inhabitants, and helps construct the souls living under her roof.

A wise woman creates a home that reflects Christ and her love for her family. A creative woman does it while making her home a fun and special place. We sometimes feel like Cinderella when it comes to daily housework, but there is a secret key to turning hated housework into willing housework. Scripture gives us tools of wisdom to rediscover this lost art of hospitality. Let's see what the Bible says about the joy of homemaking and extreme makeovers of the heart.

How Others See It

Lynn Bowen Walker

Homemaking involves people. It encompasses loving our children, nurturing their creativity, and helping them recognize their unique gifts. Homemaking is encouraging our husbands, admiring their finer qualities, and praying for them when they're going through a rough time. It's caring about the people who enter our world and nourishing them with kind word, food perhaps, and a listening ear. You and I change the lives we touch. We have the capacity to bring love and laughter and encouragement to those who enter our homes. It's a huge job.[1]

Occupation: Homemaker

TITUS 2:4–5 *Train the younger women to love their husbands and children, to be self-controlled and pure, to be busy at home, to be kind, and to be subject to their husbands, so that no one will **malign** the word of God.*

In writing to Titus and giving advice to the younger women of the early church, Paul ranked <u>homemaking</u> right up there with loving your <u>husband</u> and children.

This new life in Christ meant liberation from the oppression of the day for women. In Jewish culture they were inferior and treated as property. But for Christian women, Paul said, "there is neither Jew nor Greek, slave nor free, male nor female, for you are all one in Christ Jesus" (Galatians 3:28). They were equal with men! Still, homemaking and the traditional role of motherhood were treasured as a calling for a young woman. Paul did not see this role as demeaning or contradicting the female believer's exalted worth in the Lord.

homemaking
I Timothy 5:14
husband
Ephesians 5:33

For the first few years after our son was born and I left my career to come home, I cringed when I filled out tax forms. Why? Well, for all the same reasons you do, plus one other: On the line where you must fill in your occupation, I had to write "homemaker." I had worked hard and had a successful career. Writing that one word made me feel like I had fallen from the top of the ladder to the bottom rung. But that was before I held up the white flag and surrendered all my titles to the Boss upstairs.

Now I almost laugh out loud when I write "homemaker" as my occupation. I write it in bold letters with pride, for I know that it's one of the greatest and most challenging careers of all time. I've added some commas after my homemaker title—wife, mother, author, and speaker—but homemaker still ranks at the top of my credentials.

Examples From the Bible

In Bible times women performed homemaking chores for their families every day. Homemaking can be a calling designed by God.

- Even in days of suffering and starvation, the widow of Zarephath gathered firewood to bake bread for her family's last meal. (1 Kings 17:12)
- Another daily homemaking chore: carrying heavy pots filled with fresh water for the family, just as Rebekah (Genesis 24:15–16) and the Samaritan woman did. (John 4:1–7)
- Women worked in the fields and brought home grain, as Ruth did for her family. (Ruth 2:2)

resurrected
John 11:32–45

mosaic
small pieces of colored
tile inlaid to form a
pattern

resurrected
brought back to life
after dying

- Homemakers like Sarah prepared meals for their families and guests. (Genesis 18:1–15)
- During times of celebration, like the wedding of Cana, women prepared the feast at the home of the bridegroom. (John 2:1–11)

How Others See It

Patsy Clairmont

My favorite refrigerator magnet reads, "Mom, I'll always love you, but I'll never forgive you for washing my face with spit on your hanky." That statement is funny and effective because most of us have experienced ye ol' spit shine. It's part of our family heritage.[2]

Snapshots of Women in the Bible
Martha (John 12:1–2)

Martha woke before sunrise, took the dimly burning lamp from the shelf, and hurried down the narrow stairway that led to the kitchen in the basement. The bright yellow in the **mosaic** pavement sparkled like gold as the room brightened. There was so much to do and so little time, but she could hardly contain her excitement.

In a few hours the quiet of the morning air would be broken by the jingling of the tambourine and joyful singing and dancing. Only days before, her home had been a house of mourning, filled with sadness and wailing. But tonight they would feast and celebrate, for her brother Lazarus, who had died, now lived! The guest of honor was their dear friend Jesus, who had **resurrected** Lazarus. The whole town wanted to join in the celebration and see this dead man that walked, but her house could hold only so many. She knew that every single person she had invited would attend.

It didn't bother her today that her sister Mary still slept. She could find plenty for Mary to do later, and extra help would arrive soon. Besides, Martha thought with a smile, if Mary cooked, no one would want to eat! She would put Mary in charge of the dancers and music.

As Martha bustled around the kitchen, she nibbled on pieces of bread and cheese and popped an olive into her mouth from time to time. She had to keep up her strength; she had a busy day ahead.

Martha stood in the doorway of her small storage room and stopped for a moment to gather her thoughts. With so many guests coming, there was not enough time to bake as much bread as they would need. She would pick up her bread at the baker's shop early before they sold out. She smelled the fresh garlic that hung on the wall. It was still fresh enough. There were plenty of vegetables and onions for the stew, but she needed more wine and fresh figs. Oh, and she couldn't run out of oil; they needed so much for dipping the bread. Everything had to be perfect. Not only was a dead man dining at her table, but Jesus had spoken of leaving. She feared this could be their last meal together.

outburst
Luke 10:38–42
compassion
Matthew 9:36; 14:14

Martha felt ashamed of her <u>outburst</u> from the previous meal Jesus and his disciples had eaten there. She had been overworked, cleaning the house and slaving over a hot oven while others enjoyed his company. She had gotten so caught up in doing, she forgot to enjoy herself. Instead, she'd spent her time complaining.

But not this time. Martha looked at life a little differently since she heard Jesus call Lazarus out of the tomb, alive. When Jesus spoke, his voice pierced her soul. He not only brought her brother back to life; he resurrected her heart. She didn't resent or begrudge being the homemaker; she saw it now as a calling, a way she could serve her family and her Lord.

What she once thought was a duty was now a gift—a gift she would gladly give her Savior.

Martha forgot to slow down and enjoy the company of Jesus. Instead, she spent her time complaining, and she disappointed him. That makes me wonder how many times I've disappointed him. Does your heart need to be resurrected? Has homemaking become a catastrophe instead of a calling? Slow down—enjoy Jesus' company.

Mama's in the Kitchen

MARK 8:8 *The people ate and were satisfied.*

You may have heard of Jesus feeding a crowd of five thousand men with five pieces of bread and two small fish. Fewer people remember that Mark records a second miracle of Jesus feeding thousands of men, women, and children. Jesus being Jesus, he once again had <u>compassion</u> for the people.

For three days the multitudes had followed and listened to Jesus' teaching. Even if they had packed some lunch for the first day, by the third day they had nothing to eat.

cornerstone
Ephesians 2:19–20

There was no Jonah's Fish Fry fast-food restaurant around. Jesus and his followers were miles out of town, and he feared people would collapse if they journeyed on empty stomachs.

The disciples managed to gather up seven loaves of bread. Jesus blessed the bread, fed four thousand people, and still had seven baskets filled with leftovers.

Jesus not only cares for our spiritual needs, he cares about our physical needs as well. He and he alone can satisfy both a hungry stomach and a hungry soul.

They say the way to a man's heart is through his stomach. If that's the case, then the kitchen looms large in Mrs. Homemaker's tool kit. The kitchen is the gathering place of the home where family friendships brew, menus and parties are planned, dreams are shared, and you can whip up a fun meal to spice up family life.

If you've been involved in any building or remodeling projects, we all know the kitchen is usually the most expensive remodel—especially with the cost of cabinets. But in our heart for home makeover, your kitchen remodel won't cost you a dime, and it may prove to be the most treasured room in your home.

Growing up with four kids in the house, I felt like Mom was always in the kitchen. She made sure that no matter where we lived, we always had a big kitchen, situated beside the family room. The most important kitchen item to me was our large, well-worn kitchen table. The family and friends who pulled up a chair for casual table talk, meals, and prayers made that table mean more to my Christian heritage than any other object in the house. The table doubled as my mom's private prayer chapel. I often found her there with her cup of coffee and open Bible, silently enjoying her morning devotions.

A must in building your house is designing a special place just for you—your own private prayer chapel. You will find it to be a <u>cornerstone</u> of your house as you daily go there to pray, meditate on God's Word, and meet with him.

Author and speaker Jill Briscoe tells how as a young mother, sometimes her private time was spent in the playpen. In order to escape the children for a moment of prayer, she would take them out of the playpen, hop in, cover up with a blanket, and tell the kids it was time for Mommy to talk to God.

It doesn't matter where it is or how fancy it might be, it just matters that you have a private prayer chapel. It is there in Mama's private prayer chapel you will find renewal, refreshment, and revival as you go about the task of strengthening your family and your walk with God.

Examples From the Bible

Jesus instructed us to love, know, and obey his teachings. In order to know, we must learn and live his Word. In doing so, we experience a miracle as we pray and Jesus and the Father dwell in our hearts and lives as they make us their home.

- Jesus prayed in private. "Jesus often withdrew to lonely places and prayed" (Luke 5:16).
- Jesus prayed in times of spiritual strife. "He withdrew about a stone's throw beyond them, knelt down and prayed, 'Father, if you are willing, take this cup from me; yet not my will, but yours be done'" (Luke 22:41–42).
- Jesus prayed on the cross. "About the ninth hour Jesus cried out in a loud voice, 'Eloi, Eloi, lama sabachthani?'—which means, 'My God, my God, why have you forsaken me?'" (Matthew 27:46).
- Jesus sought direction in prayer. "One of those days Jesus went out to a mountainside to pray, and spent the night praying to God" (Luke 6:12).
- Jesus offered thanks and praise in prayer. "At that time Jesus, full of joy through the Holy Spirit, said, 'I praise you, Father, Lord of heaven and earth, because you have hidden these things from the wise and learned, and revealed them to little children. Yes, Father, for this was your good pleasure'" (Luke 10:21).
- Jesus prayed for himself. "After Jesus said this, he looked toward heaven and prayed: 'Father, the time has come. Glorify your Son, that your Son may glorify you'" (John 17:1).
- Jesus prayed for his disciples. "I am not praying for the world, but for those you have given me, for they are yours" (John 17:9). "Sanctify them by the truth; your word is truth" (John 17:17).
- Jesus prayed a prayer of intercession. "Father, forgive them, for they do not know what they are doing" (Luke 23:34).

Examples From the Bible

In Bible times the whole family ate the evening meal together. In most cases it was prepared by the mother, assisted by other family members or servants. A fun-filled kitchen will help you build your house. Let's see what's cooking in the Bible:

- Fatted calf, curds, and milk were what Abraham and Sarah prepared for their guests (Genesis 18:6–8). That sounds like the Atkins diet.
- Lentil soup was what Esau traded his birthright for (Genesis 25:29–34). That is more along the lines of the South Beach diet.
- Fish, cucumbers, melons, leeks, onions, and garlic were eaten by the Israelites during their captivity in Egypt (Numbers 11:5). That sounds a little like the Zone.
- Bread, wine, sheep, roasted grain, raisins, and fig cakes were what Abigail provided for David and his men (1 Samuel 25:18). Now, that sounds like good eats!
- Grain, wine, and olive oil were included in God's blessings (Deuteronomy 7:13). That's Italian!
- Salt was the main seasoning (Job 6:6), along with caraway and cummin (Isaiah 28:25–27). Mrs. Dash would not approve.
- Corn got Jesus and the disciples into trouble when they picked it fresh in the field (Matthew 12:1). Summer-fresh produce, right out of the garden!
- Fish for breakfast? Yes, Jesus prepared it for the disciples over an open fire (John 21:9–13). That sounds like a good campout!

We can make the kitchen a fun and special place that is always open and ready to satisfy the ones we love. Take joy in the food you prepare, knowing it will nourish and strengthen your family.

Appetite for Life

Food and memory seem to go hand in hand. An ordinary food once took me by surprise and brought back some great memories.

If you're a hamburger fan and you've dined in Southern California, I'm sure you've heard of the famous In-N-Out burger restaurants. They are known for their simple menu of hamburgers, cheeseburgers, fresh-cut fries, and thick shakes—just like the old drive-ins. Since I'm not a real fan of red meat, I never understood the big sensation about In-N-Out burgers, until this trip.

One spring when my son Philip and I were in California to visit my sister Connie, we made the obligatory trek to In-N-Out. My brother-in-law Bruce ordered chocolate shakes; Philip had a cheeseburger, fries, and shake; and I sat down to my water.

We had places to go and things to do, and as usual Philip was taking a loooong time to eat. So to help him finish, I tore off a piece of his burger and popped it into my mouth. That's when it happened. My eyes welled up with tears. I could hardly speak because I was so choked up with memories, but I managed to look at my sister and get these words out: "It's a Fair Burger!"

She looked at her husband and said, "See, I told you so!"

Now, to you that means nothing, but to my sister and me, that's a cherished memory.

Every September in our small county fair, the Lions Club sponsored a special building where the best hamburgers in the world were sold to everyone who attended the fair. It was the biggest fund-raiser for the Lions. You couldn't beat a Fair Burger. The master chef was none other than my father, affectionately known as "Boodle." He cooked with flair, adding touches such as grilled buns, grilled onions, and cheese melted right on the burger as it slowly grilled. Yum! For my sisters and me, one of the highlights of our year, every year, was assisting in the booth. I guess that was our first experience as short-order cooks. What memories!

With one bite, that burger turned into comfort food. It's no wonder my sister Sherry devours them. Even me, Miss No Burger, had an urge to stop for just one more on the way to the airport.

Fish grilled over an open fire must've been an ordinary meal that Simon Peter ate hundreds of times. I wonder how different it tasted to him after the resurrected Jesus made it for breakfast on the shore of the Sea of Tiberias. Peter had apparently given up on being a fisher of men and had returned to being a fisher of fish. John 21 gives the impression that Jesus surprised the disciples when he appeared on the shore. The Scripture says he fixed them breakfast, then afterward asked Peter, "Do you love me?" In that poignant conversation, Jesus reinstated Peter as his forgiven follower and clarified Peter's calling. From then on, whenever Peter tasted grilled fish, I'm sure he reminisced about his risen Savior and that emotional meal on the beach. Did the words "Follow me . . . feed my sheep" burn in his heart every time he tasted fish? Did each bite give him a renewed heart, a sense of mission, a new appetite for life?

Memories of past foods. Girl friend, now that's what I call comfort food!

Savor the moments!

check this out

teachers
Colossians 2:8
redemption
Hebrews 9:12
feet
John 13:5–17

sufficiency
capability; skill
redemption
Jesus paid the ransom
so we could be free
from sin.
mundane
ordinary

My Name Is Not Cinderella

COLOSSIANS 3:17 *And whatever you do, whether in word or deed, do it all in the name of the Lord Jesus, giving thanks to God the Father through him.*

The apostle Paul wrote to the Colossians because they seemed to be losing their focus. <u>Teachers</u> in Colossae were adding to their newfound Christianity elements of religions and practices they had previously been involved in. Young believers were falling away from the central theme of the Gospel: all **sufficiency** in Christ. Paul reminded them to do everything, whether in word or deed, as if doing it for Jesus. Christ was supposed to be the central focus of their new lives.

We homemakers sometimes lose our focus too. We get such close-up exposure to the Cinderella work, we can end up hating homemaking. Sometimes when I pull on the rubber gloves, rev up the vacuum cleaner, and look at the housework that is before me, I hear those mean stepsisters barking orders to sweet little Cinderella: "Cinderella, do the dishes; Cinderella, scrub the floors; Cinderella, wash the clothes. . . ." I grumble and complain just like Martha did when she whined to Jesus that she was overworked preparing food for all the guests. Like Martha, I start looking for a sister Mary to shove some of my workload on to (Luke 10:38–42).

I know my name is not Cinderella, but some days, I sure feel like her. When that happens, I need to step back, refocus the lens of my life, and examine myself to see if I've gotten away from my life's mission of being "about my Father's business" (Luke 2:49 KJV).

When Jesus said he was being about his Father's business, that business was a mission of saving the world: <u>redemption</u>. I can't save the whole world, but I can help save a little piece of it by doing what I'm supposed to be doing daily, influencing those in my home. My assignment changes on a daily basis. One day of being the best mother I can be takes priority; another day, the top task is to be the supportive spouse; or another day, the willing worker. But whatever we do, we need to remember the big picture, remain focused, and do it willfully as unto the Lord.

Was the Savior of all humanity wasting time when he washed his disciples' <u>feet</u>? No, in that **mundane** task he was showing them a divine approach to life. Just as that footwashing still impacts lives all these centuries later, household chores done with Jesus' attitude can have untold results for God's kingdom. Don't think of yourself as Cinderella. Think of

think about it

yourself as Head Overseer of the Mop Ministry. Wise women who build their houses stay focused on "being about [their] Father's business."

famine
Genesis 41–47

> ## How Others See It
> ### Joanna Weaver
> Service without spirituality is exhausting and hopeless. But in the same respect, spirituality without service is barren and selfish. We need to unite the two and do it all "as unto the Lord." When we do that, something wonderful happens to our work in the kitchen. Sinks turn into sanctuaries. Mops swab holy ground. And daily chores that used to bore us or wear us down become opportunities to express our gratitude—selfless avenues for his grace.[3]

Pray for the Best—Plan for the Worst

PROVERBS 22:3 *A prudent man sees danger and takes refuge, but the simple keep going and suffer for it.*

I'm one of those what-if people and prepare accordingly. I was caught up in the Y2K hype and was prepared for the final countdown. Fortunately, it was no big deal. My husband accused me of being disappointed that the world didn't spin out of control and that I wasn't able to use my supplies. But the jokes subsided when the following winter an ice storm brought our community to a total standstill. We were without power for two weeks, and the prepared housewife came to the rescue with all of our emergency supplies.

Emergencies come in all different forms, including natural disasters and terrorist attacks. We've all seen the total destruction and devastation of both in recent years. Just as Joseph led and prepared a nation and protected his family from a <u>famine</u> that struck Egypt, we need to prepare our families for and respond to potential emergencies.

The U.S. Department of Homeland Security advises that we should have some basic supplies on hand in order to survive for at least three days if an emergency occurs. I encourage you to make this a high priority for your family and to prepare for a disaster before it strikes.

What You Can Do

Recommended items to include in a basic emergency supply include:

- Water, one gallon of water per person per day for at least three days, for drinking and sanitation

- Food, at least a three-day supply of nonperishable food

- Battery-powered or hand-crank radio and an NOAA weather radio with tone alert and extra batteries for both

- Flashlight and extra batteries

- First-aid kit

- Whistle to signal for help

- Dust mask, to help filter contaminated air, and plastic sheeting and duct tape to shelter-in-place

- Moist towelettes, garbage bags, and plastic ties for personal sanitation

- Wrench or pliers to turn off utilities

- Can opener for food

- Local maps

Additional items to consider adding to an emergency supply kit include:

- Prescription medications and glasses

- Infant formula and diapers

- Pet food and extra water for your pet

- Important family documents such as copies of insurance policies, identification, and bank account records in a waterproof, portable container

- Cash or traveler's checks and change

- Emergency reference material such as a first-aid book

- Sleeping bag or warm blanket for each person

- Complete change of clothing, including a long-sleeved shirt, long pants, and sturdy shoes

- Household chlorine bleach and medicine dropper (when diluted nine parts water to one part bleach, the mixture can be used as a disinfectant, or, in an emergency, you can use it to treat water by using sixteen drops of regular household bleach per gallon of water)

- Fire extinguisher

- Matches in a waterproof container

- Feminine supplies and personal hygiene items

- Mess kits, paper cups and plates, plastic utensils, paper towels

- Paper and pencil

- Books, games, puzzles, or other activities for children[4]

Be informed! Finding out what can happen is the first step. Once you have determined the events possible and their potential in your community, it is important that you discuss them with your family or household. Develop a disaster plan together.

Meet with your family and discuss why you need to prepare for disaster. Explain the dangers of fire, severe weather, and earthquakes to children. Plan to share responsibilities and work together as a team.

- Discuss the types of disasters that are most likely to happen. Explain what to do in each case.

- Pick two places to meet: (1) right outside your home in case of a sudden emergency, like a fire, and (2) outside your neighborhood in case you can't return home. Everyone must know the address and phone number.

- Ask an out-of-state friend to be your "family contact." After a disaster, it's often easier to call long-distance. Other family members should call this person and tell them where they are. Everyone must know your contact's phone number.

- Discuss what to do in an evacuation. Plan how to take care of your pets.

- Write down all of these contact numbers and information on the family emergency contact card.[5]

Children and Disasters

Prepare your children for the emotions that occur during and after a disaster.

What You Can Do

Talk with your children before an emergency occurs. Reassure them with the following:

1. Disasters don't last very long. Soon things will be back to normal.

hard work
Proverbs 14:23

2. You can get a new routine if you can't go home for a while. You will settle down into a new place, and you will meet new friends.

3. Look to your parents or other trusted adults for help when you feel scared or confused. They will help you understand what is happening. Don't be afraid to ask questions such as "How long will we be in a shelter?" and "When will I go back to school?"

4. Sometimes it helps to write about your experiences or to draw pictures about what has happened. You can describe what happened and how you feel.

5. It's okay to cry during a disaster, but remember, it will get better.

6. You may be able to help out. Children of all ages can help in the shelter by baby-sitting other children or cleaning up or serving food. You can even help with sandbagging.⁶

How Others See It

Stephen Arterburn

We live in a world that has real dangers—including terrorists. As parents, we are here to teach how to be aware of things that are dangerous so you can be careful and stay safe.⁷

Where's Helpful Heloise When You Need Her?

PROVERBS 21:5 *The plans of the diligent lead to profit as surely as haste leads to poverty.*

Proverbs indicates planning is the secret to a wise woman's success. You've heard people say, "Haste makes waste." This verse is where that idea came from. If you discipline yourself and make strategic plans, your <u>hard work</u> will not go to waste—it will reward great dividends.

Pick up any women's magazine and you'll be sure to find a section on smart ideas to make life easier. We're always looking for help. I'm sure "Hints from Heloise" has rescued many a stained blouse from the rag drawer. Emilie Barnes, an author and home-management expert, can put your life together—fifteen minutes at a time.

Isn't it wonderful how God balanced the world with Organized Olivias and Disorganized Dotties? It's great for the economy too, because Olivia can make a killing off of Dottie as she zooms into Dottie's house and, like

Mr. Clean, whirls up a white tornado. Zap, zoom, zing—Dottie has an instant home makeover, and Olivia pockets a "consulting fee."

Examples From the Bible

A wise homemaker uses planning to build her house. Planning ahead helped many people in Bible times:

- God led Joseph to help Pharaoh implement plans that caused Egypt to prosper through seven years of famine. (Genesis 41:25–27)

- Jesus told the parable of ten virgins waiting for the bridegroom and the bridal party. Five were wise because they planned ahead and took extra oil for their lamps while they waited. The foolish virgins ran out of oil and went away to get more. While they were gone, the bridegroom came and the foolish virgins missed the party. This was an analogy of Christ himself, the bridegroom of the church, and his second coming. (Matthew 25:1–13; John 13:29)

- Jesus commended planning through his parable of the servant who knew his master's will and was faithful and wise, prepared and waiting for his master's return. (Luke 12:35–48)

- We can also learn from Proverbs 22:3: "A prudent man sees danger and takes refuge, but the simple keep going and suffer for it."

Say yes to planning, yes to organization, yes to uncluttered lives and schedules. Your hard work will bring you great dividends both financially and in the relationships with those you love.

How Others See It

Emilie Barnes
Simplify and unclutter your life by saying no to doing things and saving your yeses for the best things in life. Live a balanced life. Make time for yourself. Stop go-go-going. Be a person of "being" rather than a person of "doing."[8]

This Little Piggy Went to Market

There are some things you shouldn't put off. Grocery shopping just before a snowstorm hits is one of them. But honestly, I was oblivious to the snow report. Besides that, it's not supposed to snow before Thanksgiving. I just happened to have grocery shopping on my list for Monday night and moved it to the next day. I didn't know I would wake up to nine inches of snow and all my cupboards bare.

Sometimes I think I would rather go out and hunt my own food or buy a farm and raise crops and livestock than go grocery shopping. I personally don't know anyone who really enjoys this thankless task. It's time-consuming, hectic, and definitely depressing when you see your weekly grocery bill cost more than your first car.

If you watch closely, you'll see different types of shoppers. There's Mother Hubbard, who only goes to the store when there is nothing left in the house and the children are begging for bread. A friend of mine said one morning she was completely out of bread and had to resort to baking homemade biscuits. The funny thing was, her kids thought she was wonderful and wanted to know what they were celebrating.

Then there's Mrs. Busy, the one who goes shopping every day of the week, planning her evening meal in the car on the way home from work. The grocer loves her. He sees dollar signs as she bursts through the door, because research shows she'll spend a lot more money that way.

My favorite is Mrs. Commando, the shopper who declares war on shopping. Her strategy is laid out, the list completed, the menu decided weeks in advance, coupons clipped. Her weapon of choice, the pocket calculator, is grasped tightly in her hand. She marches into the store single-mindedly. She grabs a cart and begins dodging enemy fire (you know, those nice little ladies with the tempting sample carts of goodies). Mrs. Commando puts on her imaginary blinders and hustles through the store, aisle by aisle, depositing only items from her list into her cart. The yams are secured, sir! Rutabaga secured, sir! In order to avoid friendly fire, she never, ever takes her kids or husband with her, for they might try to sneak an unauthorized item into the cart.

I didn't always appreciate this shopper until she recruited me. Now I can say, I have declared war on shopping!

Since enlistment and boot camp, I too am now Mrs. Commando, saving precious hours that I spend at home with my family counting the money my new tactics saved.

Life is too short to be standing in line at the so-called Express Lane with eight items or less. This little piggy went to market, but I'd rather raid it. The battle plan: get in, get out, nobody gets hurt. "[A wise woman] is not afraid of the snow. . . ." (Proverbs 31:21 NASB).

Hospitality 101

HEBREWS 13:1–2 *Keep on loving each other as brothers. Do not forget to entertain strangers, for by so doing some people have entertained <u>angels</u> without knowing it.*

check this out

angels
Genesis 18:1–9
truth
John 14:6
hospitality
Mark 6:10–11

Hebrews was written to bring the church to a deeper understanding of the <u>truth</u> of the Gospel. The writer of Hebrews wanted those truths put into action and encouraged the believers to show love and hospitality to foreigners or strangers who needed food and shelter. Unlike today, in ancient times you couldn't find a Holiday Inn on every exit off the freeway. You couldn't even find a freeway. So it was a common practice to offer hospitality.

Jesus and his disciples depended solely on the <u>hospitality</u> of strangers as they went from village to village sharing their Good News. Hospitality is "a good thing" for building your house.

It's been said that Martha Stewart's first book, *Entertaining,* sparked the new transformation in how we welcome people into our homes. Over the past few years, Martha has had her fair share of troubles, but she seems to be back on top. I have to agree that Martha did revive the long-lost art of hospitality—and along the way built a giant "entertaining and hospitality" industry.

You might think Martha's products sell because we're a bunch of self-indulgent entertainers who want to impress others. You may have a point there. But I believe Martha's products sell because somehow in our busy lives, we never learned how to be hospitable. We sense our lack and search for the lost art. Deep down, we want to know how to serve people and make them feel warm, welcomed, and loved. And if I may borrow one of Martha's favorite sayings, "It's a good thing."

We modern women need to be reminded and encouraged to share the spirit and love of Jesus by extending hospitality to strangers, friends, and family.

How Others See It

Dee Brestin

Women can make an enormous difference by extending hospitality to those who are new in town, new at church, or new in the faith. A direct command of Scripture is for the older women to mentor younger women. Women often have a natural doorway into the world of children and can use their homes to make an eternal difference in children's lives.[9]

vision
Proverbs 29:18
leadership
Acts 20:17;
Titus 1:5

epistles
letters intended for
public circulation

Hospitality: The Warmth of the Home

1 TIMOTHY 3:4–5 *He must manage his own family well and see that his children obey him with proper respect. (If anyone does not know how to manage his own family, how can he take care of God's church?)*

Every organization needs leadership to survive. If it doesn't have someone at the helm, its members slowly lose <u>vision</u>, and it will die a slow death. This is partly why the apostle Paul wrote Timothy, a co-worker, emphasizing the need for qualified <u>leadership</u> in the church.

People who want to lead the church have to meet higher standards than "ordinary" believers. Leadership requires special skills and qualifications because new believers look to the leaders as examples and guides. Paul's **epistles** list fifteen "must have" qualifications, and the list includes hospitality (1 Timothy 3:2) and managing your household (1 Timothy 3:5). Leaders must enjoy having people in their homes and must be able to handle their own households.

You can learn a lot about someone by observing his or her family interactions. Does a leader's home reflect leadership? Do the children and spouse respect the leader? Do they love and respect God? Is God the head of their household? Paul makes a great point as he asks the rhetorical question, "How can a person lead a church, if he can't lead his home?"

Paul's question applies to us too. Put bluntly, he asks, "Do you practice what you preach?"

We can learn from the comparison of leadership in the home and the church, for many of the same skills and qualifications are needed for both. As leaders in our homes, we have higher standards to meet as our children look to us for vision and guidance. Before we offer hospitality to individuals beyond our homes, are we showing hospitality to those inside our homes?

You don't have to be as great a cook as Julia Child and serve a delicious gourmet meal every night to be a successful homemaker. As Proverbs 15:17 says, "Better a meal of vegetables where there is love than a fattened calf with hatred." The spirit of love and hospitality starts at home and is more important than the menu. A wise woman sharpens her hospitality at home before she extends it beyond her four walls.

How Others See It

Susan Alexander Yates

We need a vision. We must keep our vision of creating a family of friends clearly in mind. But remember, our vision is not ours alone. It is also that of our heavenly Father. In Him we have the unlimited resources of the universe: His wisdom, His power, and His forgiveness.[10]

Granny's Jam Cake

Fall brings back a multitude of rich memories. It has so many vivid sights, smells, and sounds: colorful harvesttime, picking just the right pumpkin in the pumpkin patch, raking (and playing in) a pile of fallen leaves. It's usually my most homesick time of the year. But one year when I learned we would have out-of-state family around our Thanksgiving table, that homesickness gave way to preparation.

I thumbed through my recipe file and found the card for the most delectable food of the season—Jam Cake. Since we moved to Seattle, I found there are those who have never even heard of this fabulous cake. Evidently it's a dish from the South, but it's a family tradition and one of my most treasured comfort foods.

The recipe was written in my grandmother's hand. My eyes stung and my heart ached, but memories of Granny and her Jam Cake brought a smile to my face. I remembered her kitchen, filled with the spicy aroma of baking nutmeg mingled with the smell of brewing coffee. I could see her fluttering around the kitchen, busy as a bee, filled with excitement and anticipation because the holidays meant a house full of friends and family.

Sometimes I mirror my grandmother—especially in the kitchen. Just like her, I start preparations weeks in advance, writing the menu in detail and compiling the grocery list. We have something else in common too: like hers, when I'm in the process of cooking, my kitchen looks as if the Pillsbury Doughboy exploded. (At his funeral, they've got to sing "When the Roll Is Called Up Yonder.") There's flour all over the countertops, utensils everywhere, and a sink full of dirty pots and pans, just like Granny's kitchen.

I hope I mirror my grandmother in other ways. No matter who gathered around her table at any time of the year, she greeted them with love and hospitality. Her hospitality went beyond the Southern tradition; it was a love she mirrored from her Creator. Acceptance. Tolerance. A radiant love that gave you a sense of warmth and security. It's no wonder everyone cherished Granny and loved coming home for the holidays.

As the fall days grow colder, the smoke and smell of a crackling fire always chase away the chill of the air and stir up some late-autumn memories for me: heartwarming memories of Jam Cake, moments with Granny, and the treasure of her love.

Heartfelt Hospitality

PHILEMON 1:7 *Your love has given me great joy and encouragement, because you, brother, have refreshed the hearts of the saints.*

"Come on in, sit a spell, and visit," were the most welcoming words of my childhood as we visited family and friends. The first runner-up to those words was the phrase that bid our visit farewell and beckoned our return, "Ya'll come back now, ya hear?" Now that's Southern hospitality! That phrase always echoed in my ears as we drove away, and it still echoes in my heart with fond memories.

The book of Philemon is a very short, personal letter from the apostle Paul to a co-worker and friend, Philemon. Paul pens this letter from prison in Rome to his friend in Colossae. He addresses what our attitudes should be toward those who are different from us.

Paul opens by thanking God for Philemon's kindness. Philemon not only had been a blessing to Paul; he had "refreshed the hearts" of God's people. **Philemon** must have been known for his generous <u>hospitality</u> and kindness throughout the city. He even opened his home for the <u>church</u> to meet there. (I'll bet if he were from southern Colossae he would say, "Y'all come back now, ya hear?")

A simple, sincere gesture of hospitality can offer hope as you refresh the hearts of those in need. As believers, we extend hospitality not because we're just really nice people, but because those who are in need see a testimony of Christ.

hospitality
Romans 12:13
church
Philemon 1:2

Philemon
a wealthy Christian
prophet
person who receives messages from God

How Others See It

Emilie Barnes

Whatever you do to your walls and windows, don't forget that the most wonderful adornment to your home is your spirit of hospitality, your willingness to share your home, and your lives with others. You don't need to wait until everything's perfect. It never will be. After all, people live in your home. Something will always need painting or recovering or replacing. You'll always want to add something here, take out something there. But share anyway! Love what you have, and invite others in to share the bounty. Your gracious welcome will fill the gaps and make the problems seem to disappear.[11]

Snapshots of Women in the Bible
The Shunammite Woman (2 Kings 4:8–37)

It became a frequent stop for Elisha. It all began as he traveled from his home in Mount Carmel to Jezreel (see Illustration #4) to consult with the king.

His reputation preceded him. But even if it hadn't, his hairy cloak gave away the fact that he was a **prophet**. Peasants and kings turned to him for help as he relayed messages to them from God.

A wealthy woman from Shunem (see Illustration #4) stopped him on his travels and persuaded Elisha and his servant, Gehazi, to eat with them. She didn't exactly need to twist Elisha's arm, since his stomach growled in hunger. He enjoyed the tasty stew, grains, and fresh fruit she provided. He left replenished, rested, and renewed for his travels.

The Shunammite woman recognized Elisha as a holy man and asked her husband to build a guest room for him. It was no king's palace, but it was better than many other lodgings Elisha had used during his travels.

hospitality
I Peter 4:9
courage
John 16:33
faith
Matthew 9:22

Elisha was so grateful for her hospitality that he sent his servant, Gehazi, to see how they could repay her kindness. Elisha offered to use his political influence to have the king protect her. She declined the offer, for there was no need; she dwelt among her people where she felt safe and secure. She expected nothing in return from this prophet.

Gehazi told Elisha they had no children. In her old age and disbelief, she was shocked when Elisha promised her a son. But as he foretold, a miracle occurred: She conceived and bore a son.

Years passed. One day her little boy went to the harvesting fields with his father in the heat of the day and collapsed, apparently from heat stroke. The father quickly had a servant carry the son to his mother.

She cradled her son in her arms. She rocked him back and forth and dipped a cloth in springwater to cool his forehead. Then his body went limp in her arms. Her heart froze and she gasped.

Her only hope was to find the man of miracles. She carried her son to the guest room, laid him carefully on the bed, kissed his forehead, and shut the door. She dropped all formality as she and a servant rushed across country to fetch Elisha.

When at last she reached Elisha at Mount Carmel, she ran and fell at his feet. Her mourning and anguish welled up as a tormented question: Why? Why did you give me this son, only to take him away?

Elisha responded as rapidly as possible. But Elisha didn't answer her question. Instead, he brought the Shunammite woman's son back to life.

The room built for a stranger's refreshment became the room where a family was resurrected.

The Shunammite woman had an open, discerning heart. When she saw a man in need, she was willing not only to feed him but also to go the extra mile and provide lodging whenever he passed by. She expected nothing in return for her generosity but was blessed through the miracle of birth and the miracle of resurrection.

In her time of crisis, she knew who to turn to—this holy man, a man of God, a man of miracles. Because of her <u>hospitality</u>, <u>courage</u>, and <u>faith</u> she received abundant gifts from God. She learned that it is truly "more blessed to give than to receive" (Acts 20:35).

Glue Guns and the Tabernacle

EXODUS 31:1–3 *Then the Lord said to Moses, "See, I have chosen Bezalel son of Uri, the son of Hur, of the tribe of Judah, and I have filled him with the Spirit of God, with skill, ability and knowledge in all kinds of crafts."*

Since God designed the **tabernacle** and gave Moses detailed instructions, it's not surprising that God also designed specific individuals with special creative abilities to fulfill his design.

God deserves and demands our best. The tabernacle was filled with gold, silver, bronze, jewels, and carved wood. Each required a skilled workman, which God provided when he had Moses send for **Bezalel** and <u>Oholiab</u>.

Generations later, as King Solomon went about his God-appointed task of building a magnificent <u>temple</u> of worship, he also needed the finest craftsmen to complete the project. Also believing God deserves only the best, Solomon negotiated with the Phoenician king Hiram of Tyre to send him skillful servants, who would be <u>compensated</u> for their work. <u>King Hiram</u> sent Huram-Abi, his very own master craftsman.

check this out

Oholiab
Exodus 31:6
temple
2 Chronicles 2:4
compensated
2 Chronicles 2:10
King Hiram
2 Chronicles 2:12–13

tabernacle
place of worship
Bezalel
craftsman that helped build the tabernacle
Oholiab
craftsman, Bezalel's assistant

Examples From the Bible

Just as God designed specific abilities in the hearts of these craftsmen, likewise, I believe he gave women special abilities to accomplish their unique tasks:

- Sheerah, a descendant of Ephraim, was mentioned as building three villages that were ancient border towns between Benjamin and Ephraim. (1 Chronicles 7:24)
- Female perfumers used their talents to make scented waters from orange trees, violets, and roses. (1 Samuel 8:13)
- Dorcas was a seamstress and sewed garments for the needy widows at Joppa. (Acts 9:36–42)

I wasn't introduced to a glue gun until I was in my thirties. I don't know how I ever lived without one; it is such a marvelous invention!

Crafts are the craze. We just can't seem to get enough. We rubber-stamp everything in sight, scrapbook every picture we can find, and tune in to the latest quilting and craft show on TV. But your own little craft corner can be more than a creative outlet for you as you design, weave, sew, glue, paint, or do whatever you do. It can also bless your family and those who admire your creations.

think about it

God created us all different. There's only one you, and you can decorate or create with your own God-given uniqueness. How would you like to display his beauty in your life? What's stopping you?

Illustration #14
Women Using a Spindle—After the flax fibers were clean and dry (right), they were drawn out by hand and wrapped around a spindle. The spindle was rotated to twist the fibers into thread (left).

How Others See It
Liz Curtis Higgs
Dear friends and others who have gifted me with their creations over the years could only guess at how their handwork has touched my life. Over a desk in our office is the cross-stitched phrase: "Working for the Lord doesn't pay much, but the retirement plan is out of this world!"[12]

Stitch by Stitch

EXODUS 35:25 *Every skilled woman spun with her hands and brought what she had spun—blue, purple or scarlet yarn or fine linen.*

There was a magnificent amount of work required in order to complete the **tabernacle**. The whole community worked together as they responded with their gifts and talents. Spinning was considered women's work in Bible times (see Illustration #14), so the women spun yarn and fine linens for the tabernacle—God's place of worship.

God opens doors for one who places her life, her heart, and her creations into his hands. You may never know how your craft touched someone, but you serve the Creator who can weave all of our gifts together into one beautiful masterpiece, the body of Christ.

tabernacle
Hebrew for "tent of meeting"

Melody's Flowers

Melody's first attempt at crafting began when her church decided to hold a craft fair and they were short on vendors. She says even though she felt she was a little short on talent, she would <u>willingly</u> see what she could throw together to fill a booth.

The response was overwhelming. The booth swarmed with customers, and she walked away with the second highest sales of the day. Her simple floral arranging not only grew into a lucrative business, but it became a creative release and a Christian outreach as well. She also volunteers her creative talents to decorate her house of <u>worship</u>. Members and visitors alike comment on how beautiful her arrangements are. They feel as if they've walked into an elegant hotel lobby.

Melody says with gratitude and humility, "I never dreamed that this would be an area that God could use me in, but I am constantly thankful that I took the risk to see what God and I could whip up together."

Whether you are creating special memories for your children, decorating a church, or sitting around a quilting frame stitching a quilt for a woman in need, you are laboring in love. Share your creativity. "She selects wool and flax and works with eager hands" (Proverbs 31:13).

willingly
Psalm 51:12
worship
2 Chronicles 2

> ### How Others See It
> **Emilie Barnes and Yoli Brogger**
> Every object in your home tells your life story. It may be a family picture when you were young or an art object from your latest vacation. Feel free to let your home be a reflection of who your family is.[13]

Final Thoughts

- A home needs to be a safe haven for its family members. As the heartbeat of the home, a woman can rediscover the lost art and joy of homemaking if she realizes the profound impact the servant heart of Christ has on people. Welcome your family home with open arms.

- The occupation "homemaker" is one of the greatest and most challenging careers of all times. It is a God-designed, treasured calling for women.

- The kitchen is the gathering place of the home. Make it a fun and special place that is always open and ready to satisfy a hungry tummy or starving soul.

- There is eternal value to our everyday endeavors. If you stay focused on being about your Father's business, every seemingly mundane thing you do will count.

- Scripture reveals hospitality as a requirement in our walk of life. Extending heartfelt hospitality not only blesses those who receive but also is a great blessing for those who give. Hospitality starts at home. Then share Christ's Spirit and love with those beyond your walls.

- Your own unique creations can serve as further expressions of God's love and glory. Being creative is part of being created in God's image, so don't hold back.

Questions to Deepen Your Understanding

1. What type of woman can build a house called home?

2. How was homemaking looked upon in the early church? (Titus 2:4–6)

3. How does the Holy Spirit help us in building our homes?

4. Martha once grumbled about her everyday duties as a homemaker. What caused a change in her life?

5. When discouraged over the hassles of housework, what can we remember to keep us from grumbling and complaining?

6. In ancient Bible times, how did one offer hospitality? How can we do the same?

7. In return for her hospitality, how was the Shunammite woman blessed?

read on

Some of Georgia's favorite books for rediscovering the lost art and joy of homemaking:

- *Busy People's Down-Home Cooking Without the Down-Home Fat,* Dawn Hall, Thomas Nelson

- *Designing Your Home on a Budget,* Emilie Barnes and Yoli Brogger, Harvest House

- *God's Good Gifts: A Scrapbooking Bible Study for Women's Groups,* Group Publishing

- *Grab a Broom, Lord, There's Dust Everywhere,* Karon Phillips Goodman, Barbour Publishing

- *Having a Mary Heart in a Martha World,* Joanna Weaver, WaterBrook Press

- *Home Warming: Secrets to Making Your House a Welcoming Place,* Emilie Barnes, Harvest House

- *Hugs for Scrapbookers,* Stephanie Howard, Howard Publishers

- *Life Management for Busy Women,* Elizabeth George, Harvest House

- *Organizing Magic: 40 Days to a Well-Organized Home and Life,* Sandra Felton, Baker Books

- *Queen of the Castle: 52 Weeks of Encouragement for the Uninspired, Domestically Challenged or Just Plain Tired Homemaker,* Lynn Bowen Walker, Integrity Publishers

- *Scrapbooking Your Spiritual Journey,* Sandra Joseph, Reminders of Faith

- Web sites for information on preparing your family for an emergency: Red Cross, *www.redcross.org;* Federal Emergency Management Agency, *www.fema.gov;* Centers for Disease Control and Prevention (biological agents), *www.bt.cdc.gov;* U.S. Department of Health and Human Services, *www.hhs.gov.*

- *A Woman of Hospitality,* Dee Brestin, Cook Communications

- *The Women's Devotional Guide to the Bible,* Jean E. Syswerda, Thomas Nelson

Part Four

Relationships and Community Involvement

Chapter 10: Touching Lives, Serving Others

Putting Your Gift to Work in the World

What's in This Chapter

- Unwrap Your Gift and Use It
- Discovering Your Spiritual Gifts
- Operation Blessing
- Who, Me, Join the Peace Corps? No Way!
- You're in the Army Now
- Career Soldier
- Things You Can Do to Encourage Your Pastor
- Encourage Our Troops and Their Families
- I Sat Next to a Legend
- Reserves Soldier

- Snapshot: Huldah
- Won't You Be My Neighbor?
- Is There Anything I Can Do?
- Neighbor to Neighbor
- Being Your Best Together With Your Church Family and Friends
- Sisterhood of Believers
- The Symbol of Friendship
- Church Makes an Eternal Difference
- Women's Role in the Early Church and Today
- Snapshot: Dorcas

Here We Go

I wish someone would come up with a better recruiting mascot than Uncle Sam. As a child I got nightmares from that picture of a mean-spirited, tight-lipped, finger-pointing old coot. I could never imagine being a willing recruit for him.

In the spring of 1997, volunteerism got a jump-start as Colin Powell chaired the president's Volunteerism Summit in Philadelphia. (Good choice for a recruiter. He's a lot better looking than Uncle Sam.) Celebrities, past United States presidents, and CEOs all jumped in, waving the volunteer flag and encouraging Americans to pull up their bootstraps, join hands, and volunteer. After all, it's our civic duty! As hoped, thousands of ordinary citizens volunteered their time and energy.

Little did they know, but Colin Powell and the Volunteer Summit began laying the groundwork for the army of volunteers needed to respond to catastrophic events that followed: in 2001 the terrorist attacks on 9/11, in

Holy Spirit
Galatians 4:6
gifts
Romans 12:6–8
spiritual
Ephesians 4:7–11

2004 the tsunami that struck Indonesia, and in 2005 the hurricane Katrina, the most costly disaster-relief operation in our nation's history.

I believe it is our civic duty to volunteer. More important, however, is our Christian duty to touch lives and serve others as we follow the example of Christ, our tender, loving, and caring Master. He commanded us to "love one another as I have loved you" (John 15:12 NKJV). Now that's a great recruiting slogan! You (yes, you!) can make a difference in the lives of others.

Service is not reserved for a designated group of people to do. The act of serving is for everyone. Once we discover our own special abilities and spiritual gifts, we can put them to work and make a difference in the lives of others if we are willing to serve.

Serving may be as simple as responding to a next-door neighbor's crisis, being involved in a community canned food drive, or implementing your gifts at your local church. Your service may be a lifetime of committed involvement, or your situation may only permit you to commit to a short-term mission trip. Regardless of what shape it takes in each of our lives, we must reach out to others. When all is said and done, a whole lot more is said than done. We need to put more "show" in our Gospel "show-and-tell."

Let's see what the Bible says about touching lives by serving others.

Unwrap Your Gift and Use It

1 Corinthians 12:4–6 *There are different kinds of gifts, but the same Spirit. There are different kinds of service, but the same Lord. There are different kinds of working, but the same God works all of them in all men.*

As Paul writes the church at Corinth (see Illustration #13 on page 180), he zooms in on problems relating to how the world views our actions. In this particular Bible passage he deals with how we discover and use our gifts to further the work of the church.

When Jesus left to return to his Father, he gave us the gift of the <u>Holy Spirit</u> to dwell within us. The Spirit in turn gives us <u>gifts</u> that we can use in ministering to one another. These may come in the form of an added bonus to our traits, temperaments, and abilities, or they may be <u>spiritual</u> gifts. Whatever the gift, Paul encourages us to discover, unwrap, and put our gifts to work in the world.

Discovering Your Spiritual Gifts

1 Corinthians 12:7–11 *Each person is given something to do that shows who God is: Everyone gets in on it, everyone benefits. All kinds of things are handed out by the Spirit, and to all kinds of people! The variety is wonderful:*

> *wise counsel*
>
> *clear understanding*
>
> *simple trust*
>
> *healing the sick*
>
> *miraculous acts*
>
> *proclamation*
>
> *distinguishing between spirits*
>
> *tongues*
>
> *interpretation of tongues.*

All these gifts have a common origin, but are handed out one by one by the one Spirit of God. He decides who gets what, and when. (MSG)

spiritual gifts
1 Corinthians 12:1–31;
Romans 12:1–8;
Ephesians 4:1–16
for the common good
1 Corinthians 12:7
God hates division
Proverbs 6:16–19

canon
Latin for the Greek work *kanon*, means rule or standard

<u>Spiritual gifts</u> are more than talents someone may possess. Each of us, in our DNA, has special abilities or talents—we are all unique individuals. The term "spiritual gifts" implies that they are in addition to your individual uniqueness—the "God power" given to us when we become followers of Christ. The intended purpose of any gift is "<u>for the common good</u>." These gifts are not given for us to boast of special gifts, or to receive praise and self-adoration. When we receive a spiritual gift(s), we are to receive it in humility and love and use this gift to serve others. It's a testimony of who God really is.

Let me get a little theological here. There are volumes written on this subject, but I just want to share "a little something." There are two camps on this topic of spiritual gifts, which has caused division in the church (and, by the way, <u>God hates division</u>). This is my simplified version—but remember, I like to keep things simple. One camp argues that the gifts of miraculous acts, healing, and tongues ended with the apostles and the completion of the **canon** of the New Testament Scriptures. They base this on 1 Corinthians 13:10: "but when perfection comes, the imperfect disappears."

Jesus returns
John 14:2–3; 21:22;
I Thessalonians
4:14–17;
I Corinthians
15:51–52;
Matthew 24:32–34,
24:44;
Acts 1:7

same united purpose
Ephesians 4:1–16

live in him
2 Corinthians 3:18;
Ephesians 2:1–10, 22;
4:24;
Colossians 1:27;

believers were corrected
2 Corinthians 13:1–10

The other camp tends to believe "when perfection comes" refers to the second coming of Jesus Christ, and all gifts are still freely distributed by the Holy Spirit until <u>Jesus returns</u>.

Over the past twenty-six years I've spent in ministry, I've seen the good, the bad, and the ugly of both camps. To simplify it a little more (I'm sure my Bible professors are cringing as they read this simple section), I think humans often are guilty of dismissing something if they haven't personally experienced it for themselves. But the Scripture is clear that not all of us have the same gifts—but all of us are to use our intended gifts for the <u>same united purpose</u>. This is a testimony of who God really is, and each gift is to be used for the common good.

I was raised in the first camp, where I was taught that those miraculous gifts ended with the apostles and the completion of the canon of the New Testament Scriptures. But as I've matured on my own spiritual journey, I have found that some of the godliest individuals I have ever known speak or pray in tongues and have experienced miraculous acts and healings. They are also some of the same individuals who have the most intimate relationships with God. They <u>live in him</u>. Everyone sees Jesus in them. Sometimes I think that when we see someone with that intimate relationship with God and they have a specific spiritual gift, we want that specific gift. But their gift doesn't make them any more spiritual; it's their intimate relationship with God that they have nurtured, a relationship we all can experience.

But be aware, just as in the early church <u>believers were corrected</u> because of their ignorance and their succumbing to the influence of pagans, we have believers today who need to be corrected who either do not have gifts they claim to have or are using spiritual gifts for their own good and not for their intended purpose.

What You Can Do

Here are things you can do to determine your best spiritual gifts (again, I'm taking the simplistic approach):

1. Use the Word of God to discern spiritual gifts. Does your ability align with the spiritual gifts mentioned in Scripture?

2. Pray that God will give you the discernment to know the difference between a talent and your spiritual gift, but use both.

3. Access your abilities. Write everything down that you enjoy doing. Is there a specific ability that you acquired after you became a believer? We have God-given talents from birth, but those talents can also blossom into spiritual gifts once you turn your life completely over to God.

4. As you go about your daily walk, what area of service do you feel that God is blessing? Are you leading a Bible study where others gain understanding and knowledge? Does your heart ache for those in desperate need? Do those you minister to feel blessed by your actions? Do they make positive comments?

5. Go to a spiritual mentor and ask for his or her wisdom and discernment. Sometimes we don't see ourselves clearly. It's wise to acquire another viewpoint.

6. Get plugged into the local church body. Does your spiritual gift match up with any of the following ministries?

A. *Encouragement gifts* strengthen and encourage those who are weary and build up the faithful.
- Recovery Ministry
- Prison Ministry
- Counselors
- Premarriage/Marriage Mentors
- Moms Support Groups

B. *Teaching gifts* teach and apply the Scripture in order that the student will fully understand the message.
- Children's Ministry
- Youth Ministry
- Bible Study Leaders

C. *Leadership gifts* are areas of ministry that motivate and lead a group in a focused direction.
- Chairperson
- Organize/Develop Programs
- Finances/Accounting
- Missions

D. *Hospitality gifts* are areas of service that welcome newcomers and serve the existing body of the church through practical provisions.

- Greeters/Information Booth
- Parking Crew
- Communion Preparation
- Creative Decorating
- Meal Preparations for Shut-Ins

These are just a few of the vital ministries in the local church you can become involved in. What are you waiting for? Get plugged in.

Operation Blessing

"We would be homeless and in a shelter without Rachel," says George Weatherby. For two decades, Rachel Sparkowich has been running Operation Blessing, a nondenominational Christian ministry that gives away clothing, furniture, housewares, and food in Portsmouth, New Hampshire. About two thousand families walk through the center's doors each year, referred by shelters, churches, and welfare organizations.

On a typical day at Operation Blessing, Rachel, a tall, thin, cheery woman, spends most of her time in the office organizing the center's seventy volunteers, making arrangements for various pickups, and offering guidance and encouragement to people who ask for it.

Merriel Thomas, a volunteer, said, "Operation Blessing met my physical needs. Some people come in here wondering if God exists. When they leave, they know he does."[1]

I'm sure if you asked Rachel, she would readily admit that her work could not be completed without volunteers. Any director of a nonprofit organization would probably tell you the same. Some organizations are so short on help, they recruit almost frantically. The key to a successful volunteer is matching their unique God-given gifts with the appropriate ministry task.

What You Can Do

You have your very own special gift or gifts. There are ministry recruiters out there sitting on the edge of their seats waiting for the phone to ring as they pray for the perfect willing servant. Here are a few organizations that can use your gifts of service:

- Habitat for Humanity is always looking for serving hands that can handle a hammer and help build a home.

- Crisis pregnancy centers around the country are looking for women with tender hearts and listening ears who care not only about the unborn, but the unwed as well.

- Homeless shelters need cheerful, smiling faces to offer food, shelter, and a ray of hope for lonely lives.

- The Salvation Army (and some church ministries) could use skilled mechanics to repair cars that have been donated for single mothers in need of reliable transportation.

- Samaritan's Purse emergency relief programs provide desperately needed assistance to victims of natural disaster, war, disease, and famine. They are looking for volunteer teams of up to fifteen people, minimum age sixteen, who are willing to serve for at least three workdays for cleanup and repair.

Opportunities surround you in your community. What are you waiting for? Unwrap your spiritual gift and put it to use so the world can see Christianity in action.

Lydia
a businesswoman who was converted by Paul

Dorcas
a woman disciple who died and was miraculously brought back to life by Peter

Phoebe
a first-century deaconess

Examples From the Bible

As we see the acts of women in the Bible, we can examine their stories and see what spiritual gifts these women most likely possessed. Here are some examples of women who had serving gifts:

- Hospitality is the God-given ability to welcome and graciously care for and serve both strangers and guests through a receptive and warm attitude (1 Peter 4:9).[2] **Lydia** used her gift of hospitality by inviting the apostle Paul into her home and providing practical provisions of fellowship, food, and shelter (Acts 16:13–15).

- Helps, or service, is the God-given ability to complete practical and necessary tasks, thereby allowing others to succeed in their own giftedness (Romans 12:6–8).[3] **Dorcas** used her gift of helps as she made garments for the needy widows (Acts 9:36). **Phoebe** used her gift of helps as she assisted Paul in delivering his letter to the church at Rome. She also was known for helping others in her own church home at Cenchrea (Romans 16:1–2).[4]

- Faith is the God-given ability to trust that, in response to prayer, God will do what he says he is going to do (1 Corinthians 12:9).[5] **Mary** the mother of Jesus used her gift of faith as she trusted God to fulfill his promise of a virgin birth through her (Luke 1:38, 45; 2:19).

joy and crown
Philippians 4:1

humble
I Peter 5:5–6

please
John 8:29

Priscilla
a Christian woman
who served with Paul
in Corinth

humble
not proud; not self-
assertive

- Teaching is a God-given ability to comprehend, clearly explain, and apply the Word of God to the lives of those who listen (Romans 12:7).[6] **Priscilla** used her gift of teaching when she and her husband helped Paul teach the churches and as they instructed Apollos in the full message of Christ (Acts 18:18–19, 24–28).

- Prophetesses are special women who are God's spokespersons; persons who receive and deliver messages from God. These messages do not contradict Scripture or the principles of the Scripture. Deborah was a prophetess and fourth judge of Israel after Shamger. She judged for forty years (Judges 4:4, 14). Huldah was a teacher and prophetess of Israel during the time of Josiah. She is known for recognizing the authenticity of the Book of the Law found when rebuilding the temple. Anna was a prophetess who lived when Jesus was dedicated at the temple. She was the first to recognize and proclaim Jesus as the Messiah (Luke 2:36–38). Philip's daughters were the four single daughters of the evangelist Peter who helped him during his ministry (Acts 21:9).

How Others See It

Sheila Walsh

It is clear that the gifts have little to do with the recipient and everything to do with the Giver. Every gift comes by the grace of God and is equal in His sight. The trouble is, they are not usually equal in our sight. Some gifts have more curb appeal than others in our culture.[7]

Who, Me, Join the Peace Corps? No Way!

PHILIPPIANS 2:3–5 *Do nothing out of selfish ambition or vain conceit, but in humility consider others better than yourselves. Each of you should look not only to your own interests, but also to the interests of others. Your attitude should be the same as that of Christ Jesus.*

If the apostle Paul had a favorite church, I think it would be the church at Philippi, which he referred to as his "<u>joy and crown</u>." This church followed Christ and served others.

But like children we need to be reminded from time to time how to get along in life. Paul called the Christians in Philippi to **humble** themselves, to look inward, and to examine their motives. In other words he asked, "Why are you doing your good works? Is it to build yourselves up in the eyes of man or is it to <u>please</u> God and honor his kingdom? Is it for your own selfish desires or for the joy your service will bring to others?" (paraphrased by Georgia). Service is outward expression of inward compassion.

Examples From the Bible

Humility is lowliness, meekness, and mildness; a freedom from pride.

- Jesus made humility a cornerstone of character. (Matthew 18:4; 23:12)
- Jesus by his humility drew men to himself. (Matthew 11:28–30; John 13:12–17)
- Paul emphasized the humility of Jesus. (Philippians 2:3–5; 2 Corinthians 8:9)
- Paul commended us to be humble toward one another. (Romans 12:10; 1 Corinthians 13:4–6)[8]

soldier
Numbers 1:3; 2:2; 10:14
called
Genesis 14:1–24

philanthropy
charity; generosity

During the Volunteer Summit I mentioned earlier, **philanthropy** reigned. Many large corporations not only organized their army of employee volunteers, but also donated big bucks. As I read the news coverage each day, I thought it was going to turn into a "Look at me, I gave more money than you" contest.

You may not have the time or the special calling on your heart to sign up for a hitch with the Peace Corps and serve abroad in an underdeveloped area, but whatever vehicle you choose for your service, let your attitude be the same as Jesus when you reach out to help others. Take a good look inward to understand your motives. As important as the gesture of service is the spirit of service.

In ancient Israel, every man above the age of twenty was called to be a <u>soldier</u>; they were on permanent reserve duty. Just as Abraham <u>called</u> his men and gathered a posse to rescue Lot, a tribal leader could call on men in his tribe for service at any time. Each man had to submit and humble himself for his time of service. Under God's leadership, we must be willing to submit and humble ourselves for acts of service.

How Others See It

Bill Hybels

Self-indulgence is a dead-end road. Look around and you will see example after example of shattered lives resulting from a "me first" mindset. Jesus wants his followers to know that true fulfillment comes only through faithful service to God and humble service to others. This is the only sensible way to live.[9]

You're in the Army Now

They lined the fireplace mantel like soldiers standing at attention. The yellow, tattered covers beckoned me to draw closer. I couldn't resist. Old books have always intrigued me, especially when I know that a relative of ages ago once turned those same pages.

A few summers ago, Mom and Dad placed several antique books from my grandfather's and father's collection on the mantel. But every time I was at home on a visit, time passed by too quickly to sit down and enjoy them. But I finally stopped long enough to skim through a few pages in one little book.

The cover title read War Department: Basic Field Manual—Soldier's Handbook, July 23, 1941. It was my dad's manual from the service. It contained everything a soldier needed to know from what to wear and when to wear it to how to load, carry, and fire arms. But the most beneficial information was recorded in the foreword. In detail it described five characteristics of the good soldier.

I'll share a condensed version:

*1. **Be obedient**—Obedience means to obey promptly and cheerfully all orders of your commissioned and noncommissioned officers. At first you cannot be expected to know the reason for everything you are ordered to do. As you remain longer in service and you understand more of the reasons for military training, you will find that everything has been figured out as the result of experience in the past.*

*2. **Be loyal**—Loyalty means that you must stand by your organization through thick and thin.*

*3. **Be determined**—Determination means the bulldog stick-to-it-iveness to win at all costs; determination to win means success in battle.*

*4. **Be alert**—Always be on your guard. A good soldier may be pardoned for failure, but never for being surprised.*

*5. **Be a member of the team**—Teamwork means that each man gives everything in his power to make for the success of the whole unit. Unless you play your own special part, the team may not win.*

As I read through the manual my eyebrows rose as I thought to myself, "They could be on to something here." Those characteristics of a good soldier not only could build strong platoons, but the same principles would benefit families, businesses, and churches. It's no wonder in the early church they often referred to fellow believers as soldiers.

My dad was a good soldier, and he continues to follow those same principles throughout his life. I think I'll take the time to finish that little old manual. I could use some tips on making myself a more efficient soldier for God's army.

"Endure hardship with us like a good soldier of Christ Jesus" (2 Timothy 2:3).

Career Soldier

LUKE 18:29–30 *"I tell you the truth," Jesus said to them, "no one who has left home or wife or brothers or parents or children for the sake of the kingdom of God will fail to receive many times as much in this age and, in the age to come, eternal life."*

When Jesus said this, he had just looked deep inside the rich young ruler and seen money on the throne of his heart instead of God. This young man was single-minded toward his riches, but not his God. Jesus wasn't saying you couldn't have riches and still be a follower. Money itself wasn't the problem; it was a heart condition that kept the wealthy young man away from God's kingdom.

Those listening thought people got rich because God approved of their lives, and thus poured out his blessings in wealth. Jesus corrected them and explained that those who leave all to follow him would be blessed abundantly, not only now but also in eternity.

A career soldier is a soldier who has committed to a lifetime of service in the military. As soldiers for Christ, many believers become involved in a short-term service. Then, once they have a taste of the action, they enlist for a lifetime of service. They become career soldiers under the authority and leadership of Christ the King.

Jesus could have meant that his followers would receive a spiritual blessing, or he could have been describing riches in the physical realm. I've experienced both. Over the years we followed God's lead even when it meant leaving our extended families and moving out of our comfort zones. Blessings have always followed. Sometimes wealth, but always spiritual blessings.

think about it

———————

Mother Teresa of Calcutta made a lifelong commitment to serve others. Through the Missionaries of Charity she touched thousands of lives by giving hope to the hopeless and dignity to the dying. Mother Teresa

everyday insights

was blessed with both spiritual and material riches. Although she lived in poverty, through her recognition and commitment to her cause she was blessed with funds that provided for her worldwide organization that continues to touch lives and serve others.

Countless lesser-known persons share in a lifetime, full-time commitment of serving others for God. In your very own church and community, dozens of men and women work relentlessly to fulfill their calling in ministry. Use your spiritual gifts to support them in their calling. Take every opportunity to pray for them and find ways to help encourage, revitalize, and renew their spirits.

If you feel God calling you to dedicate your life to a full-time commitment in Christian service, I would encourage you to take that step of faith. It's a fulfilling journey you will never regret.

How Others See It

Paula White

God called me to preach with that motor mouth! He is the One who gave me a fluency of speech and ideas and an ability to speak in a powerful way to convey His powerful truths. Very often what other people see as your faults or foibles are the very things that God sees as your foremost assets waiting to be redeemed, strengthened, and fashioned in such a way that they bring glory to Him.[10]

Things You Can Do to Encourage Your Pastor

Pastors and their families live under incredible pressures. Their lives are played out in a fishbowl, with the entire congregation and community watching their every move. They are expected to have ideal families, to be perfect people, to be always available, to never be down, and to have all the answers we need to keep our own lives stable and moving forward. Those are unrealistic expectations to place on anyone, and yet most of us are disappointed when a pastor becomes overwhelmed, seems depressed, lets us down, or completely burns out. That's why God has instructed us to recognize his servants.

"The elders who direct the affairs of the church well are worthy of double honor, especially those whose work is preaching and teaching" (1 Timothy 5:17).

There are two ways to help your pastors and their families feel appreciated:

- *Figure out what you can do personally* to recognize and honor these leaders. A simple card, an invitation to lunch, a promise to pray for them or an offer to baby-sit, wash a car, or mow a lawn make wonderful statements.

- *Share the concept of Clergy Appreciation Month with others in your congregation and challenge them to join you* in some kind of formal planning. You might consider a special service of affirmation, a potluck event, or planting a tree in their honor. The sky is the limit![11]

Encourage Our Troops and Their Families

Not only are we to minister to families in full-time Christian service, but we also need to be a source of strength and encouragement for military families as these committed soldiers, both active duty and reserve, protect our freedoms and defend our democracy.

It's important to keep those still deployed—and the families they've left behind—from feeling forgotten or emotionally isolated.

There are several ways churches can help military families feel appreciated:

- *Post prayer reminders* in church bulletins listing parishioners or their family members still in action, and hold a special service to honor them. Mail copies of postings to those deployed so they know they're being spiritually uplifted.

- *Ask families and Sunday school classes to adopt military members.* Give pictures and addresses of deployed members to parishioners who commit to pray for and write to them—and check on their loved ones. Also, add their names to the church calendar. "As the war drags on, many tend to forget to send letters and offer help."

- *Take donations for care packages* containing practical supplies like sunscreen and toiletries. (The Department of Defense recommends using Operation USA Care Package, *www.usocares.org.*) Include items that help those overseas stay connected to their community, like the local sports section, church bulletins, prepaid long-distance cards (available at *www.operationuplink.org*), tape recordings of friends' greetings, or a picture of those praying for them. (Camouflage, pocket-sized New Testaments and devotionals are available from Campus Crusade for Christ's Military Ministry, *www.milmin.org.*)

- *Provide practical help* for military spouses left behind through volunteer teams that offer free baby-sitting, car maintenance, and yard services. Also establish a hotline for spouses who have emergencies.

- *Start support groups* for spouses of deployed members. If they're used to attending church as a couple, they may need this extra encouragement to stay involved.[12]

How Others See It

Ellie Kay

If Bob knows that when he returns from his mission he will have a loving family waiting for him, he is better equipped to perform at the height of his capabilities. When he believes that his family will have people in the community who will assist them through the uncertain weeks and months ahead, he rests a little better when he contemplates the stars in a darkened sky half a world away. And in many ways, these families, as well as their communities, have contributed to our national defense, as have all the supportive families of other airmen, sailors, and soldiers.[13]

The church body has many parts, yet is still one <u>body</u> with one central <u>focus</u>. Whether we serve in part-time, short-term, or full-time ministry, we are all essential to the function of the body.

Examples From the Bible

The Bible gives examples of men and women who became career soldiers for God as they spent a lifetime of service in ministry:

- The twelve disciples left families, occupations, and homes to follow Jesus and teach his Word. (Matthew 4:18–22; 10:1–4; 11:1)

- Eli, the high priest of Israel, lived at Shiloh in a dwelling adjoining the tabernacle. He gave a lifetime of service to God. (1 Samuel 1–4; 14:3; 1 Kings 2:27)

- John the Baptist lived as a Nazirite in the desert. He dedicated his life to preaching repentance in preparation for the coming of the Messiah. (Matthew 11:12–14; Luke 1:15–17; 3:4–9)

- Anna lived and worked in the temple as she dedicated herself to serving God. (Luke 2:36–38)

Mother Teresa

We must grow in love, and to do this we must go on loving and loving and giving and giving until it hurts—the way Jesus did. Do ordinary things with extraordinary love: little things like caring for the sick and homeless, the lonely and the unwanted, washing and cleaning for them.[14]

I Sat Next to a Legend

coffee break

His Bible fit in his hand like an old worn glove. Creased and cracked leather showed years of extended use. Only a few flecks of gold leaf remained on the tattered edges. The pages had a distinct and unusual curve in the middle. He lifted it. His thumb fit perfectly in the curve. With one flick of the wrist, pages that years ago were once stiff and crisp floated by like feathers.

This was a great moment for me, for I sat next to a legend.

While visiting my sister in Kentucky, I had the opportunity to attend church services in Grayson, Kentucky, home of my alma mater, Kentucky Christian College. I walked into the auditorium and saw one of my favorite professors, Dr. Donald Nash, who instructed my Greek and New Testament courses.

I invited myself to sit with Dr. Nash and his wife. Before church we chatted for a few minutes and caught up on what he had been doing over the few years since his retirement. Suddenly, organ music filled the air and halted our conversation. A silence fell over the audience and services began, but I was reminiscing about days gone by.

As a young college student, I didn't realize the credentials and status my professors held. Usually I was too busy gossiping about their quirks to appreciate the knowledge they possessed. But as time has passed and I've lived life, I hold individuals like Dr. Nash in high regard. Before my visit, while doing research for a writing assignment, I had just reread one of his books. I was in awe of his writing ability and the insights I gained from him.

Funny thing is, I read that particular book years earlier in college. It was required. I don't remember it having the same effect on me then. I'm sure as it sat on my library shelf, crushed between other college reference books collecting dust, the content didn't magically change. Thank goodness, I did.

check this out

judgment
Romans 14:10;
2 Corinthians 5:10

grace
Ephesians 2:8–9

Son
John 14:6

good deeds
Matthew 5:16

judgment
punishment for sin; a
reference to the last
day, when all people
will stand before
Christ to be judged by
him.

The minister presiding over the church service, also a former student of this great teacher, began reading a passage of Scripture. I watched as Dr. Nash held his Bible and followed along. Knowing Dr. Nash, the constant wear on his Bible was not only from teaching his students, but from his personal walk with Christ. I wondered if years from now my Bible would show the same signs of use.

Dr. Nash is a master of his trade. He believes passionately in the subjects he has taught and written about. As a young man Dr. Nash unwrapped his spiritual gift of teaching and, as he committed himself to a lifetime of Christian service, gave it away. Thousands of men and women have learned about the Bible in his classroom. Then as these students went out into the world sharing the gospel and serving others, countless more individuals have been indirectly touched by this one man.

I thank God for granting me a spiritual heritage that includes men of Dr. Nash's stature. Our prayer should be that we will be a part of someone's spiritual heritage as God uses us to touch the lives of others.

Thank you, Dr. Nash.

Reserves Soldier

MATTHEW 25:34–36, 40 *Then the King will say to those on his right, "Come, you who are blessed by my Father; take your inheritance, the kingdom prepared for you since the creation of the world. For I was hungry and you gave me something to eat, I was thirsty and you gave me something to drink, I was a stranger and you invited me in, I needed clothes and you clothed me, I was sick and you looked after me, I was in prison and you came to visit me. . . . I tell you the truth, whatever you did for one of the least of these brothers of mine, you did for me."*

In Matthew, Jesus spoke about the importance of doing good deeds. Looking to the coming **judgment** and the end of time, Jesus identified himself with those in need and taught the importance of making a difference in the lives of others through social involvement.

However, Jesus also explained that good works alone will not ensure someone a place in heaven. We can't board a chartered "Works Plane" to get us to heaven; God's <u>grace</u> through the death of his <u>Son</u> is our only vehicle. However, our actions and <u>good deeds</u> are proof of our faith, love, and commitment to Christ.

A reserve soldier is part of the country's armed forces, subject to call in an emergency. Like a reserve soldier, this may be a time in your life when you can serve only if an emergency arises. You may be able to carve out only a couple of hours of your week to offer help, or set aside a week of your vacation for a short-term involvement. However small it may be, make a commitment to serve.

Our nation called upon its army of volunteers when in 2005 Hurricane Katrina hit the Gulf Coast. Hurricane Katrina was immediately met by the largest Salvation Army deployment in its disaster relief history. More than 1.6 million people throughout the country have been assisted by the Salvation Army alone since the storm made landfall. Nine months later the Salvation Army had received donations in excess of $363 million that were used to meet the needs of those in the hardest hit areas along the Gulf Coast as well as survivors who evacuated to other parts of the country.[15]

Franklin Graham, president of the Christian relief agency Samaritan's Purse, urged Christians to work wisely and in unity in the Katrina aftermath. Immediately, he went to the airwaves and challenged Christians not only to pray for the victims of Katrina but to share our homes, our finances, and our hope found only in Jesus. Christians across the country answered that call as churches and homes opened their doors to evacuees and sacrificially sent millions and millions of dollars for relief.

Margaret McLaughlin, a certified social worker, took a team of Bible college students from Kentucky Christian University to assist a small church seven miles east of Baton Rouge. Calvary Baptist Church and Pastor Rhett Major opened the doors of their small congregation to 128 people who found shelter sleeping in their Sunday school rooms and sanctuary. They did not have the financial resources, but God provided exactly what was needed on a day-to-day, often minute-by-minute, basis. Margaret's team was able to assist by serving food, cleaning, sorting clothes, and, as social workers, listening to people share their loss. Knowing victims of trauma experience acute stress disorder, Margaret knew her team could help these victims in the first step of healing as they shared their traumatic stories with these counselors in training. At the request of the evacuees, Pastor Major began sharing every night about the love of Christ, and several evacuees accepted Christ.

Their kindness did not go unappreciated. Weekly, the church receives cards and letters thanking them for caring enough to make that horrific time a little easier through their warm smiles, helping hands, and encouraging words.

The need was too great for any government agency to adequately meet. You've read story after story or even experienced firsthand similar acts of kindness as individuals and churches stepped up to share the love of God. We were a shining example to the world as reporters wrote about the overwhelming response of Christians and the church.

Every little bit helps. It's better to serve in small segments of time than no time at all.

Snapshots of Women in the Bible
Huldah (2 Kings 22; 2 Chronicles 34:22)

It didn't surprise Shallum when five of the king's messengers showed up at his doorstep. As the keeper of the king's wardrobe, he was used to receiving members of the king's court. But never had the king sent a chief priest and a scribe for wardrobe business.

It wasn't wardrobe business. The king's representatives wished to speak to Huldah, Shallum's wife! They had a request from the king.

When King Josiah's workmen were busy repairing the temple that Solomon had built more than three hundred years before, they discovered a treasure. It was customary to place important documents in the foundations of buildings. The workmen came across the Book of the Law (see Illustration #15), the scrolls containing the laws of Moses. They were convinced that Solomon must have placed the scrolls in the cornerstone of the temple.

During the reign of King Josiah's father, Manasseh, copies of the scrolls had been destroyed when Manasseh turned away from God and began worshiping false gods. Now, the succeeding generation was not very familiar with the Law, but the king's men knew Huldah had studied the scrolls and the laws of Moses.

Huldah had made friends with Josiah's mother, Jedidah. Over the years Josiah had watched Huldah and found her to be wise and dedicated to God. He respected the women in his life and now wanted Huldah to tell him if his discovery was authentic.

Shallum watched as his wife studied the Book of the Law. Huldah's years of preparation proved valuable. She found the scrolls totally authentic and used her gift of prophecy to give the king a message.

Huldah boldly foretold that the Lord would bring evil upon Judah because the country had turned to idols. But she assured King Josiah that because of his tender heart he would be spared; that he would be gathered unto his <u>fathers</u> before this doom would occur. He would not suffer.

Assured that these scrolls really held God's Law, King Josiah proclaimed them publicly and immediately put them into action.

check this out

fathers
2 Kings 21:15, 21

Illustration #15
Dead Sea Scrolls—The Book of the Law was believed to be the scroll of the "law of Moses," the core of the book of Deuteronomy. It was a great discovery and would have looked just like the Dead Sea Scrolls discovered in 1947 that were fragments of every book of the Hebrew Bible except Esther. The scrolls were found in caves near Qumran, on the northwestern shore of the Dead Sea.

Huldah had access to the palace through her husband's work for many years. How long did the king know of her? Did he know and respect her as he grew from a boy to a man? God uses us where we are and with what gifts we possess.

Huldah, as a woman, could have been intimidated by suddenly being thrust into the highest level of Judah's politics. But she followed her calling and, through her service, national revival ensued. Huldah let God use her in a mighty way.

A neighbor is anyone in need.

words to live by

loving
Deuteronomy 6:5
neighbor
Leviticus 19:18
parable
Luke 10:25–37

Won't You Be My Neighbor?

LUKE 10:27 *He answered: "'Love the Lord your God with all your heart and with all your soul and with all your strength and with all your mind'; and, 'Love your neighbor as yourself.'"*

Once when Jesus taught, a student of the laws of Moses stood up and asked what he must do to inherit eternal life. Jesus' response was like a first-century version of *Jeopardy*, since Jesus answered a question with a question. (Obviously, this is where Merv Griffin, *Jeopardy*'s creator, got the idea.) He answered by asking the young man, "What is written in the Law [and] how do you read it?" (Luke 10:26).

The law student knew that Jesus knew the correct answer, and may have believed that Jesus was looking for a way to trip him up. To play it safe, the law student quoted the Old Testament law concerning <u>loving</u> God and loving your <u>neighbor</u>. Ding! Jesus said they were the right answers. The student gained a thousand points and control of the board.

But that wasn't enough to win, and you know how lawyers hate to lose. So he asked a Double Jeopardy question: "Who is my neighbor?"

This time instead of playing a game of questions, Jesus answered with a story. It was the <u>parable</u> of the Good Samaritan, a traveler who helped a stranger he found beaten, naked, and left for dead beside the road. Religious leaders passed the victim by, but the Samaritan provided food, shelter, and medical care, expecting nothing in return.

So who is my neighbor? The correct *Jeopardy* response is, "Who is anyone in need?"

Jesus' answers always had a way of getting to the root of the problem. We often don't want to take time to help people, even those we know. Jesus' parable shows how important it is to stop to help everyone, even those we don't know or like.

For many reasons we have an aversion to getting to know our neighbors. Sometimes we even joke about it. We laughed as Tim, the "Tool Time" handyman on the sitcom *Home Improvement*, never saw his neighbor's face for seven years. We saw the neighbor's fishing hat and his eyes from time to time. He was great at giving "through the fence" advice, but he never actually reached over the fence.

If we are to love our neighbor, we're going to have to reach over the fence to touch a life. Simple acts of kindness make a difference in the lives of others. Yes, that means our neighbor might see us as we really are. But can't you put up with a slight drop in privacy in order to inherit eternal life?

There were how-to instructions built into the commandment Jesus gave the young man: Love your neighbor as yourself. We don't need to ask how to treat ourselves. Most of us never have a problem loving ourselves. One little nudge will provide me an excuse to pamper myself, and I'm off to Bath and Body Works for a refill of Tropical Stress Relief Bubble Bath so I can soak my worries away. We treat ourselves to a night on the town. If we're sick, we demand the best health care available. Yes, we love ourselves . . . and I need to love others as much as I love "little ol' me." If we all loved our neighbors as Jesus commanded, they would roll out the red carpet whenever they saw us coming.

Nicodemus
John 3:1–21; 19:39
delay
Deuteronomy 21:23;
Acts 25:17
washed
Acts 9:37
myrrh
Matthew 2:11;
Mark 15:23;
John 19:39

Sanhedrin
the official group of ruling priests and Levites among the Jews during New Testament times
myrrh
an expensive, pleasant-smelling plant used to make perfume

> ## How Others See It
> ### Joel Osteen
> If you want to live your best life now, you must make sure that you keep your heart of compassion open. We need to be on the lookout for people we can bless. We need to be willing to be interrupted and inconvenienced every once in a while if it means we can help to meet somebody else's need.[17]

Is There Anything I Can Do?

LUKE 23:55–56 *The women who had come with Jesus from Galilee followed Joseph and saw the tomb and how [Jesus'] body was laid in it. Then they went home and prepared spices and perfumes.*

Jesus spoke his last words. He breathed his last breath. He hung on the cross dead. Joseph of Arimathea, a wealthy member of the **Sanhedrin** and a secret follower of Christ, mustered up the courage to go to Pilate and ask for the body.

Joseph and Nicodemus, another secret follower, took away his body, and, in the Jewish tradition, without delay washed it, wrapped it in linens with spices of **myrrh** and aloe, and laid Jesus' body in Joseph's tomb, a cave carved out of a rocky hillside.

Mary Magdalene and Mary the mother of Jesus followed them to the tomb to see where Jesus was buried, with plans to return and anoint him with spices. Did they not know Nicodemus had already used seventy-five pounds of spices, an amount only a king would receive? Or were they simply trying to find something they could do to help the family in this

time of sorrow?

Too many times when a crisis hits the home of a friend or neighbor, we don't know what to do, so we do nothing. We may even ask how we can help, but in the midst of the storm they can't come up with a specific task. But "nothing" can be the worst thing to do. We need to offer simple acts of kindness to show we care—to show that God cares.

Simple acts of kindness usually do not take a significant amount of time but make a significant impact upon the lives of those in crisis. Do any simple thing that you can do (without barging in and taking over). Listen to what your friend or neighbor in crisis is saying, ask God for wisdom, and respond as you feel led. Your acts of kindness will not go unnoticed or unappreciated as you touch another's life.

What You Can Do

Georgia's list of simple acts of kindness:

1. Send a card with encouraging words.

2. Prepare a tray of food for quick bites.

3. Offer to watch the children.

4. Pick up some groceries.

5. Make phone calls.

6. Smile and wave.

7. Let a car go in front of you in a traffic tie-up.

8. Hold the door open for someone.

Neighbor to Neighbor

The bold headlines faded but returned when the judge sentenced the youth in the following week. One troubled youth, David Dodge, had viciously taken the life of twelve-year-old baby-sitter Ashley Jones, whom her father referred to as "a flower." A community was in shock, a family agonized over the murder of their daughter, and I'm sure the parents of the killer were devastated that their own flesh and blood could commit such a horrendous crime.

I read all the coverage from day to day and produced a radio show for my husband's talk show, *America Today with Phil Ling*, on the subject "Unprecedented Surge in Youth Crime." The research was disturbing. The October 1997 murder in Stanwood, Washington, is repeated in similar acts of crime across America daily. Callers to the radio show were outraged and tried to offer solutions to juvenile crime.

On the show the goal was not to merely talk about the problems but to interview individuals who are making a difference, and offer biblically based solutions to issues and challenges America faces. Following the calls, our guest was Lisa Barnes Lampman, president of an organization called Neighbors Who Care, the first national Christian victim assistance program and a subsidiary of Prison Fellowship. Lisa is also author of a book on the same subject, *Helping Neighbors in Crisis*. Neighbors Who Care springs from the story of the Good Samaritan, who cared for a crime victim. Jesus finished the parable with the admonition to "go and do likewise." The organization recruits and trains volunteers to provide assistance to victims: crime-scene cleanup, property repair, transportation, filling out claim forms, referral to local church support groups, follow-up calls, home visits, and more. That's what I call a neighbor who cares.

In the newspaper coverage of the tragic death of Ashley Jones, I was impressed with the community's outpouring of love and support for the Jones family—their neighbors in crisis. But from the interview with Lisa Lampman, we found out that the positive reaction from the Stanwood community was rare. Most individuals do not understand, or they are unsure how to respond to pain and grief, and they ignore or avoid the needs of those who are hurting.

I had to agree with Lisa when she said, "God calls us to minister one-on-one with each other. That's what makes an impact and a difference. We can't leave it up to the government anymore. We must, as a church, love our neighbor as ourselves."

Being Your Best Together With Your Church Family and Friends

My watching of *Saturday Night Live* ended twenty-seven years ago when I graduated from college, entered the real world, and couldn't stay up so late. But I have seen clips of comedian Dana Carvey's character the *Church Lady*. She looks outdated, as if she had stepped out of the early episodes of *The Andy Griffith Show*, with puckered lips, an old-fashioned house-

church
Acts 2:42–47
mansion
John 14:1–6

dress, and a black Bible she carries on her crusade against Satan. I have to admit, Dana Carvey made me laugh. (I've even known a few church ladies just like that in my time.)

You don't have to look or act like the *Saturday Night Live Church Lady* to be part of a church. (Thank goodness!) But being plugged into a church community is a vital part of growing in our walk with God. He intended the <u>church</u> to come together to learn, pray, and worship as one body.

"Therefore, my dear brothers, stand firm. Let nothing move you. Always give yourselves fully to the work of the Lord, because you know that your labor in the Lord is not in vain" (1 Corinthians 15:58).

As believers in the early church faced persecution, the apostle Paul reminded them of the hope we have in Christ's return and our resurrection. The fear of persecution and death should no longer have a grip on our lives, for more awaits us beyond this life—rooms in the heavenly <u>mansion</u> Jesus has prepared for us.

Paul encouraged the Corinthian Christians to have no fear and to remember that what really mattered was their service for the cause of Christ.

There is no better place of service than with your local church body. Look what happened when Christ recruited twelve willing workers—they turned the world upside down! With your acts of service, the church can have an eternal impact. We can change our families, our communities, and the world as we minister to one another and spread the news and love of Christ. "And whatever you do, whether in word or deed, do it all in the name of the Lord Jesus, giving thanks to God the Father through him" (Colossians 3:17).

Sisterhood of Believers

PHILEMON 1:1–5 *To Philemon our dear friend and fellow worker, to Apphia our sister, to Archippus our fellow soldier and to the church that meets in your home: Grace to you and peace from God our Father and the Lord Jesus Christ. I always thank my God as I remember you in my prayers, because I hear about your faith in the Lord Jesus and your love for all the saints.*

There are three sisters in my family—Sherry, Connie, and me, Georgia. My dad always refers to us as Number One Daughter,

Number Two Daughter, and Number Three Daughter. (Then there's the baby of the family—the only boy, David—and Dad calls him Number One Son—that's a whole different story.) I also would respond to ShConGeorgia when my parents or teachers tried to recall my name, jumbling all three names together.

Yes, I admit it, I was the bratty, tattletale little sister, especially to my mean oldest sister, Sherry. I'm surprised I survived childhood. It became a constant pattern. I would threaten Sherry that I would divulge her secrets to Mom and Dad. She would retaliate by attempting to smother me with a pillow or knock me down the stairs. All the while our parents never knew of this sibling rivalry. It became the "sister dance"—a dangerous dance that I knew the steps to all too well. Along the way, Connie—Daughter Number Two—observed quietly at a safe distance to avoid any conflict or friendly fire, and then after we called a cease-fire, she helped bandage up the wounds.

Over the years, the sister squabbles somehow evolved into sister serenity as we became forever friends. I love my sisters. They are my best friends!

I know we're not the only family with that familiar story. There are plenty of sisterhood stories out there. Sisters have a way of overcoming the conflicts of childhood and being best friends the rest of their lives. I think it's the common bond. As sisters we shared so much history—the same childhood experiences, the same spiritual heritage, the same joys and sorrows. We even shared some of the same college days together. We shared life. We're family.

adopted into God's family
Ephesians 1:5
children of God
1 John 3:1

That's why I think the Bible refers to the church as "God's family." We have a common bond—Jesus' Great Commission—"Go and make disciples of all nations, baptizing them in the name of the Father and of the Son and of the Holy Spirit, and teaching them to obey everything I have commanded you. And surely I will be with you always, to the very end of the age" (Matthew 28:19–20). We have been <u>adopted into God's family</u>. When we surrender our lives to him, we become <u>children of God</u> to build his church on earth—we are converted into brothers and sisters in Christ.

Examples From the Bible

God created mankind to be part of his family:

- From the beginning God wanted to adopt us into his family. (Ephesians 1:5)

- We are called "children of God" (1 John 3:1).

- "If we are children, then we are heirs—heirs of God and co-heirs with Christ" (Romans 8:17).

- We have an eternal "family" (Ephesians 3:14–15).

- We have a family "inheritance" (1 Peter 1:4).

- Living in "God's household . . . the church of the living God" (1 Timothy 3:15).

- Believers are "fellow citizens with God's people and members of God's household" (Ephesians 2:19).

- We are to be "devoted to one another in brotherly love" (Romans 12:10).

- Jesus said, "For whoever does the will of my Father in heaven is my brother and sister and mother" (Matthew 12:50).

God created us. He knows all about the special bond we share with other women—especially women in the sisterhood of the church.

On my life's journey when my biological sisters were not close at hand and I needed more support than a phone call, I knew I could always rely on my adopted sisters in God's family. He's provided me with special Christian sisters for each and every path in my journey.

He has provided me with (I'm not listing names here, that would take up a whole chapter—they know who they are):

- *Salutation sisters* who took on the role of Welcome Wagon women and from coast to coast have greeted this stranger into their homes and made me "feel at home."

- *Serving sisters* who've shared mission trips with me and willingly volunteered to serve as the hands and feet of Jesus.

- *Faith-filled friends*, those women of faith who share with me in the gift of teaching and are dedicated to teaching the Word of God.

- *Singing sisters* who have joined their voices with me in worship and praise.

- *Suffering sisters* who have shared in each other's darkest sorrows—even walking together down the dark valley of the shadow of death.

- *School sisters*, who "do life" with each other during our children's school days. Carpooling, childcare, play dates, homeroom moms, field trips, and sports sisters.
- *Special delivery sisters*, my friends who offer a voice for the unborn babies and share Jesus' love with expectant mothers in Crisis Pregnancy Centers.
- *Political pals*, my godly friends who speak up and challenge our culture. Together we use our influence for what is moral and right in the sight of God.
- *Writing women*, my friends "in the business" who network with one another and help keep those creative juices flowing.
- *Spa sisters*, who know how to soothe the soul with a day trip to the spa.
- *Fun friends* who take it upon themselves to make every day a Disney adventure.
- *Sanctifying the saints' sisters*, my Pastors' Wives friends who encourage and strengthen each other as we help our husbands edify the saints.

close friends
Matthew 26:37

My life has been enriched by my friends. We are not meant to live life isolated. Even Jesus had his special circle of <u>close friends</u>. If you've been isolating yourself from others, I encourage you to take that step of faith and join with other church ladies and not only find a friend but be a friend.

> ## How Others See It
>
> ### Leslie Parrott
> What matters is that you have a small chorus of female voices to speak into your life. A group of women who know that your life and each of theirs matters. A group of women who are invested in helping you and every other member make a difference.[18]

The Symbol of Friendship

The fresh-baked aroma of bread always draws me to the bakery in the supermarket. It's as if it has long, thin fingers beckoning me to the counter as it fills my nostrils. If I have a weakness when it comes to food, without a doubt, the answer is bread. I love it any way you slice it.

Throughout the world bread is a staple of most diets. It also carries symbols and legend with it. In ancient times, many cultures believed bread was a gift from God. The Spanish saying is, "All sorrows are less with bread." Italians say, "Bread is all food, the rest is merely

*accompaniment." To the Germans bread is a symbol of home and fam-
ily. And Russian folklore declares, "Bread is the symbol of friendship."*

*That must be where my favorite bread gets its name: "friendship
bread."*

*While living away, whenever I would take a trip home to visit my
family in Kentucky, I indulged in my favorite friendship bread. Linda,
one of my sister's friends, sends it for us to enjoy. And that's just what
I do. Enjoy it for breakfast, lunch, dinner, and between meals.*

*This particular bread is called friendship bread because you give it
away to friends.*

*It's a yeast bread that takes a starter (usually given to you by a
friend). You feed it on a regular basis, and it grows and grows. It is
baked several times a week, and since your own family can't devour
that much bread, you give it away to friends. I might add, it gets the
friend addicted, anticipating week-to-week visits from a friend bearing
bread gifts, joyfully unwrapping the loaf and sharing it over a cup of
coffee.*

*Our friendships are much like friendship bread. Friendships are
formed by a starter. It may be a brief introduction with a smiling face,
or a common ground or interest like a small-group Bible study, neighbors, or car pool. The list could go on and on. But the starter is there,
and someone takes the initiative to develop friendships. You never
know, God may have let your paths cross for a very special reason.*

*Like bread, we have to feed our friendships in order for them to grow
and not wither away. We need to show our love in abundant ways, and
be there when asked for help, even if it's sacrificial.*

*Our friendships are not gifts until we unwrap them and give them
away, time and time again for all to enjoy. Friendship bread—a simple starter for making abundant friendships.*

Friendship. I can honestly say I love it—even more than bread.

Church Makes an Eternal Difference

MARK 16:15 *[Jesus] said to them, "Go into all the world and preach the
good news to all creation."*

The gospel of Mark ends with Christ giving his followers their marching
orders to go into the entire world with his message. After Jesus' resurrection, he ministered for four more days on earth before his **ascension** into
heaven.

The final **commission** to go into the entire world seems to have been uttered to the eleven at Jesus' ascension. It may, however, have been a summary of final instructions that Jesus repeated over and over during his forty-day post-resurrection ministry. In substance, it is recorded four times: (1) here, in connection with his first appearance to the disciples; (2) at his Galilean appearance (Matthew 28:18–20); (3) at his final appearance in Jerusalem (Luke 24:47); and (4) at his ascension (Acts 1:8).[19]

commission
charge, command

When unbelievers face crises or turning points in their lives, they search for answers from authentic believers who may have shared the same struggles. In most cases, they silently observe day by day with inquiring minds, listening to your conversations and keeping a watchful eye on how you handle life's struggles and disappointments. People are looking for an authentic relationship with God. They look to see if your personal relationship with God makes an authentic difference.

In one week I read the flowing stories:

- *A youth worker molested an eight-year-old boy. The family was devastated, angry, and confused.*

- *A physician was fired unjustly from his position at a local clinic. His wife was depressed and uncertain of what the future held.*

- *A teen was arrested on drug charges. The parents were broken-hearted and needed wisdom and advice for their situation.*

- *A father driving across a mountain pass with his thirty-two-year-old son witnessed his son's sudden death from a heart attack. With no civilization around for miles, he continued his journey to the next town with his son's lifeless body. Grief-stricken and shattered, he sought help and comfort in his time of crisis.*

These were all local headline news stories, but I knew of them personally because they were real hurting people who made their way to our church. They each had something else in common. Each situation involved non-Christians who, in crisis, turned to a Christian neighbor, a Christian teacher, or a Christian co-worker.

Are non-Christians searching for what we have? Absolutely! It is our mission to go into the entire world and preach the good news to all creation. When tragedy hits our neighborhood, we can offer our neighbors the

peace
John 14:27;
Philippians 4:7;
Ephesians 2:14

peace that passes all understanding—the only good news that can make an eternal difference in their lives.

> How Others See It
>
> ### Bill Hybels
>
> A way we can expand the horizons of servanthood is by sharing our skills and abilities with others. The Bible clearly communicates that in the family of believers we should not only share our gifts with one another, but we should also be enthusiastically and eagerly sharing our talents, learned skills, and abilities with others.[20]

Women's Role in the Early Church and Today

GALATIANS 3:26–28 *You are all sons of God through faith in Christ Jesus, for all of you who were baptized into Christ have clothed yourselves with Christ. There is neither Jew nor Greek, slave nor free, male nor female, for you are all one in Christ Jesus.*

Well, let's just jump headfirst into the issue of a woman's role in the church. There are volumes and volumes of written opinions on this subject. Once again, I'm going to take a simplistic approach and condense it into a mini version of different views.

There are several camps:

1. Some churches believe women are to be totally silent—they can be seen but never heard.

2. Other churches allow women to do works of service behind the scenes but in no way, shape, or form serve in any role of leadership.

3. There are churches that go one step further and allow women to lead or teach women or children only, but may allow some exceptions for teaching men and women if it is approved by the male leadership.

4. In some churches women are allowed to use their God-given spiritual gifts to further the advancement of God's kingdom in any arena.

Those are the basics, but I think I've covered most general ideas represented in churches today. Now let's take a look at the Bible and see what it has to say about women's roles in the church.

What was Jesus' attitude? Jesus brought freedom and dignity to women. In a time and culture where women were treated as property and maintained a low level in society—totally subordinate to men—Jesus elevated women as he reached out and touched their lives—including them in his days of ministry. He ministered to them as they ministered with him. He introduced a radical faith and radically changed their lives:

- God used Anna, a prophetess, to first proclaim Jesus as the Messiah. (Luke 2:36–38)

- Contrary to what Pharisees taught in his day, which was not to speak to a woman, especially a Samaritan woman, Jesus not only spoke to a woman, but he also chose the Samaritan woman at the well to be the first person to whom he revealed that he was the Messiah. (John 4:1–26)

- Women accompanied Jesus and his disciples. (Luke 8:1–3)

- Jesus allowed women to sit at his feet and learn alongside the disciples, when it was customary for men and women to be separated. (Luke 10:38–42)

- Jesus commended Mary for choosing to seek him instead of banishing herself to the traditional role of a woman. (Luke 10:42)

- Women helped financially support Jesus and the disciples' journey. (Luke 8:3)

- Jesus forgave sinful women, and they became followers. (Luke 7:36–50)

- Jesus gave women significance and purpose to their lives. (Luke 10:38–42)

- Jesus was sensitive to medical issues specific to women and healed them. (Matthew 9:20–22)

- Jesus commended the poor widow with her mite. (Luke 21:4)

- Women were the last to leave the cross and the first to witness Jesus' resurrection. (Luke 24:1–12)

Examples From the Bible

These are examples of women in the Bible who played a vital role in the early church and the spreading of the Gospel:

- The disciples continued Jesus' attitude of inclusion of women in the early church. After Jesus' ascension, the disciples gathered together with women constantly praying. (Acts 1:14)

- As prophesied by Joel the prophet and Jesus, the Holy Spirit was given to both men and women. (Acts 2:1–21)
- Both men and women were baptized. (Acts 8:12; 16:14)
- The disciples did not segregate women in worship as did the Jews in synagogues and temple worship. (Acts 12:12; 1 Corinthians 11:2–16)
- Both men and women were persecuted for their beliefs. (Acts 8:3; 9:1–2)

There are examples of specific women in the Bible as well:

- **Euodias and Syntyche** worked by Paul's side in spreading the Gospel. (Philippians 4:2)
- **Tryphena and Tryphosa** were called "those women who work hard in the Lord." (Romans 16:12)
- **Philip's four unmarried daughters** prophesied and assisted their father in spreading the Gospel. (Acts 21:9)
- **Apphia** was a "sister" in Christ at Colossae and wife of Philemon, who worked with Paul. (Philemon 1:2)
- **Mary of Rome** was mentioned by Paul as a laborer in the church "who worked very hard." (Romans 16:6)
- **Persis** "worked very hard in the Lord." (Romans 16:12)
- **Rufus's mother** was the spiritual mother of Paul and a worker in the church. (Romans 16:13–15)
- **Junia** was listed as "outstanding among the apostles." (Romans 16:7)
- **Lydia** was Paul's first convert and hosted the church at Philippi in her home. (Acts 16:14–15, 40)
- **Damaris** was listed with the male philosophers who converted to Christianity. (Acts 17:34)
- **Phoebe** "our sister" was a "servant [deaconess] of the church in Cenchrea." (Romans 16:1)
- **Chloe** had a house church, and Paul addresses her the same as he addresses male leaders. (1 Corinthians 1:11)

A couple of Scripture verses are used today to keep women silent in the church and out of leadership roles, specifically 1 Timothy 2:11–12: "A woman should learn in quietness and full submission. I do not permit a woman to teach or to have authority over a man; she must be silent."

These verses were included in the letter written from the apostle Paul to Timothy, a young minister, giving him advice on how to handle issues that had developed in the church. As you can see in the previous list, women in the early church were evangelists, teachers, and deaconesses; they prophesied and were listed alongside elders; they were missionaries and martyrs. With this said, 1 Timothy 2:11–12 contradicts Paul's other writing, actions, and attitudes toward his fellow women servants. I, along with many Bible scholars, interpret this as an immediate correction for a particular situation—not a command to be passed down for ages to come. It involved the relationship between husbands and wives—not the relationship of the church.

Women at Ephesus (1 Timothy 1:3) were being deceived by false teachers, as Eve was deceived by Satan (1 Timothy 2:13–14). It appears that a problem arose where husbands and wives were arguing issues in public. Evidently it was chaotic. Paul was addressing the specific issue, saying women needed to "quiet themselves," submit to the authority of their husbands, and learn before they were able to teach. The word *quiet* is also used in 1 Timothy 2:2, where Paul encouraged everyone to live "peaceful and quiet lives."

If this is a big issue in the church you attend, I would suggest, above all else, don't cause division. (Remember, God hates a divisive spirit.) If you feel you are unable to fulfill what God has called you to do, you can either (1) find a church that allows you to use your spiritual gifts with no gender restrictions, or (2) stay at your church and willingly choose to lead women. Bloom where you are planted! God can use you and your gifts in a mighty ministry to and for women. You may be exactly where he wants you in this season of your life.

How Others See It

Rick Warren

Being included in God's family is the highest honor and the greatest privilege you will ever receive. Nothing else comes close. Whenever you feel unimportant, unloved, or insecure, remember to whom you belong.[21]

Snapshots of Women in the Bible
Dorcas (Acts 9:36–42)

Dorcas, also called Tabitha, enjoyed meeting God in prayer at daybreak on the flat roof of her home overlooking the Mediterranean Sea. The cool sea breeze was invigorating. The sun glistened on the waves that danced and crashed against the rugged rocks of the coastline. The sea had calmed after a week of fierce winds. Dorcas watched a group of women walk the beach. She knew their mission; she had witnessed it dozens of times before.

The group gathered around a dark object on the shore. They were there to identify the body of a fisherman lost at sea. The waves that took his life

commands
Exodus 22:22–24;
Deuteronomy
10:18–19
service
Romans 12:4–8

also returned his body home to the sandy beaches of Joppa.

Widows accompanied other women who searched for missing husbands. The widows had walked those same steps, felt their loss, and known their pain. They were there to lean on. Dorcas could pick out individual widows who returned month after month with newly worried women. Dorcas noticed that as the widows struggled to survive, their clothes slowly turned to rags. She prayed for a way to help, and God answered her prayers. She knew what she must do. There was only one talent she had, but she did it well. She could sew. She could use her needle and thread to sew clothes for the widows. After all, God <u>commands</u> us to take care of orphans and widows. Dorcas knew her <u>service</u> would please God and lift the lonely widows' spirits.

Dorcas began to sew and sew and sew. The widows in the community grew to know her well. They loved her generous gifts, loving heart, and listening ear. She became their friend as she shared their burden of sorrow and offered simple gifts of love to help mend their broken lives.

It was a normal day as she worked on a beautiful tunic for a woman who had recently been widowed. Dorcas couldn't wait to see the smile on the woman's face when presented with these new clothes. Then a shooting pain took her by surprise. Suddenly she felt faint. There was no strength in her arm. She dropped her needle and thread, clutched her chest, and everything went dark.

The women arrived in the afternoon at the time Dorcas had specified, but when they knocked no one answered the door. Fearing foul play, they eventually forced their way into her home. They found Dorcas slumped over, lying on the floor amid the fabric of unfinished clothes. She looked as though she slept, but they knew she had died. They gently picked her up, washed her body for burial, laid her on the bed, and began to mourn the loss of their dear friend.

Some didn't lose hope. They knew of the miracles her fellow believers were performing. They sent two men for the disciple Peter and asked him to come at once. Peter rushed to her home and found the house filled with widows weeping the loss of their closest friend. They showed him the garments Dorcas had blessed them with.

Peter instructed them to leave the room. He knelt by her bed and prayed. Dorcas heard someone call her name. She opened her eyes and saw Peter stretch out his hand. She felt his strong, rough fisherman grip as he helped her up. She had no pain. She walked out of the bedroom and heard the gasps and delighted squeals of her friends. It didn't take her long to discover that she was a miracle—Peter had raised her from the dead, just as Jesus had given him the <u>power</u> to do.

power
Matthew 10:8

The news spread quickly in Joppa about this woman who was always doing good and helping the poor. She had served the Lord, the Lord had rewarded her, and many believed in the Lord.

Strong friendships with other "church ladies" are vitally important because they have a special way of bringing out the best in each of us. No matter how small or large a church you attend, you can gain spiritual support and grow your soul as you minister to others. I'm sure you'll be proud when the world calls you a "church lady."

People are watching to see how God works in and through us.

Final Thoughts

- The gift of serving touches hearts, nourishes souls, and fuels ministries that share the love of Christ.

- Serving is for everyone. We each have special abilities and God-given gifts we can share with others. We need to look beyond ourselves, unwrap our gifts, and commit to the act of serving. But do it for God, not for personal glory.

- Yes, you can make a difference in the lives of others. No act of kindness, no matter how great or small, will go unnoticed by God. Whether you can only carve out a small piece of time or you decide to commit to a lifetime of service, whatever you do will enrich not only your life, but those you touch.

- Our neighbor is anyone who is in need. It could be our next-door neighbor, a community member, or someone across the continent. Make a special effort to reach out to a neighbor in their time of crisis through your simple acts of kindness. Let them know that you and God truly care.

- The church needs you! You need the church! Believers are the fuel for ministries. Twelve willing workers changed the world, but they did it together. If you've been staying on the fringes of the body of Christ, find a church and get involved.

Questions to Deepen Your Understanding

1. Why is it our duty as believers to volunteer and serve?

2. What motive should we have in serving?

3. How do we prove our Christian commitment to the world?

4. King Josiah had Huldah check the Book of the Law for authenticity. What credentials did Huldah possess to complete such a task?

5. Do believers have special gifts? How are we to discover them?

6. The Jewish lawyer asked how he could inherit the kingdom of God. What was Jesus' response?

7. Why is your work in the Lord not in vain, even if it seems to go unnoticed?

8. What instrument did Dorcas use in her service to God?

Some of Georgia's favorite books for putting your gift to work in the world:

- *Building an Effective Women's Ministry*, Sharon Jaynes, Harvest House

- *Chicken Soup for the Volunteer's Soul: Stories to Celebrate the Spirit of Courage, Caring, and Community*, Jack Canfield, Health Communication

- *Deal with It!* Paula White, Nelson Ignite

- *Discovering Your Spiritual Gifts*, Women of Faith Bible Study Series, Phyllis Bennet, Zondervan

- *Focus on the Family Women's Ministry Guide*, Gospel Light

- *What's So Spiritual About Your Gifts?* Henry T. Blackaby and Mel Blackaby, Multnomah

- *Here I Am, Lord . . . Send Somebody Else*, Jill Briscoe, Thomas Nelson

read on

- *Heroes at Home: Help and Hope for America's Military Families,* Ellie Kay, Bethany

- *Just Walk Across the Room: Simple Steps Pointing People to Faith,* Bill Hybels, Zondervan

- *Love in Action: Experience the Joy of Serving,* Interaction Series, Bill Hybels and Kevin Harney, Zondervan

- *The Purpose-Driven Church,* Rick Warren, Zondervan

- *Renewal on the Run: Embracing the Privileges and Expectations of a Ministry Wife,* Jill Briscoe, New Hope Publishers

- *Taking the High Ground,* Colonel Jeff O'Leary, Cook

- *We Are Sisters,* Dee Brestin, Life Journey/Cook Communications

- Web sites for information on humanitarian relief: Samaritan's Purse, *www.samaritanspurse.org;* Habitat for Humanity, *www.habitat.org;* Salvation Army, *www.salvationarmy.com;* Crisis Pregnancy Center National Referral, *www.heartlink.org;* World Vision—United States, *www.WorldVision.org.*

- *Learning a Lifestyle of Service: Pursuing Spiritual Transformation,* John Ortberg, Laurie Pederson, and Judson Poling, Zondervan

Chapter 11: Speaking Out on Cultural Issues

Using Your Voice to Improve Your Community

What's in This Chapter

- From the PTA to the Oval Office
- Passing Along Your Political Heritage
- Send Me?
- We Are Out Here
- Overcoming Hurdles
- A Friend in the News
- Snapshot: Esther
- Protecting Your Family's Future
- Snapshot: Shiphrah and Puah
- She Wasn't in the Count
- Speak the Truth in Love
- You Can Be Persuasive
- Why Christians Should Vote
- Remember Who You Are

Here We Go

It's no secret that over the centuries women have played a major role in politics and leadership. American history books are filled with women who made a difference through involvement in politics. **Susan B. Anthony** helped win the fight for the American woman's right to vote in the nineteenth century. Rosa Parks, an African-American passenger on a bus, decided in December 1955 that she was tired of the injustice of **segregation** and refused to move to the back of the bus. Rosa Parks became a hero in the **civil rights** movement.

Women who voice their biblical beliefs can change lives, shape communities, and transform a nation. We have to be willing to stand up, speak out in love, and do our part to protect our families. It's guaranteed we will face opposition, but with God's strength and <u>guidance</u> we can make a difference.

Let's see what the Bible has to say about women and our involvement in politics.

guidance
Psalms 25:9; 32:8;
Isaiah 58:11;
John 16:13

Susan B. Anthony
early activist in American **temperance** and antislavery movements

temperance
anti-alcohol

segregation
the practice of separating racial groups from each other

civil rights
rights guaranteed to individuals by the Constitution of the United States and other acts of Congress

captivity
Exodus 13–15

Miriam
Hebrew prophetess

prophetess
a woman who is
inspired to speak the
will of God

Deborah
a prophetess,
counselor, judge
of Israel

Esther
queen of Persia and
Media

Examples From the Bible

Bible women were very involved in their communities and their governments.

- **Miriam**, the first Hebrew **prophetess**, accompanied her brothers Moses and Aaron as they led the children of Israel out of Egyptian <u>captivity</u>.

- **Deborah** was a woman of great power as she served the children of Israel in the role of counselor, judge, and deliverer in time of war. When no man had the courage to take action, Deborah rallied troops, inspired them, and led them to victory, which was Israel's first united action in 175 years. (Judges 4)

- **Esther**, a courageous orphan Jewess who became queen of Persia, was faced with a choice to speak out and possibly die, or remain silent and deny her faith. When she learned of the plot to kill all the Jews in the kingdom, she risked her life revealing that she was a Jew. By speaking out she was able to save her people from massacre. (Esther 2–10)

From the PTA to the Oval Office

ROMANS 13:1 *Everyone must submit himself to the governing authorities, for there is no authority except that which God has established.*

Throughout the book of Romans, the apostle Paul gives us guidance in our everyday lives and shows the purpose of God's laws and God's grace. Paul gives us the answer as to why we, God's children, should obey man's government. Paul explains that the government was established by God, and we are subjects under God.

Scripture records that God set up three institutions:

1. God established the home and family (Genesis 1:28) to increase humanity's numbers and to subdue the earth. (Genesis 2:22–24)

2. God established the church to increase the number of disciples and spread the Good News of Christ and salvation. (Acts 2:42–44, 47)

3. God established the government to be accountable unto God and to keep his commandments and laws. (Genesis 9:5–8)

Examples From the Bible

Leaders in government in Bible times who loved God and his laws, and made a positive impact on society include:

- Joseph: became ruler of Egypt under Pharaoh and saved his family and a nation from a famine. (Genesis 37:1–50:26)

- David: the second king of Israel followed God's direction during his reign. His descendant, Jesus, was the Messiah. (1 Samuel 16:13, 19–23)

- Josiah: a young king who "did what was right in the eyes of the Lord and walked in all the ways of his father David, not turning aside to the right or to the left" (2 Kings 22:2). Josiah led his kingdom back to the Law of God and renewed the nation's covenant with God.

Some leaders in government in Bible times disobeyed God's laws and had a negative impact on society.

- Athaliah: ruled for six years over Judah. She was extremely wicked and worshiped Baal (see illustration, page 40). She nearly destroyed all of the royal House of Judah, her own blood relations, but missed one boy. (2 Chronicles 22:10–12)

- Jezebel: wife of King Ahab who persecuted prophets of God. She tried to force her worship of Baal on God's people. (1 Kings 16:31—2 Kings 9:37)

- Saul: the first king of Israel disobeyed God. God, in turn, rejected Saul. "The Lord was grieved that he had made Saul king over Israel" (1 Samuel 15:35).

- Herod Antipas: king of the regions of Galilee and Perea during the time of Christ. He had John the Baptist beheaded and took part in Jesus' trial. (Luke 3:1; Mark 6:17–29)

Whether joining the **PTA** or running for the Oval Office, if believers incorporate God's laws and grace into their home, church, and government, they will have a life-changing and eternal impact on our world. The question should not be "Why should we be involved in government?" The question is "Why not be involved in a God-ordained government?"

How Others See It

Billy Graham

If America is to survive, we must elect more God-centered men and women to public office—individuals who will seek Divine guidance in the affairs of state.[1]

Passing Along Your Political Heritage

My blood runs red, white, and blue. I'm sure it's in my DNA. I somewhat inherited my love and involvement in the political arena from my dad. He was a strong believer in public service and in ordinary citizens leaving their political thumbprint on the world.

I was too young to remember when he served as mayor of our little Kentucky town, but I do remember when he ran for the seat of state representative. It was a big deal. It became a family project. We had our own little war room in Dad's office, complete with tactical plans. Mom and Dad divided the troops to cover more ground. We piled in separate cars loaded down with campaign posters, nails, and hammers. The journey took us down winding back roads that snaked through counties in our district. By the time we were through, Dad's face was posted on the outside walls of every little country store, sides of barns, and every telephone pole within our reach. It was exciting! And with the whack of that hammer, another politician was born.

The only event that topped the excitement of campaigning was election day. School was called off, the courthouse overflowed with voters, and I even witnessed a few bribes take place with the change of a handshake and whiskey. (Of course, that wasn't my dad.) It was also the first time I was allowed to go behind the curtain and "pretend vote" as I watched Dad pull the lever on the newfangled voting machine. I loved every minute of it.

Sorry to report, when all the votes were tallied that evening, he didn't win the race. But he wasn't a loser. He won me over. I was never more proud of him. He was sporting a beard that year—he was my Abraham Lincoln. He held his ground and stood firm for what he believed. Even though public speaker was a weaker trait, he spoke with strong conviction and integrity. And he passed on the legacy of being "salt and light" in our community.

I don't think it was coincidental that my husband and I share the same convictions of being involved in the political arena. We're two peas in a pod, supporting and joining each other in our civic endeavors. In God's timing, I'm sure one of us will hold a political office someday.

Since Dad's campaign so many years ago, I've been trying to make a difference. Along the way I've sat behind rickety tables and registered voters, I've organized fund-raisers and campaigned for or against causes that affect the moral fiber of our country. I've joined other political sisters to pound the pavement, knock on doors, and hand out leaflets. I've pulled the lever, punched the chads, and cast my vote with a touch on a computer screen for people of faith—candidates that hold the same biblical principles, morals, and values that I hold dear—the same principles of our Founding Fathers.

It's been an honor, privilege, and duty to be part of our democracy.

It all began when Dad took his family on his campaign trail—win or lose. He passed his political heritage down to the next generation to continue Christ's command to be <u>salt and light</u> in our world.

Send Me?

Isaiah 6:8 *Then I heard the voice of the Lord saying, "Whom shall I send? And who will go for us?" And I said, "Here am I. Send me!"*

Isaiah preached in Jerusalem, the capital of **Judah**, during a time when King Uzziah had brought the nation to great prosperity. But the nation must've suffered from spiritual heart disease, for they turned away from God.

Isaiah saw a **<u>vision</u>** of God seated on his throne with angels praising him by saying, "Holy, holy, holy is the Lord Almighty" (Isaiah 6:3). When Isaiah saw the glory and **righteousness** of God and his own unrighteousness, he repented of his unclean lips. Isaiah clearly saw the poor spiritual condition of his own heart and the heart of his people, and he grieved for his nation.

God asked whom he could send to deliver his message. Isaiah willingly said, "Here am I. Send me!"

Over the years this passage of Scripture is used in reference to missionary work, but we can be used in mission work in our own backyard if we, like Isaiah, willingly become a voice for God to our community.

Since God established the government, the most active citizens should be Christian citizens. We should have input into leadership, the laws of our land, and in the enforcement of those laws.

salt and light
Matthew 5:13–14
vision
Isaiah 6:1–13

Isaiah
"the salvation of Jehovah"
Judah
The twelve clans, or tribes, of Israel were divided into two nations. The two tribes in the south were called Judah; the ten tribes of the north organized as Israel.
vision
a prophecy or revelation in which a person sees something that God wants him or her to see
righteousness
harmony with God, his will, and with others

witnesses
Acts 1:8

Examples From the Bible

Women of the Bible who willingly followed God's lead:

• Sarah left her home and country and faithfully followed her husband to a land of the unknown. God blessed her as the "Mother of Nations." (Genesis 21:1–13)

• Rahab hid the spies of Israel, which led to the capture of the city of Jericho. God spared the life of Rahab and her family. (Joshua 2:1–24; 6:1–25)

• Mary the mother of Jesus was willing to face possible death by being unwed and pregnant as she became God's handmaiden and bore the Son of God. (Luke 1:25–38)

• Jesus was Jewish, and Samaritans regarded Jews as their political enemies. The Samaritan woman said yes to Jesus and opened the door of Samaria to Jesus and his message. (John 4:4–26)

Our society is screaming out for answers and boundaries. As <u>witnesses</u> of Christ we can implement spiritual values in our governing body and impact our communities with the spiritual truths of the Scriptures.

How Others See It

Elizabeth Dole

My grandmother taught me that what we do on our own matters little—what counts is what God chooses to do through us. She stressed the importance of ministering to others and Jesus' instruction to his followers to "Feed my sheep." Public service is a part of that.[2]

We Are Out Here

Remember how 1998 started? Maybe this sounds familiar: "In breaking news from the White House . . . ," "Stay tuned for the latest developments in the sex scandal," and, "It's all a vast right-wing conspiracy." Whew! You heard it from all sides, from CNN to Entertainment Tonight to radio talk shows.

I raise the subject not because of the scandal itself, but because of the allegations made against other Americans during the scandal. I heard one local talk show host say, "Every American male has committed adultery. If that [not committing adultery] was a prerequisite for being elected President of the U.S., no one would qualify." Now, that's ridiculous! Contrary to that commentator's absurd opinion, there are moral individuals out here living lives of character.

Kathleen Parker's editorial in USA Today (2/1/98) examined the women involved in the White House scandal. Ms. Parker was really depressed that there were no more "classy women" or "great broads" left in this country. She said, "What ever happened to privacy and discretion, sophistication and class?" She continued, "I'm talking about the kind of woman who, if she's had an affair, doesn't feel compelled to share the experience with CNN." She wasn't concerned about the moral fiber of this nation. Her concern was merely whether women who kiss, tell!

Speaking on behalf of all the women of character, sisters in Christ who dare to live their lives and raise their children on biblical truths, who preserve their marriages living by the book, and make a difference by sharing their truths and principles with others—we are out here! We are saying to God, "Here I am, send me!" We're praying for our families, our church, and our country, knowing that when the media frenzy is over, lives will be broken, our country wounded, and conservative thinking bruised.

But unlike the doomsayers, I have hope. I have a heritage of faith—faith in the same God our Founding Fathers placed their trust in when they developed America. A heritage of faith that's been tested through time and still stands. This faith has always played a role in the history of our nation. Faith in God is our only hope and the future of this nation.

establishing
Romans 15:19, 23
training
I Thessalonians 4:1–12
instructed
Matthew 10:14

Gentiles
non-Jews
Barnabas
"son of encouragement"

Overcoming Hurdles

ACTS 13:50 *But the Jews incited the God-fearing women of high standing and the leading men of the city. They stirred up persecution against Paul and Barnabas, and expelled them from their region.*

On Paul's missionary journeys he worked in the cities establishing churches and training new believers.

As Paul preached about Christ, many received his message with open hearts and spread the exciting news throughout the city. However, the Jewish leaders opposed Paul because he included the **Gentiles** in his invitation to hear about Christ. Out of envy, the Jewish leaders stirred up many leading men and women of the community to persecute Paul. They cast him and his missionary companion **Barnabas** out of the city. As they left, Paul and Barnabas shook the dust off their sandals, just as Jesus had instructed his disciples to do when their message was rejected.

persecution
2 Timothy 3:11;
Acts 14:19–20

When Paul faced <u>persecution</u> for carrying the message of Christ, the Lord protected him. Can we be as brave as Paul? When we take a stand for biblical principles in our governing bodies, we will face resistance and will have to overcome the hurdles. But remember, "the foolishness of God is wiser than man's wisdom, and the weakness of God is stronger than man's strength" (1 Corinthians 1:25).

Some think that gaining a voice in the political arena is the biggest hurdle women have to overcome. Yet we're better off than we were three decades ago. In the United States in 2006, 8 of 50 governors are women, 14 of 100 senators are women, and 67 of 435 House members are women. In state legislatures, city councils, and county commissions, women represent 20 to 25 percent of elected officials. And who knows? We may someday soon be referring to our commander in chief as Madam President.[3]

A Friend in the News

In 2005, Washington State hit the news with a first for women in politics. It became the first state to have both a woman governor and two women serving in the United States Senate.

There's another woman in Washington State who has been in the news for the past nine years. Years ago I served on the advisory board of our women's ministry, and we were searching for a full-time women's minister. Our women's ministry intern came to me with what she thought would be the perfect candidate for the position. The candidate's name was Val Stevens. At that time Val served as a Washington State director and national board member of Concerned Women of America. I remember commenting that it looked like Val was right where God wanted her to be—in the political arena. Little did I know how prophetic those words were. Soon Val felt a calling from God, and she tossed her hat in the ring. She ran for a state representative seat and won her district. Val has since been in political office for nine years, four as a state representative and the last five as a senator.

Val and I became friends through our involvement in politics. I saw firsthand that she is a respected senator. Val has faced her critics graciously; she's stood strong and held fast to her principles, and she is an example of a woman of integrity. Val is an ordinary wife, mother, and grandmother making an extraordinary difference. She had other things she could spend her days accomplishing, but she felt God's calling to use her abilities in the political arena. She stepped up, answered the call, and said, "Here I am, send me!"

Concerned Women for America is a group established nationwide to defend traditional family values.

If you have stood up and said, "Send me," don't let opposition and fear stop you. God is not a God of <u>fear</u>. He has given us the power of love. As God-fearing women, we can accomplish <u>anything</u> he calls us to do. Expect opposition when standing up for what is right, but remember, God empowers us to stand for him.

fear
2 Timothy 1:7
anything
Philippians 4:13
bowed
Exodus 4:31; 32:8–9

Esther
orphan girl, chosen to be queen
Mordecai
Esther's cousin
virgin
a person who has never had sex

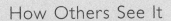

How Others See It

Beth Moore

We just have to keep believing that . . . God is who He says He is. God can do what He says He can do. I am who God says I am. I can do all things through Christ. God's Word is alive and active in me.[4]

Snapshots of Women in the Bible

Esther (Esther 1–10)

Esther's family was taken into captivity under King Nebuchadnezzar's reign. She once lived a life of nobility, but now she was a Jewish orphan raised by her cousin **Mordecai**.

The provincial king, Xerxes, was looking for a replacement for his queen. Queen Vashti had refused one of Xerxes' requests, so he banished her and ordered that a new queen be found. So the search began throughout 127 provinces for a new queen.

Mordecai served in the royal court. As soon as he heard news of the search, he sent for Esther. Out of all the **virgins** presented to the king, Xerxes chose Esther and placed the royal crown on her head. Esther became loved and respected throughout the palace and the kingdom as she enjoyed the status of her new title.

But all was not well in the palace, for Mordecai was hated by the king's chancellor, Haman. The king respected Haman and ordered everyone to bow down to him. But Mordecai <u>bowed</u> down only to God and refused to bow to Haman.

Because of Haman's wounded pride, he decided to kill Mordecai and all other Jews in the empire. Until this time, for her own protection, Queen

fast
Ezra 8:23;
Daniel 9:3;
Zechariah 7:3

eunuchs
men who have been
castrated

Esther had kept her Jewish heritage a secret. When she found out that the king plotted to eliminate the Jews, she was faced with an awful dilemma.

Mordecai asked Queen Esther if she would go to the king to save their people. Esther's former guardian told her that this may be the very reason she sat on the royal throne. Maybe this was her purpose in life. Maybe God placed her there "for such a time as this" (Esther 4:14), for there was no one else close to the king who could stop the slaughter.

No one could go to the king uninvited, not even the queen. Esther feared she was placing her own life in danger, but knew she had to speak up. She said, "If I perish, I perish" (Esther 4:16).

Knowing she could not do this alone, she called for all the Jews to <u>fast</u> and pray for three days as she prepared to meet the king. Esther went before the king unannounced. The penalty should have been death, but instead he welcomed her into his court and asked what her request would be. She first made a small request that the king and Haman would join her for a banquet.

At the banquet the king once again asked what request she had. Esther did not feel the timing was right and asked the king to return the next day.

That evening the king was restless and could not sleep. He asked a courier to read from the book that recorded memorable deeds of his people. Mordecai's name was recorded as one who had revealed that two **eunuchs** plotted to kill the king. His speaking up had saved the king's life. It was also recorded that Mordecai had never been rewarded. The king resolved to reward Mordecai for his acts. The next morning as Haman came to ask for permission to kill Mordecai and the Jews, he was surprised by the king's order to honor Mordecai.

Later at the banquet, Xerxes met with Esther and asked what he could do for her. She fell at his feet in tears and begged for the lives of her people. When Haman's plot was revealed, the king ordered that Haman be hanged from the very gallows that Haman had built for Mordecai.

The king instructed Esther to write a contradictory order that would stop the annihilation of the Jews. He signed it and sealed it with the royal seal.

Esther was a woman who would not tolerate the injustice for her people. She would not stand by and do nothing. Esther stood up for God and her people and spoke up to her ruler. Esther's actions saved her people from extermination. One woman made a difference for an entire race.

Protecting Your Family's Future

EPHESIANS 6:10–11 *Finally, be strong in the Lord and in his mighty power. Put on the full armor of God so that you can take your stand against the devil's schemes.*

The apostle Paul reminded the believers in Ephesus to remember who we are at war with—<u>Satan</u>.

From earliest times, mankind wore devices for protecting the body in battle. These devices varied and were made of different material, from heavy leather to hardened steel. Usually armor consisted of a shield carried on one arm, a coat or breastplate, leather or iron casings for the legs and feet, and a helmet for the head.[5]

Satan
Matthew 4:10;
2 Corinthians 11:3;
Revelation 9:11

Satan
"adversary" or enemy

Illustration #16
Armor of God—Just as this Roman soldier is protected by his armor, Paul told the Ephesian Christians to put on the full armor of God as described in Ephesians 6:11–17.

Paul compares a soldier armed and ready for battle to our spiritual walk, encouraging us to put on our "full armor of God" (see Illustration #16) and prepare for battle.

In our society we are at war over man's values versus God's values. Our children are caught in the middle of that war as we try to protect them. In order to protect our families we must be ready for battle. Armor, anyone?

The Full Armor of God

Article of Armor	Scripture
Sword of the Spirit	Hebrews 4:12
Belt of Truth	John 14:6
Breastplate of Righteousness	Isaiah 59:17
Feet Fitted With Readiness and Peace	Acts 14:10
Shield of Faith	Mark 11:22
Pray in the Spirit	Colossians 4:2

It took me forever to join the online world. I was unusual because more than 40 percent of the Internet's growth is attributed to women connecting.

I've been navigating the wonderful, wacky world of cyberspace for years now. But I'm one of those unfortunate individuals who lives too far out in the country to have broadband, so while you're surfing at the speed of sound, I'm staring at the screen, treading water, waiting patiently for something to pop up. But that's okay. I like the peaceful sound of "silence" out in the country.

Home computers and the Internet have become as common as TV and toasters. I had a computer for years, but I was one of those who thought the Internet was too scary to join. But with my writing career, it got too embarrassing to tell editors I wasn't online, so I gave in.

It's been great, but it definitely has its disadvantages. You have sexual predators who ride the Internet into our homes, porn access 24/7, hackers, viruses, and spammers. Chat lines can lead to online and face-to-face affairs. And cyberspace bullies can intimidate you or your children. It's no wonder I was afraid to join!

Some might wonder why believers would even be in cyberspace, but it's a great way to be salt and light on this information superhighway. Plus, the more we're involved, the more we can actually help influence how cyberspace will develop in the future. It's a fact. Computers are here to stay. Computers have altered the way we work, play, learn, and communicate. Since they're an essential part of our future, don't you think we should help chart the course?

"See to it that no one takes you captive through hollow and deceptive philosophy, which depends on human tradition and the basic principles of this world rather than on Christ" (Colossians 2:8).

What You Can Do

Practical tips on how to safeguard our families from the destructive influence of the Internet include:

1. Install a software package filter that not only protects each member of your family by blocking out unwanted Internet sites but also protects your family's financial investment with your PC by blocking viruses.

2. Have "online use" guidelines written out for your family. Go over them with each member of your family and make sure they understand the whys and hows of the rules on Internet use and the consequences for breaking those rules. If the rules are broken, follow through on the consequence.

3. Have your computer in an out-in-the-open gathering place. You wouldn't send your kid to play in a dangerous street or allow your teens to go to a bar and chat with strangers, so don't invite strangers into your home. Sexual predators do not have to break down the door to get into our homes—the Internet lays out a welcome mat.

4. Chat rooms or instant messaging should be allowed only with individuals you and your children both know. Let your child know that you will check their online activity and e-mails from time to time.

5. Join forces that are dedicated to making the Internet safe for children and guarding them from the effects of illegal, hard-core pornography.

How Others See It

Mary Manz Simon

Today's PC immersion is potentially dangerous. The violent themes in media desensitize views. Sexual immorality is a recurring theme in socially irresponsible entertainment. These are especially critical concerns for children and you, who are vulnerable to outside influences while they develop a framework for personal views and values they will hold forever.[6]

What You Can Do

Practical advice on navigating the current influences that affect your family include these tips:

1. Stay connected. Kids, even tweens and teens, care about what parents think. Use sports, music, movies, or other relevant topics to launch new levels of connectedness with your child. Learn by listening. Grow by observing.

2. Develop new touchpoints with your child. As children age, their interests mature. Their skills of observation deepen. Their attention becomes more focused. Be honest with your child when he crosses a threshold of appropriateness. Then instruct by influencing and modeling, not lecturing.

3. Parents and older kids often link through parallel activities. Shovel the driveway with your child, clean out a closet together, or even sort coupons side by side. Find comfortable times to talk together. Discussing a recent movie or headline issue is less threatening when you and your child work as partners and conversation evolves naturally.

4. Spending time together is critical. Your child is inundated by pop culture at every turn. Media teach. Entertainment informs. The Internet influences. You can and should teach, inform, and influence too. However, that can happen only if you and your child intersect frequently.[7]

Snapshots of Women in the Bible
Shiphrah and Puah (Exodus 1:15–21)

Shiphrah and Puah loved the sound of a newborn baby's cry. As midwives, they had delivered dozens of babies, but tears welled up in their eyes with each new birth.

The pharaoh, however, did not share the midwives' joy over each new life. He feared the Hebrews he held in captivity would soon outnumber the Egyptians. He devised a plan to have all the Hebrew newborn males killed during childbirth, and called for the midwives to be brought before him.

Shiphrah and Puah wondered why they would be ordered before the pharaoh. Had they done something wrong? They went to his court with great uncertainty. Their hearts were troubled as they heard his orders. He commanded them to kill all the baby boys at birth, but to let the girls live.

Shiphrah and Puah knew that children were a gift from God, <u>loved</u> by him. They refused to murder children.

Moses, the great prophet, would have been a victim of the command if Shiphrah and Puah had obeyed Pharaoh's laws instead of <u>obeying</u> God's laws. In this snapshot, two women took a stand against murder and stood for their beliefs. They <u>feared</u> God more than man, and God rewarded and <u>blessed</u> them.

Today across America women involved in crisis pregnancy centers take a stand for God as they try to protect children from **abortion**. Lives are saved and hearts are mended as they share Christ's message of life and love.

loved
Luke 17:2
obeying
1 John 2:4–5
feared
Exodus 1:17
blessed
Exodus 1:21

abortion
ending a pregnancy by removing an unborn child from the mother's uterus

She Wasn't in the Count

It was Thursday afternoon, and at our house that's skate-deck afternoon. If Philip is caught up on his homework, we meet his friends for two hours of in-line skating fun as they chase each other around and around the rink.

Every now and then the moms abandon the snack tables, lace up the ol' skates, and get some exercise. Of course we have to be very careful not to skate too close to our children, or even act like we know them. So we skate incognito, zooming by our own children without saying a word.

One day we invited some friends to join the crew. They have a four-year-old named Taylor who tried with all of her might but just couldn't keep up with the big kids. That didn't bother her. She scooted around the rink with a big smile on her face and enjoyed every minute. Her mom was busy with her big sister, so when Taylor had a big spill I slowed down, helped her up, and asked if she wanted some company. Hand in hand we skated around the rink, stopping occasionally when Taylor tumbled.

Like most preschoolers, Taylor is a little talker. She chitchatted away, her little brown locks of hair blowing in the wind when speedsters whizzed by. She's an adorable, sweet child you just want to squeeze every time you see her. As she looked up at me with her beautiful sparkling blue eyes, I silently thanked God for ministries like Special Delivery.

Special Delivery is a pregnancy help center in Kirkland, Washington. Like other pregnancy centers across the country that reach out to girls

newness
Romans 6:4

and women with unplanned pregnancies, they offer an alternative to abortion. After receiving help from this crisis pregnancy center, Taylor's biological mother chose life and placed her in an adoptive home. Taylor was to join a wonderful, loving Christian family, who, unable to have children of their own, had already adopted a big sister (who anxiously awaited Taylor's arrival from the hospital).

She's only four, so January 22 holds no special meaning to her. But that January 22, 1998, just a couple of weeks from the day we skated, marked the grim twenty-fifth anniversary of Roe v. Wade, the Supreme Court decision that legalized abortion. Twenty-five years later, thirty-five million babies were dead.

I thank God for organizations like Special Delivery and for willing servants who share their lives and spiritual gifts with others. I support and pray for ministries on the front lines that make a loving effort to help women choose life. I thank God someone chose to make a difference so my little friend and her sister were not counted among the thirty-five million.

Without a shadow of a doubt, I know one day my skating partner will understand that life is a precious gift from God. When she hears her story, she will be overwhelmed by the abundant love that was poured out by so many to keep her out of the death count. I held her little hand that day because someone became a servant and chose to make a difference.

Speak the Truth in Love

1 PETER 3:15–16 *But in your hearts set apart Christ as Lord. Always be prepared to give an answer to everyone who asks you to give the reason for the hope that you have. But do this with gentleness and respect, keeping a clear conscience, so that those who speak maliciously against your good behavior in Christ may be ashamed of their slander.*

The apostle Peter deals with Christians and their relationship with the world. First, God must be the center of a believer's life. He must be first in your heart. You must know the Word and be ready and prepared not only to defend your position, but also to tell why you have hope in your message. We must present ourselves with gentleness and respect, not hatred or violence. Peter encourages us to live correctly, to walk in the newness of life with clear consciences before God, so our lives witness of Christ's love to the world.

check this out

How Others See It

Joni Eareckson Tada

I don't want America to move into the future with a heart of stone. Christians are charged with the only message that can change the heart of the bus driver, restaurant owner, and employer. We are commissioned to shake salt in newspaper editorial columns or at the market, dry cleaners, PTA, or university classrooms. We have the message—and God has given us the means—to speak to ethicists who promote the idea that people are "better off dead than disabled." It is fundamentally at this level that a nation's heart is healed.[8]

lack
Hosea 4:6
overcome
Romans 12:21

homosexual
person with sexual desires for those of the same sex

As you become an active Christian citizen, you must remember your commission to "be about [your] Father's business"—it's not our business, it's God's business. We are only his representatives. Not only should we know the truth of the Word, we must know the truth behind referendums, bills, special education programs, and issues that are being placed in our communities. We can be destroyed within from the <u>lack</u> of knowledge. If the issue is dealing with a hot topic such as abortion or **homosexual** marriage, we must know the ills that they place on society, the consequences, and the reason for our beliefs. All must be done in a Christlike manner, in order that evil can be <u>overcome</u> with good.

Scripture Concerning Abortion

Scripture Reference	Verse
Exodus 20:13	You shall not murder.
Psalm 139:13–14	For you created my inmost being; you knit me together in my mother's womb. I praise you because I am fearfully and wonderfully made; your works are wonderful, I know that full well.
Proverbs 24:11–12	Rescue those being led away to death; hold back those staggering toward slaughter. If you say, "But we knew nothing about this," does not he who weighs the heart perceive it?
Jeremiah 1:5	Before I formed you in the womb I knew you, before you were born I set you apart; I appointed you as a prophet to the nations.

Scripture Referring to Homosexuality

Reference	Verse
Romans 1:24–27	Therefore God gave them over in the sinful desires of their hearts to sexual impurity for the degrading of their bodies with one another. They exchanged the truth of God for a lie, and worshiped and served created things rather than the Creator—who is forever praised. Amen. Because of this, God gave them over to shameful lusts. Even their women exchanged natural relations for unnatural ones. In the same way the men also abandoned natural relations with women and were inflamed with lust for one another. Men committed indecent acts with other men, and received in themselves the due penalty for their perversion.
1 Corinthians 6:9–10	Do you not know that the wicked will not inherit the kingdom of God? Do not be deceived: Neither the sexually immoral nor idolaters nor adulterers nor male prostitutes nor homosexual offenders nor thieves nor the greedy nor drunkards nor slanderers nor swindlers will inherit the kingdom of God.
Leviticus 18:22	Do not lie with a man as one lies with a woman; that is detestable.

In *Roe v. Wade*, Norma McCorvey fought for and won the right to secure an abortion. She became the poster child for the abortion movement. On August 8, 1995, twenty-three years later, headlines shocked the world with her conversion to Christ, complete with a photo of her baptism. In her book *Won by Love*, Norma tells how a little girl's affection, a mother's trust, and a gregarious man's friendship surprised her and led her to Christ.

She wrote, "After years of working in a cauldron of hatred, factional infighting, bitterness, and resentment, I was won by a people of love. Their love included telling me that I was a sinner, that abortion was an offense to God, and that I would someday pay for this activity if I did not repent. But it was a love that also showed me there was a way out, an opportunity to experience forgiveness, grace and mercy. I was won by love."[9]

You Can Be Persuasive

> **2 CORINTHIANS 5:11** *Since, then, we know what it is to fear the Lord, we try to persuade men. What we are is plain to God, and I hope it is also plain to your conscience.*

The apostle Paul, writing the Christians in Corinth, was looking toward life after death and the judgment each of us will receive "according to what he has done, whether good or bad" (2 Corinthians 5:10 NASB).

Death frequently knocked at Paul's door as he faced persecution, bodily harm, and imprisonment. At times he realized it would have been easier to <u>die</u>, knowing in death he would see Christ face-to-face and dwell in his presence. Humans fear judgment on this earth, but we are responsible to the judgment of God for all that we do and say as we persuade others of his message of forgiveness, love, and eternal life.

die
Philippians 1:21, 23

As believers we have a huge load on our shoulders. We carry the weight of persuasion. Like Paul, at times we just wish it would all be over and God would just take us home. We look around and see the mess our world is in, and we are tempted to think that what we do in society doesn't matter, what happens in the world doesn't affect us, and when we all face judgment, God will take care of everything.

Don't give up. It does matter. We must remember our first goal is to fill our bus and take as many people to heaven as we possibly can. And second, God will hold us responsible for our actions or the absence of our actions.

You can be persuasive and make a difference in our world.

What You Can Do

One person can influence the opinions of many people:

1. *Use the power of the press:* The editorial section of the newspaper is a great place to present your thoughts, facts, and convictions on an issue. You don't have to be an expert to get in print. The letters column is open to everyone. You can persuade thousands of people who read your words.

2. *Call in to your local radio talk show:* Radio is not just all talk. Thousands upon thousands of listeners tune in to hear what's on the mind of John and Jane Doe. Live radio is a little more nerve-racking than writing to a newspaper, so I suggest you write your thoughts on paper before calling in and be prepared to defend your statements. Try to have fun!

3. *Write your legislators:* Did you know that your representatives view each letter received as representing at least one hundred other constituents? Write only about one issue at a time. Be sure to include the bill number and title. Bring it to a personal level and tell why this bill would affect you, your family, and your community.

4. *Call your legislator's hotline with the same information you would include in your letter.* If you don't talk directly with your representative, your message will be recorded and given to him or her.[10]

Why Christians Should Vote

It is absolutely critical that Christians be registered, be informed, and vote our values. As believers, we have a duty to be involved in the democratic process.

- *Honor, Privilege, Duty.* Americans are blessed to have a "government of the people, by the people, and for the people." But democracy has one key requirement: our participation. When you vote, you help determine who will lead our nation, make our laws, and protect our liberties.

- *The Influence of Faith.* Our faith in God should influence our values in life, and that includes the political arena. These ideas come from moral standards, which help prevent a free society such as ours from sliding into social chaos.

- *The Ministry of Voting.* That's right. Your vote can be a form of ministry. After all, when you vote, you are directly and indirectly having an impact on people's lives. By the people you select and the ballot measures you support, you are making a practical difference—for good and bad—in the lives of unborn children, impressionable youth, married couples, and hurting souls.[11]

Examples From the Bible

The Bible gives us many examples of faithful people who made a difference for God through their persuasive words. You can be persuasive and make a difference in our world. Listed are just a few who spoke up for God:

- **Daniel** the prophet lived seventy years under Babylonian rule, yet did not compromise his convictions. He resisted political pressure. When called upon by the king, he spoke the truth of God's Laws and was placed in leadership in the glorious city of Babylon. (See Illustration #17; Daniel 5:18–21.)

- **Jeremiah** was a prophet who stood up for God's Laws as he preached to a wicked nation of disobedient Jews. He wrote God's warnings and impending disasters out on a scroll. Even though imprisoned, persecuted, and hated by those he dared to confront, Jeremiah remained faithful and foretold a new law that would be written on men's hearts. (Jeremiah 24:7; 31:31–34; Hebrews 8:1–9:28)

- **Stephen's** preaching caused many to accept the Word of God. Scripture records, "Now Stephen, a man full of God's grace and power, did great wonders and miraculous signs among the people" (Acts 6:8). Though Stephen was falsely accused before the Sanhedrin, he defended his belief in Jesus. "All who were sitting in the **Sanhedrin** looked intently at Stephen, and they saw that his face was like the face of an angel" (Acts 6:15). Even after Stephen's **stoning**, the church grew as persecution scattered the believers throughout the Roman Empire, where they preached the Word.

Sanhedrin
powerful Jewish ruling council, comparable to Congress and the papacy combined

stoning
method of capital punishment where the accusers hurled rocks at the condemned

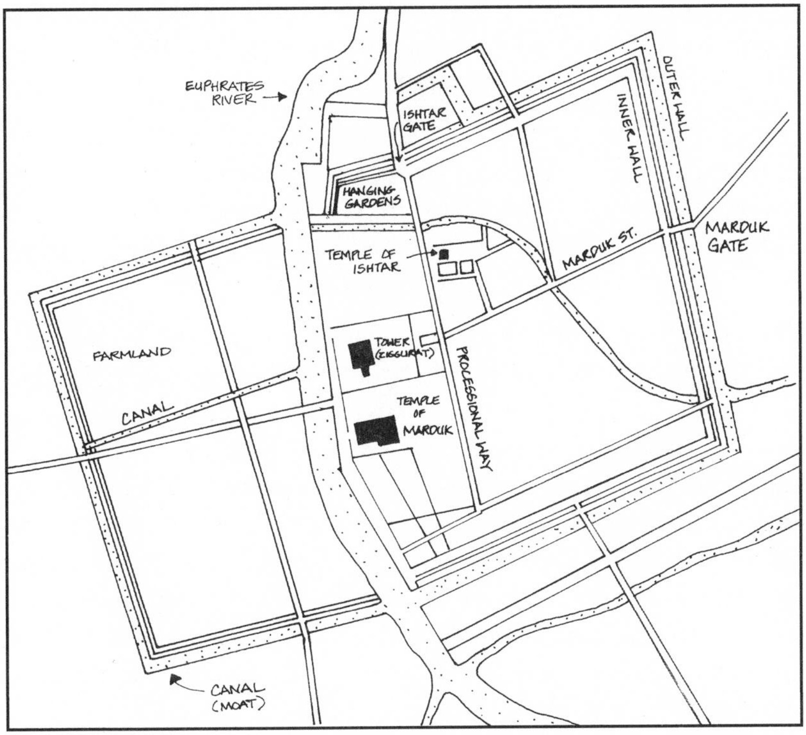

Illustration #17
Ancient City of Babylon—One of the greatest cities of all times. The palace alone took up more than six square miles, and the Hanging Gardens were one of the Seven Wonders of the World.

Remember Who You Are

One of my favorite old television shows is *The Waltons*. I love it! It reminds me of the stories my dad and grandparents would share about growing up in the hills of Kentucky during the Depression. There was one episode where John Boy is going away to college. It's a proud moment; he's the first Walton to go away and further his education. His dad takes him down in the old pickup truck to the train depot. They are having an emotional moment; it's one of those awkward times between a father and son. They want to hug and embrace, but at the same time you can tell his dad is thinking that John Boy is not a boy anymore; he's a man going off to college. Kind of teary-eyed, his dad is struggling for something to say, and the only thing that comes blurting out of his mouth is, "John Boy, remember who you are."

As a nation, our spiritual heritage has helped mold us into the great country we are. But it's easy as a nation to forget just who we are. That's why we have anniversaries to remember events like 9/11. It's a time to call us back—to simply remember just who we are as a nation.

On September 11, 2001, as the towers came down and the day wore on, we all watched the live coverage in horror. But through all those horrific scenes I saw two images of hope. I'll never forget the firefighters raising the flag over the site, and in the background stood the Statue of Liberty with the smoke lingering in the air around her as she held her torch high. But there in the midst of all that destruction stood a chapel—right beside where the Twin Towers once stood. You couldn't see it before, the towers overshadowed it, but there it was, immovable, and on its dome was a cross standing tall and pointing to the sky. It was as if it were reminding us to lift our eyes to the heavens, where our strength comes from (Isaiah 40:26–31).

As believers in this unique country called America, we are called to be salt and light to a dark and decaying world. We need to help hold up the true eternal light—the light of Jesus Christ.

Always look to God's advice for being your best. Be women in faith. Faith can build strong families. Faith can restore relationships. Faith can carry you through struggles and sorrows. And faith can influence the culture.

Remember who you are, but more important, remember whose you are as you place your life in the hands of God.

WHAT'S IN THE BIBLE FOR WOMEN

"God's wisdom is something mysterious that goes deep into the interior of his purposes. You don't find it lying around on the surface. It's not in the latest message, but more like the oldest—what God determined as the way to bring out his best in us" (1 Corinthians 2:7 MSG).

Final Thoughts

- Women have made an impact in leadership across the centuries. The Scripture records how God used women and men to accomplish his goal of turning hearts back to God. It's our duty as believers to be involved in government as we try to have a life-changing and eternal impact on our world.

- Our actions are a witness of Christ to the world. As we go about the great commission of teaching about Jesus, we must always speak "the truth in love" (Ephesians 4:15).

- In order to protect our families, we must be ready for battle as we put on the full armor of God. We must constantly be in the Word, walk with Christ, place our faith in God, and devote ourselves to prayer.

- You can make a difference right where you are as you go about sharing God's Word with others. As Esther, Deborah, Shiphrah, and Puah did in ancient days, today we women of faith can make a difference if we stand up, speak up, and reclaim the soul of America for God. Get active.

Questions to Deepen Your Understanding

1. Why should we obey man's government?

2. What three institutions did God establish?

3. What did Isaiah do that allowed God to use him?

4. Are Christians immune to opposition?

5. What did Esther do that made such an impact on her nation?

6. What gave Esther the strength to go to the king and possibly face death?

7. How can we protect our families as we battle societal values that contradict God's values?

8. Why did Shiphrah and Puah disobey a direct command from the pharaoh?

9. In what attitude are we to speak out against the injustices of society?

10. To whom are we ultimately responsible for our actions?

read on

Some of Georgia's favorite books for using your voice to improve your community:

- *America: The Last Best Hope,* William J. Bennett, Thomas Nelson

- *America's Christian Heritage,* Gary DeMar, Broadman & Holman

- *Answers to Your Kids' Questions,* Chuck Colson, Tyndale

- *The Faith of America's First Ladies,* Jane Cook, AMG Publishers

- *Fighting for Dear Life: The Untold Story of Terri Schiavo and What It Means for All of Us,* David Gibbs and Bob DeMoss, Bethany

- *How to Be a Christian in a Brave New World,* Joni Eareckson Tada and Nigel M. de S. Cameron

- *The Journey: How to Live by Faith in an Uncertain World,* Dr. Billy Graham, Thomas Nelson

- *Lies That Go Unchallenged in Popular Culture,* Chuck Colson, Tyndale

- *The Light and the Glory,* Peter Marshall, David Manuel, Baker

- *Marriage Under Fire,* Dr. James C. Dobson, Multnomah

- *The 360° Leader: Developing Your Influence From Anywhere in the Organization,* John C. Maxwell, Thomas Nelson

- *Trend-Savvy Parenting,* Dr. Mary Manz Simon, Tyndale

- Web sites for information on using your voice to improve your community: Joni Eareckson Tada's ministry to the disabled, *www.joniandfriends.org*; Ethics and Medicine, *www.ethicsandmedicine.com*; National Right to Life Committee, *www.nrlc.org*; Family Research Council, *www.frc.org*; Focus on the Family Action Organization, *www.focusaction.org*; Bsafe Internet Filters, *www.bsafehome.com*.

- *Why You Can't Stay Silent,* Tom Minnery, Tyndale

Appendix A • The Answers

Chapter 1: Spiritually Fit

1. God's Word is perfect and true. It makes us wise and brings us joy in life if we follow its guidelines. It leads us to do right and satisfies the appetite of our souls. (Psalm 19:7–11)

2. Sarah put her faith and trust in God by following his instructions. She left her homeland and followed her husband, Abraham. (Hebrews 11:11)

3. Mary surrendered her time (Luke 10:39), her sorrow (John 11:32), and her precious possessions (John 12:1–11) to Jesus.

4. We should worship God, obey God, and praise God daily. (Psalm 86:11–12)

5. Elizabeth walked with God in service, in prayer, in praise, in obedience, and by faith. (Luke 1:8–25, 39–45)

6. Our souls are satisfied by God's words recorded in the Scripture. (Matthew 4:4)

7. The Samaritan woman found Jesus, who gave her the Living Water of the Holy Spirit. (John 4:4–26; 7:37–39)

8. Prayer nurtures your relationship with God as you communicate with him continually. (Romans 12:12)

Chapter 2: Rainy Days and Mondays

1. Jeremiah told the children of Israel to keep living, be patient, and wait on God's plans for "hope and a future." (Jeremiah 29:1–32)

2. Jesus knows our suffering souls. When we turn to Christ in the midst of our suffering, we no longer live for ourselves but for God. (Matthew 27:1–66; John 10:14)

3. The widow of Zarepath followed Elijah the prophet's instructions and shared what she thought was her last meal with him. (1 Kings 17:1–24)

4. The apostle Paul advised the Ephesians to restrain and control their anger. We can express our feelings of frustration and anger, but we are not to let anger turn to hatred and bitterness. (Ephesians 4:26)

5. They all listened and followed God. Noah's wife found relief and happiness when the floodwaters receded and the survivors built an altar to praise God (Genesis 8). Hagar was comforted by an angel and found strength to continue (Genesis 6). Naomi stayed true to God, and he blessed her with the companionship of Ruth. (Ruth 1)

6. The psalmist was honest with himself and his state of mind and cried out to God for help in prayer. (Psalm 69:1–2)

7. Laughter gives you a break from your pain. Your heart may still ache, but laughter gives relief. (Proverbs 14:13; 17:22)

8. When we suffer, we can gain relief by allowing others to help us. (1 Corinthians 12:25–26)

9. Rahab harbored two spies from Israel's army and saved her family. She left behind her immoral life and believed in God as she joined the Israelites. (Joshua 2:1–21; Hebrews 11:31)

Chapter 3: From Burnout to Balance

1. Do not worry, trust him (Jesus).

2. Make "knowing Christ" first in your life.

3. Pray and seek God's guidance, look to his Word to see if the activity is God-honoring and fits into his purpose for your life.

4. Dwell on whatever is true, noble, right, pure, lovely, praiseworthy. (Philippians 4:8)

5. Self-reflection/evaluate their schedules.

6. They went to a quiet place for rest and solitude away from the crowds.

7. Pray, read Scriptures, and listen to your children's fears.

8. Eunice remained faithful to God and instructed Timothy in the same faith. She influenced the church through Timothy as he became a leader in establishing the early church and spreading the gospel.

9. He literally saved them from perishing in the desert as he provided a well to replenish Hagar and her son Ishmael. He gave them comfort and hope for their future.

Chapter 4: Mom Factor

1. We are to impress upon our children that they should love the Lord with all their hearts, with all their souls, and with all their strength. (Deuteronomy 6:5–7)

2. The older women were to teach the younger women to love their husbands and to love their children. (Titus 2:3–4)

3. Hannah continually prayed for Samuel and turned his life over to God's hands. (1 Samuel 1:1–3:21)

4. The key advice parents should give children is to love the Lord and "walk in his ways" (1 Kings 2:2–4).

5. Samson's mother was obedient to the faith as she loved, prayed, confronted, and instructed Samson in the way of the Lord. (Judges 13:6; 9:23; 14:3)

6. God gives us the gift of the Holy Spirit, which dwells in our hearts when we accept Jesus as the Lord of our lives. (1 Corinthians 13:8, 13)

7. Eunice remained faithful to God and passed her faith along to Timothy as she instructed him in God's commands and principles. (2 Timothy 1:1–6)

Chapter 5: Home Front or Battlefront?

1. God is the foundation we must build our families and marriages upon. (Psalm 127:1)

2. Recommit your covenant to God and to one another. Let God be the foundation of your marriage. (Matthew 7:24)

3. Rebekah showed two exemplary qualities: She was willing to leave the familiar behind, and she made a lifelong commitment to her marriage. God rewarded Rebekah with a husband who loved her and with twin boys. (Genesis 24:1–67)

4. The Bible permits divorce in the case of sexual unfaithfulness by a spouse (Matthew 5:31). The intended goal of separation is reconciliation. (Colossians 1:19–20; Matthew 5:21)

Chapter 6: Relationships in the Family Tree

1. We need to acquire wisdom and understanding to live a blessed and happier life.

2. The spiritual nourishment we need to help us handle difficult relationships is the law of the Lord—God's Word and the fruits of the Spirit—love, joy, peace, patience, kindness, goodness, faithfulness, gentleness, and self-control. (Galatians 5:22–23)

3. Miriam, Moses, and Aaron all had the same goal and purpose—to obey, worship, and glorify God.

4. Martha displayed traits of the Perfect Melancholy as she desired organized perfection and was pessimistic.

5. Abigail's husband was mean-spirited, foolish, and a drunk.

6. Jethro suggested that Moses act as judge only in the hardest cases and that he return to his calling of leadership and teaching.

7. It is first the responsibility of the widow's family to care for and provide for her needs. If she has no family, then the church is to provide for her needs.

Chapter 7: Money, Money, Money

1. The borrower is a servant to the lender. (Proverbs 22:7)

2. The prophet's widow went to the wise prophet Elisha seeking advice. (2 Kings 4:1–7)

3. Godliness with contentment unlocks the door to plastic prison (1 Timothy 6:6–10). Contentment is found in Christ.

4. The world is watching and our lives are a beacon of Christ and his power in our community. (Philippians 2:1–15)

5. More was not enough for Lot's wife. (Genesis 19:1–26)

6. The widow gave all that she had. The devotion behind her gift was what mattered to Jesus. (Luke 21:3–4)

7. We are to give cheerfully and willingly, not reluctantly. (2 Corinthians 9:6–8)

Chapter 8: All I Do Is Work, Work, Work

1. Work is designed by God and work is good. God's Son even worked while on earth. (Genesis 1:26; Mark 6:3)

2. Paul encouraged the Colossians to put Christ first and work as if they worked for the Lord. (Colossians 3:23)

3. God sent Paul to teach them about Jesus and a fuller understanding of the Scripture. Because of Lydia's willingness to follow the message of Jesus, Christianity spread throughout Europe. (Acts 16:13–15)

4. Our actions should reflect the love of Christ. We should get along, live in harmony, and not pay back evil for evil. (1 Peter 3:8–9)

5. As salt in the workplace, we can stop the decaying morals that surround us, flavor lives with the love of Christ, and create a thirst for God. (Matthew 5:13–15)

6. She first and foremost feared and honored God. (Proverbs 31:31)

7. He knew God's laws and chose not to sin against God. (Genesis 39:9)

8. Their business provided funds for themselves and Paul as he stayed with them and assisted them in tentmaking. Part time, they helped Paul in various teaching ministries and as a result the gospel continued to spread. (Acts 18:18–28)

9. A wise woman listens and adds to her learning. (Proverbs 1:5)

Chapter 9: I Have a Glue Gun and I'm Not Afraid to Use It

1. A wise woman builds a house called home. (Proverbs 14:1)

2. Homemaking was a treasured calling for a young woman. (Titus 2:4–6)

3. The Holy Spirit is the comforter and helper of those who love Jesus. (John 14:23)

4. Jesus rebuked her and encouraged her to take more time to commune with God. (Luke 10:41–42)

5. We are to be about our heavenly Father's business and do everything as unto the Lord. (Luke 2:24)

6. Hospitality meant providing lodging and food. (Hebrews 13:1–2; Genesis 18:1–2)

7. The Shunammite woman was blessed with a son, and the added miracle of her son being brought back to life. (2 Kings 4:8–37)

Chapter 10: Touching Lives, Serving Others

1. Christ commanded us to "love each other as I have loved you" (John 15:12).

2. To please God and honor his kingdom. (Philippians 2:3–5)

3. Our actions and good deeds are proof of our faith. (Matthew 25:35)

4. Huldah was a prophetess whom God used as a messenger. She studied the laws and taught others. (2 Kings 22)

5. Every believer has at least one gift. To discover it, consider Scripture, seek God's wisdom as you look inward, and notice what you enjoy and are good at when you serve the church. (1 Corinthians 12:4–6; Romans 12:3–8; Ephesians 4:7–11)

6. Love God and your neighbor as you love yourself. (Luke 10:27; Deuteronomy 6:5; Leviticus 19:18)

7. What really matters is pleasing God. As a bonus, eternal reward awaits when you are obedient to God and his Word. (1 Corinthians 15:58)

8. Dorcas sewed garments, so her instruments were needle and thread. (Acts 9:36–42)

Chapter 11: Speaking Out on Cultural Issues

1. God established the government. (Romans 13:1–2)

2. God established the home (Genesis 2), the church (Acts 2), and the government. (Genesis 8:20–9:7)

3. Isaiah repented of his own unrighteousness and volunteered willingly by saying, "Here am I. Send me!" (Isaiah 6:8)

4. No. The early church faced persecution as we do today around the world. (Acts 13:50)

5. Esther remained true to her faith and her heritage as she spoke up to the king and revealed a plot to massacre all of the Jews in the kingdom. (Esther 1–10)

6. Esther called the Jews to pray and fast for three days as she sought strength from God. (Esther 4:15–17)

7. We receive spiritual protection when we put on the full armor of God. (Ephesians 6:10)

8. They chose to obey God's Laws over man's commands. (Exodus 1:17)

9. We are to speak out in gentleness, respect, and love. (1 Peter 3:15–16)

10. We each will be judged by God. (2 Corinthians 5:11)

Appendix B • The Experts

Arterburn, Stephen—Cofounder and chairman of New Life Treatment Centers, founder of the Women of Faith movement, and author of over thirty books, including several bestsellers.

Barnes, Emilie—Nationally known home-management expert and popular speaker. Her fifteen books, including *More Hours in My Day, The 15-Minute Organizer,* and *If Teacups Could Talk,* have sold more than one million copies.

Brestin, Dee—Speaker at large retreats on the topic of women's friendships and author of *The Friendships of Women, We Are Sisters,* and a best-selling line of Bible study guides.

Briscoe, Jill—Known throughout the world for her Bible study and speaking ministry. Jill is director of Telling the Truth media ministries and has authored a number of books.

Chapman, Gary, PhD—Directs marriage seminars throughout the country and is host of the nationally syndicated radio broadcast *A Growing Marriage.* He is author of the bestselling books *The Five Languages of Love* and *The Five Love Languages of Children.*

Clairmont, Patsy—Author of many books including *It's About Home.* She is a popular speaker.

DiMarco, Haley—Author of the bestselling *Dateable, Mean Girls, Mean Girls Gone,* and *Mean Girls All Grown Up.* Haley helps organizations communicate with teens and adults with a postmodern mindset through her company, Hungry Planet.

Dobson, James, PhD—Psychologist, bestselling author, and president of Focus on the Family ministries.

Dole, Elizabeth—Outspoken Christian woman and wife of Bob Dole, past Senate Majority Leader. She served as president of the Red Cross, the world's largest humanitarian relief agency, and presently serves as a U.S. congresswoman.

Eldredge, Stasi—Coleader of the women's ministry of Ransomed Heart and is passionate about women discovering their identity as the Beloved of Christ. She is the bestselling author of *Captivating.*

Ellis, Gwen—Writer, editor, speaker, and consultant who, following her retirement from the publishing world, established her own company, Seaside Creative Services, Inc. Her books include *Thriving as a Working Woman: 101 Ways to Make Money at Home* and *Simply Fun for Families.*

Ethridge, Shannon—Bestselling coauthor of *Every Woman's Battle,* as well as wife, mother, speaker, and lay leader.

Feldhahn, Shaunti—Bestselling author of numerous books, including *For Women Only;* nationally syndicated newspaper columnist; and public speaker.

George, Elizabeth—Bestselling author of *A Woman After God's Own Heart* and *Life Management for Busy Women,* and popular teacher and speaker at Christian women's events.

Graham, Billy—"America's pastor." Dr. Graham has preached before eighty million people worldwide and has seen three million people commit their lives to Christ at his crusades. He is the author of numerous bestsellers, including his latest release, *The Journey: How to Live by Faith in an Uncertain World.*

Hart, Archibald D., PhD—Dean of the Graduate School of Psychology and professor of psychology at Fuller Theological Seminary in Pasadena, California. He has authored several books including *Stress and Your Child, Overcoming Anxiety,* and *The Hidden Link Between Adrenaline and Stress.*

Higgs, Liz Curtis—Author, speaker, and nationally known humorist. She has a monthly column in *Today's Christian Woman* magazine.

Hunt, Mary—Author of *Debt-Proof Living* and founder and publisher of *Cheapskate Monthly,* a newsletter to encourage financial confidence and responsible spending.

Hunter, Brenda, PhD—Psychologist, internationally published author, and passionate defender of the mother-child bond. She has defended hands-on mothering on *The Today Show, CBS This Morning,* and *Larry King Live.* She authored *A Mother's Love and Home by Choice.*

Hunter, Lynda—Author and founding editor of Focus on the Family's *Single Parent Family* magazine. She is a popular speaker and writer of a syndicated newspaper column for single parents.

Hybels, Bill—Pastor of Willow Creek Community Church, known worldwide for its "seeker sensitive" approach. He is the author of a number of books and Bible study series, including *Too Busy Not to Pray and Making Life Work*.

Kay, Ellie—Regular guest on CNBC's Power Lunch, national magazine columnist, international speaker, and national radio commentator for *Money Matters*. She is the author of *A Mom's Guide for Family Finances and Heroes at Home*.

Littauer, Florence—International speaker and popular author. She and her husband, Fred, conduct marriage and personality seminars and are the founders of CLASS.

Littauer, Marita—President of CLASS (Christian Leaders, Authors, Speakers Services) and author of many books. She is an international speaker.

Lotz, Anne Graham—Daughter of Billy and Ruth Bell Graham, founder of AnGel Ministries, and author of several bestselling books, including *Heaven: My Father's House, Just Give Me Jesus,* and *Why?*

Maxwell, John C.—Internationally known speaker on the topic of personal and corporate leadership development. He is the author of several books and the founder of Injoy Ministries.

Meyer, Joyce—Bible teacher since 1976 and in full-time ministry since 1989. She is the bestselling author of more than fifty inspirational books, including *Battlefield of the Mind* and *In Pursuit of Peace*. Joyce's *Enjoying Everyday Life* radio and television programs are broadcast around the world.

Moore, Beth—Writer and teacher of bestselling books and Bible studies whose public speaking engagements carry her all over the United States. A dedicated wife and mother of two, Beth lives in Houston, Texas, where she leads Living Proof Ministries and teaches an adult Sunday school class.

O'Connor, Lindsey—Author, freelance journalist, speaker, and—her favorite role—mother of five. She has worked in broadcast news, including a stint as a news anchor. She writes on family and women's issues, end-of-life issues, and faith. Her books include the bestseller *If Mama Ain't Happy, Ain't Nobody Happy*. Lindsey and her family live in Colorado.

Omartian, Stormie—Bestselling author of *The Power of Praying* books (more than 4.5 million copies sold). Stormie and her husband, Michael, have been married for more than twenty-eight years and live in Tennessee.

Osteen, Joel—Senior pastor of Lakewood Church in Houston, Texas, one of America's largest and fastest-growing congregations, and bestselling author of *Your Best Life Now*.

Parrott, Les—Internationally known bestselling author. He and his wife, Dr. Leslie Parrott, have been featured on *Oprah, CBS This Morning, CNN, The View,* and in *USA Today* and the *New York Times*. The Parrotts are authors of the award-winning *Saving Your Marriage Before It Starts,* and *Becoming Soul Mates,* among many others. Les and Leslie are currently serving as governor's marriage ambassadors for the Oklahoma ten-year Marriage Initiative.

Parrott, Leslie—Marriage and family therapist and codirector with her husband, Dr. Les Parrott, of the Center for Relationship Development at Seattle Pacific University. She is the author of *You Matter More Than You Think* and coauthor with her husband of several bestselling books, including *I Love You More*.

Partow, Donna—Author of devotional and practical advice books, including *No More Lone Ranger Moms*.

Ramsey, Dave—Bestselling author of *Financial Peace, More Than Enough,* and *Money Makeover*. He is founder of the Lamp Group, Inc., and popular host of the nationally syndicated radio talk show *The Dave Ramsey Show*.

Silvious, Jan—Cohost (with Kay Arthur) of Precepts Ministry's national radio program, *Precepts With Kay and Jan*. She is an author, a counselor, and a popular speaker.

Simon, Mary Manz—Popular media personality, speaker, and practical parenting specialist. She is the bestselling author of many children's books and *Trend-Savvy Parenting*.

Sittser, Gerald L., PhD—Professor of religion and philosophy. A former pastor, he is the author of four books, including *A Grace Disguised,* and many book reviews and articles for popular and scholarly journals.

Smalley, Gary—America's relationship doctor and cofounder and chairman of the board of the Smalley Relationship Center. He is the author and coauthor of more than forty books, including the bestselling *Marriage for a Lifetime, Secrets to Lasting Love,* and *The DNA of Relationships*.

Stoop, David—Founder and codirector of the Center for Family Therapy. He is writer and coauthor of several books, including *130 Questions Children Ask About War and Terrorists,* and is an ordained minister. He and his wife, Jan, lead marriage and family seminars across the country and abroad.

Swindoll, Charles R.—President of Dallas Theological Seminary. He is also president of *Insight for Living,* a radio broadcast ministry aired daily worldwide. He was senior pastor of the First Evangelical Free Church in Fullerton, California, for almost twenty-three years and has authored numerous books on Christian Living.

Swindoll, Luci—Vice-president of public relations at Insight for Living. She is a popular speaker and the author of six books, including *Notes to a Working Woman* and *I Married Adventure*.

Tada, Joni Eareckson—Author of more than twenty books. She serves as president of JAF Ministries, a Christian organization that advances Christ's kingdom among the world's 550 million people with disabilities.

Teresa, Mother—Started her own order, the Missionaries of Charity, in 1950. She won the Nobel Peace Prize and was acclaimed internationally for her work among the destitute and the dying.

Tobias, Cynthia—Founder and president of Learning Styles Unlimited, Inc. She is a popular speaker and bestselling author of *The Way They Learn* and *Every Child Can Succeed*.

Trent, John—President of the Center for Strong Families and StrongFamilies.com, an organization that trains leaders to build and lead marriage and family programs in their communities. He has authored and coauthored more than a dozen award-winning and bestselling books.

Troccoli, Kathy—Award-winning singer, songwriter, and author. She is the author and coauthor of several books, including the bestseller *Falling in Love With Jesus* and *Live Like You Mean It*.

Walker, Lynn Bowen—Stanford graduate who was trained as a journalist, but who chose instead to dedicate herself to raising a family and building a strong home. She has written for many magazines, including, *Today's Christian Woman* and *Glamour*. She is the author of *Queen of the Castle*.

Walsh, Sheila—Past host of *The 700 Club*. She is a popular speaker, vocalist, and author of several books, including *Honestly, Outrageous Love*, and *I'm Not Superwoman*.

Warren, Rick—Bestselling author of *The Purpose-Driven Life* and *The Purpose-Driven Church*. He is the founding pastor of Saddleback Church in Lake Forest, California, one of America's largest and best-known churches.

Weaver, Joanna—Author, pastor's wife, and mother of two. She is an award-winning author of the wedding gift book *With This Ring*.

Whelchel, Mary—Founder of the national radio program *The Christian Working Woman*. She is an author and popular speaker.

White, Paula—Pastor, teacher, and speaker. She is known for her dynamic Bible teaching and preaching with delivery as an exhorter and motivator. She is also the host of the nationally syndicated program *Paula White Today*. She is the author of *Deal With It!*

Winfrey, Oprah—Considered one of the most influential women in media. She is host of the *Oprah Winfrey Show* and owner of Harpo Productions and *O, the Oprah Magazine*.

Yates, Susan Alexander—Columnist and regular guest on the radio program *On Your Mark*, broadcast in Boston and Washington. She is a popular speaker and author.

Endnotes

Chapter 1

1. Joyce Meyer, *Look Great, Feel Great* (New York: Warner Faith, 2006), 111.

2. Jill Briscoe, *Women in the Life of Jesus* (Wheaton, IL: Victor Books, 1986), 69.

3. Anne Graham Lotz, *I Saw the Lord* (Grand Rapids, MI: Zondervan, 2006), 52.

4. Dee Brestin, *A Woman of Worship Bible Study* (Colorado Springs, CO: Cook Communications, 2006), 49.

5. Kathy Troccoli, *Live Like You Mean It* (Colorado Springs, CO: WaterBrook Press, 2006), 58.

6. Bill Hybels, *The God You're Looking For* (Nashville, TN: Thomas Nelson, 1997), 147, 152.

7. Joyce Meyer, *Battlefield of the Mind* (New York: Warner Faith, 1995), 163.

8. Robert Sullivan, "Discovery: Sleepless in America," *Life* magazine (February 1998): 56.

9. Stormie Omartian, *The Power of a Praying Woman* (Eugene, OR: Harvest House, 2002), 28.

Chapter 2

1. Elisabeth Kübler-Ross, *On Death and Dying* (New York: Macmillan, 1969), quoted by Joyce Landorf, *Mourning Song* (Old Tappan, NJ: Fleming H. Revel, 1974), 16.

2. Anne Graham Lotz, *Why?* (Nashville, TN: W Publishing Group, 2004), 78.

3. Joni Eareckson Tada and Steven Estes, *When God Weeps* (Grand Rapids, MI: Zondervan, 1997), 50.

4. Gerald L. Sittser, *A Grace Disguised* (Grand Rapids, MI: Zondervan, 2004), 56.

5. Lisa Beamer, *Let's Roll!* (Wheaton, IL: Tyndale, 2002), 242.

6. Jill Briscoe, *The New Normal* (Colorado Springs, CO: Multnomah, 2005), 46.

7. Sheila Walsh, *Outrageous Love* (Nashville, TN:). Countryman, 2004), 86.

8. Joni Eareckson Tada, *31 Days Toward Overcoming Adversity* (Sisters, OR: Multnomah, 2006), 73.

9. Walsh, *Outrageous Love*, 108.

10. SmithKline Beecham *Pharmaceuticals, A Health Education Material* reviewed favorably by the American Academy of Family Physicians Foundations, "Symptoms of Depression," 3–4.

11. Verdell Davis, *Let Me Grieve, but Not Forever* (Dallas, TX: Word, 1994), 59.

12. Sue Buchanan, *I'm Alive and the Doctor's Dead* (Grand Rapids, MI: Zondervan, 1994), 128.

13. Jan Silvious, *Look at It This Way* (Colorado Springs, CO: WaterBrook Press, 2003), 20.

14. Evelyn Husband with Donna Vanliere, *High Calling* (Nashville, TN: Thomas Nelson, Inc., 2003), 186.

15. Sittser, *A Grace Disguised*, 74.

Chapter 3

1. Rick Warren, *What on Earth Am I Here For?* (Grand Rapids, MI: Zondervan, 2004), 5.

2. Joyce Meyer, *Look Great, Feel Great,* 136.

3. Joanna Weaver, *Having a Mary Heart in a Martha World* (Colorado Springs, CO: WaterBrook Press, 2002), 180.

4. John and Stasi Eldredge, *Captivating* (Nashville, TN: Thomas Nelson, 2005), 28.

5. Elizabeth George, *Life Management for Busy Women* (Eugene, OR: Harvest House, 2002), 202.

6. Archibald D. Hart, *Stress and Your Child* (Dallas, TX: Word, 1992), 68.

7. Ibid., 31.

8. Stephen Arterburn and David Stoop, 130 Questions Children *Ask About War and Terrorists* (Wheaton, IL: Tyndale, 2002), xviii.

9. Cynthia Yates, *Living Well as a Single Mom* (Eugene, OR: Harvest House, 2006), 205.

10. Sheila Walsh, *I'm Not Wonder Woman: But God Made Me Wonderful* (Nashville, TN: Thomas Nelson, 2006), 134.

11. Gwen Ellis, *Thriving As a Working Woman* (Wheaton, IL: Tyndale, 1995), 36–37.

Chapter 4

1. Brenda Hunter, Ph.D., *The Power of Mother Love* (Colorado Springs, CO: WaterBrook Press, 1997), 1.
2. Oprah Winfrey, *O, the Oprah Magazine* (May 2003): 290.
3. Quotes from *USA* and *Business Week* magazine (May 2003).
4. James C. Dobson, *The Strong-Willed Child* (Wheaton, IL: Tyndale House, 1978), introduction, x.
5. Cynthia Ulrich Tobias, *Every Child Can Succeed* (Colorado Springs, CO: Focus on the Family), preface.
6. George Washington, in *A Mother's Love*, based on the painting by Ron Dicianni, Caesar Kalinowski, ed. (Nashville, TN: Broadman and Holman, 2000), 44.
7. Donna Partow, *No More Lone Ranger Moms* (Minneapolis, MN: Bethany House Publishers, 1993), 31.

Chapter 5

1. John Maxwell, *The Success Journey* (Nashville, TN: Thomas Nelson, 1997), 178.
2. John and Stasi Eldredge, *Captivating* (Nashville, TN: Thomas Nelson, 2005), 26.
3. Bob Russell, *Marriage by the Book* (Cincinnati, OH: Standard Publishing, 1992), 20.
4. Washington Citizen Newsletter, "Five Things You Can Do to Strengthen Your Marriage" (Bellevue, WA: Washington Family Council, March 1999), 3.
5. Les and Leslie Parrott, *I Love You More* (Grand Rapids, MI: Zondervan, 2005), 28.
6. Gary Smalley, The *DNA of Relationships* (Wheaton, IL: Tyndale, 2004), 94.
7. Gary Chapman, *Loving Solutions* (Chicago, IL: Moody Press, 1998), 51.
8. Smalley, *The DNA of Relationships*, 83.
9. John Trent, *Breaking the Cycle of Divorce* (Carol Stream, IL: Tyndale, 2006), 135.
10. Chapman, *Loving Solutions*, 135, 142.
11. Ibid, 30.
12. Jan Silvious, *Foolproofing Your Life* (Colorado Springs, CO: WaterBrook Press, 1998), 178.

Chapter 6

1. Gary Smalley, *The DNA of Relationships* (Wheaton, IL: Tyndale, 2004), 83.

2. Paula White, *Deal With It!* (Nashville, TN: Nelson Ignite, 2004), 7.
3. Florence and Marita Littauer, *Personality Puzzle* (Grand Rapids, MI: Revell, 1992), excerpts 24, 81.
4. Ibid.
5. Susan Alexander Yates, *A House Full of Friends* (Colorado Springs, CO: Focus on the Family, 1995) 140.
6. Charles Swindoll, *Growing Strong in the Seasons of Life* (Portland, OR: Multnomah Press, 1983), 349.
7. "Aging Parents and Children Together," *www.ftc/gov/bcp/conline/pubs/service/apact.*
8. Joni Eareckson Tada, *The Life and Death Dilemma* (Grand Rapids, MI: Zondervan, 1995), 22.
9. Betty Benson Robertson, *Changing Places: A Christian's Guide to Caring for Aging Parents* (Kansas City, MO: Beacon Hill Press of Kansas City), 24.
10. Anne Graham Lotz, *Heaven: My Father's House* (Nashville, TN: W Publishing Group, 2001), 97.

Chapter 7

1. Joyce Meyer, *In Pursuit of Peace* (New York: Warner Faith, 2004), 167.
2. Dave Ramsey, *Financial Peace* (New York: Viking, 1997), 90.
3. Ibid., 92.
4. Mary Hunt, *Debt-Proof Living* (London: Faithworks, 2006), 11.
5. Dave Ramsey, *More Than Enough* (New York: Viking, 1999), 69.
6. Les and Leslie Parrott, *I Love You More,* 108.
7. Judith Couchman, *Celebrating Friendship, Women of Faith Bible Study Series* (Grand Rapids, MI: Zondervan, 1998), 29, 77.
8. Ellie Kay, *A Mom's Guide to Family Finances* (Grand Rapids, MI: Revell, 2004), 128.
9. Edith Dean, *All the Women of the Bible* (New York: Harper and Row, 1955), 353.
10. Joel Osteen, *Your Best Life Now* (New York: Warner Faith, 2004), 256.
11. Mary Hunt, *The Financially Confident Woman* (Nashville, TN: Broadman and Holman, 1996), 54.

Chapter 8

1. Elizabeth George, *Life Management for Busy Women* (Eugene, OR: Harvest House, 2002), 232.
2. *Clarity Magazine*, (October/November 1998).
3. "Money Makers" by Maria Bartinomo in *Reader's Digest* (May 2006): 53.
4. Ibid., 54.

5. Luci Swindoll, *Notes to a Working Woman* (Nashville, TN: W Publishing Group, 2004), prologue, xii.

6. Hayley DiMarco, *Mean Girls All Grown Up* (Grand Rapids, MI: Revell, 2005), 130.

7. Ibid., 25.

8. Ibid., 29.

9. Ibid., 30.

10. John Maxwell, *Winning People* (Nashville, TN: Thomas Nelson, 2004), 245.

11. Dee Brestin and Kathy Troccoli, *Forever in Love with Jesus* (Nashville, TN: W Publishing Group, 2004), 30.

12. J. D. Douglas, ed., *The New Bible Dictionary,* (Grand Rapids, MI: Eerdmans Publishing), 510–11.

13. Shannon Ethridge, *Every Woman's Battle* (Colorado Springs, CO: WaterBrook Press, 2004), 13.

14. Shaunti Feldhahn, *For Women Only* (Sisters, OR: Multnomah, 2004), 71.

15. Jan Silvious, *Foolproofing Your Life* (Colorado Springs, CO: WaterBrook Press, 1998), 171.

16. Mary Whelchel, *The Workplace Questions Women Ask* (Portland, OR: Multnomah), 28.

17. Lindsey O'Conner, *A Christian's Guide to Working From Home* (Eugene, OR: Harvest House, 1997), 10.

18. Lynda Hunter, *Parenting on Your Own* (Grand Rapids, MI: Zondervan, 1997), 22.

19. Swindoll, *Notes to a Working Woman,* 150.

Chapter 9

1. Lynn Bowen Walker, *Queen of the Castle* (Franklin, TN: Integrity Publishers, 2006), 5.

2. Patsy Clairmont, *Sportin' a Tude* (Wheaton, IL: Tyndale, 1997), 169.

3. Joanna Weaver, *Having a Mary Heart in a Martha World* (Colorado Springs, CO: WaterBrook Press, 2002), 86.

4. Emergency Supply List, U.S. Department of Home Land Security, *www.ready.gov* (accessed August 10, 2006).

5. American Red Cross, "Terrorism—Preparing for the Unexpected," *www.redcross.org* (accessed August 10, 2006).

6. FEMA for Kids: "What You Might Feel in a Disaster," *www.fema.gov/kids/feel.htm* (accessed August 10, 2006).

7. Stephen Arterburn and David Stoop, 130 *Questions Children Ask About War and Terrorists* (Wheaton, IL: Tyndale, 2002), 28.

8. Emilie Barnes, *Creative Home Organizer* (Eugene, OR: Harvest House, 1995), 14.

9. Dee Brestin, *A Woman of Hospitality* (Colorado Springs, CO: Cook Communications, 2005), 85.

10. Susan Alexander Yates, *A House Full of Friends* (Colorado Springs, CO: Focus on the Family, 1995), 31.

11. Emilie Barnes and Yoli Brogger, *Designing Your Home on a Budget* (Eugene, OR: Harvest House, 2006), 159.

12. Liz Curtis Higgs, *Only Angels Can Wing It* (Nashville, TN: Thomas Nelson, 1995), 175.

13. Barnes and Brogger, *Designing Your Home on a Budget,* 8.

Chapter 10

1. Meadow Rue Merrill, "Operation Blessing" in *Family Circle* (February 16, 1999): 15.

2. Phyllis Bennet, *Discovering Your Spiritual Gifts, Women of Faith Bible Study Series* (Grand Rapids, MI: Zondervan, 1998), 39.

3. Ibid., 40.

4. Ibid., 43

5. Ibid., 28.

6. Ibid.

7. Sheila Walsh, *I'm Not Wonder Woman, But God Made Me Wonderful,* 133.

8. *The New Compact Bible Dictionary* (Grand Rapids, MI: Zondervan, 1981), 236.

9. Bill Hybels, *Putting God and Others First, Serving Lessons, Small Group Series* (Grand Rapids, MI: Zondervan, 1998), 21.

10. Paula White, *Deal With It!* (Nashville, TN: Nelson Ignite, 2004), 155.

11. "Clergy Appreciation," The Parsonage, a Web site of Focus on the Family, *www.parsonage.org* (accessed August 2006).

12. Adapted from How to Encourage Our Troops and Families, CITIZEN Web site of Focus on the Family, *www.family.org/cforum/citizenmag/webonly/a0025489.cfm* (accessed August 2006).

13. Ellie Kay, *Heroes at Home: Help and Hope for America's Military Families* (Minneapolis, MN: Bethany House, 2002), introduction.

14. Mother Teresa, *A Simple Path, compiled by Lucinda Vardey* (New York: Ballantine Books, 1995), 99.

15. Salvation Army Web site "Army Prepared for 2006 Hurricane Season," *www.salvationarmy.com* (accessed August 2006).

16. Rick Warren, *The Purpose-Driven Life* (Grand Rapids, MI: Zondervan, 2002), 289.

17. Joel Osteen, *Your Best Life Now* (New York: Warner Faith, 2004), 241.

18. Leslie Parrott, *You Matter More Than You Think* (Grand Rapids, MI: Zondervan, 2006), 101.

19. *Halley's Bible Commentary* (Grand Rapids, MI: Zondervan, 1965), 483.

20. Hybels, *Putting God and Others First*, 47.

21. Warren, *The Purpose-Driven Life*, 121.

Chapter 11

1. Billy Graham in "Why Christians Should Vote," publication/brochure (Colorado Springs, CO: Focus on the Family, 2006).

2. Jennifer Ferrant, "Elizabeth Dole" in *Christian Reader* (May/June 1999): 23.

3. "Office Holders" (New Brunswick, NJ: Center for American Women and Politics, Eagle Institute of Politics, Rutgers, The State University of New Jersey), *www.cawp.rutgers. edu/Facts/Officeholders/firsts.html* (accessed August 2006).

4. Beth Moore, *Believing God* (Nashville, TN: Broadman and Holman, 2004), 229.

5. *The Layman's Bible Encyclopedia* (Nashville, TN: The Southwestern Company, 1964), 63.

6. Mary Manz Simon, *Trend-Savvy Parenting* (Carol Stream, IL: Tyndale, 2006), 88.

7. Ibid., 89.

8. Joni Eareckson Tada and Nigel M. De S. Cameron, *How to Be a Christian in a Brave New World* (Grand Rapids, MI: Zondervan, 2006), 82.

9. "Why Christians Should Vote," publication/brochure (Colorado Springs, CO: Focus on the Family, 2006).

10. Ibid.

11. Ibid.

Index

Creator, 12, 46, 100, 186, 238
Crete
    definition, 89
crisis pregnancy centers, 52,
    250, 270, 296, 298
crucifixion, 50, 104, 168, 190
    definition, 36
cultivate genuine, deep
    friendships, 196
culture, 4, 14, 116, 252, 270
curse, 178
cursed
    definition, 186
customs, 2, 118
cyberspace, 294

D

"dainty one," 168
dangerous, 192, 228, 268, 294
David and Michal, 120, 130
Davis, Verdell, 46
Dead Sea Scrolls
    discovered in 1947, 262
    illustration, 262
dead to sin and alive in Christ
    definition, 6
deathbed, 94, 150
Deborah, 50, 70, 210, 284
    definition, 284
debt-proofed life, 170, 184
decaying morals, 196
deceitful desires, 96
deceitful woman, 100
deceptive philosophy, 294
decrees, 144, 200
    definition, 94
defining your top priority, 60,
    62, 64
dehydration
    definition, 46
Delilah, 100, 168, 176
    definition, 169
deliverance, 6, 40, 100, 144,
    154, 168
deliverance of Israel, 100
democracy mixed with
    servanthood, 212
denial, 30, 34, 58
depraved generation, 172
depression

symptoms of, 44
Depression, the, 102
"desolate woman," 138
despair, 8, 44, 48, 58, 120,
    122, 154
destructive marriage, 128
detachment
    definition, 131
devil
    definition, 40
devil's schemes, 292
DiMarco, Hayley, 194, 195,
    214
disappointed, 6, 72, 90, 218,
    224, 256
disappointments, 30, 32, 34,
    40, 44, 48, 58, 120, 272
disaster, 30, 60, 70, 224, 226,
    246, 250
disciple who betrayed Jesus,
    168
discontentment, 53
discouragement, 44, 122
disgrace, 138
disloyalty, 136
Disorganized Dotties, 228
distinguishing between spirits,
    246
divide big jobs into many
    smaller ones, 77
divorce, 128
divorce court, 172
divorced, 72
DNA, 132, 136, 158, 246, 286
Dobson, James, 93
Dole, Elizabeth, 288
don't let money pull you apart,
    172
Dorcas, 76, 237, 244, 251,
    276, 278, 280
    definition, 251
    an early deaconess in the
        church, 76
    ministered to other widows
        by making tunics and
        garments, 76
doubt, 8, 40, 191
doubtful, 141, 178
"do you practice what you
    preach?" 232

draw upon spiritual resources,
    128
dump debt, 166
dyers
    definition, 199

E

earthquakes, 227
easygoing phlegmatic, 177
economy, 182, 228
effective mother, 92
Egyptian maidservant, 41
Egyptian pharaoh, 55, 138
Eldredge, John, 65
Eldredge, Stasi, 65, 109
Eliezer, 116
Elijah, 34, 39, 40, 166, 233
Elijah's travels
    illustration, 40
Elimelech, 153, 154
Elizabeth, 14, 15, 16, 20, 102
emergency supplies, 225
emotionally abused, 127
emotionally and mentally
    stimulated, 202
emotional states, 201
    found 166 times in scripture,
        201
emotional ties, 129
Emperor Claudius, 208
    employee/employer
        relationships, 188
empty your heart of pride,
    anger, and resentment,
    168
encouraged the imprisoned,
    179
encouragement gifts, 249
endurance, 112
    definition, 26
entertain strangers, 231
enthusiastic, 22, 144
enthusiastic spirit, 115
environment of encouragement,
    99
Ephesus, 41, 58, 277, 293
Epistle
    definition, 232
epitaph
    definition, 14

hospitality is "a good thing" for building your house, 231
hospitality was practiced in the Bible, 233
hospitals built and helped the needy, 179
hot flashes, 4
household, 146
"how can a person lead a church, if he can't lead his home," 232
Huldah, 25, 252, 262, 263
human hearts hardened, 128
humanity, 21, 36, 129, 130
humble
    definition, 252
humble, be, 164, 194, 252
humbled
    definition, 87
humility and harmony, 157
humility is, 111
    freedom from pride, 253
    lowliness, 253
    meekness, 151, 253
    mildness, 253
Hunt, Mary
    on a debt-proof life, 171
    on the act of giving, 180
Hunter, Brenda, 84, 85
Hunter, Lynda, 210
Huram-Abi, 237
Huram's mother, 75
Hurricane Katrina, 246, 261
Hybels, Bill
    on God's guidance, 17
    on self-indulgence vs. humility, 253
    on servanthood, 274
hypobranchial gland, 199
hypocrisy, 194

I

idle, 187
idolatry
    definition, 32
"If I perish, I perish," 292
immoral life, 55
impacted
    definition, 128
impress them on your children,

89, 181
impulse, 170, 177
incestuous union, 153
incognito
    definition, 94
ineffective, 91
infidelity
    definition, 127, 205
information superhighway, 294
inheritance, 148, 157, 188
inherit eternal life, 263
in-laws, 120, 143, 144, 146
insecurity, 23
installment debt, 170
integrity, 96, 202, 203, 286
Internet, 24, 294, 295, 296
interpretation of tongues, 247
intimate faith, 4, 15
intimate relationships, 3, 20, 24, 36, 65
"into each life a little rain must fall," 32
inventors, 99
invest confidently and consistently, 171
invisible barrier, 177
Isaac, 17, 26, 54, 116, 117, 121
    definition, 6
Isaiah, 45
    definition, 287
Ishmael, 54, 73
"Is life really worth living?" 188
isolation, 36, 38, 73, 102
items to help you get over the bad romance, 204
it is a privilege to be a grandparent—and a great responsibility, 147

J

jar of oil, 167
jealously, 53, 194, 195
Jedidah, 263
Jehosheba, 71
Jericho
    definition, 55
Jerusalem
    definition, 5, 84

Jerusalem's temple
Jesus
    definition, 6, 84
Jesus at the temple
    illustration, 86
Jesus granted women dignity, 118
Jesus paid the ransom so we could be free from sin, 224
Jesus prayed
    on the cross, 221
    for direction, 221
    for himself, 221
    for his disciples, 221
    to offer thanks and praise, 221
    and praised God, 25
    a prayer of intercession, 221
    in private, 221
    the psalms, 13
    in times of spiritual strife, 221
Jesus'
    disciples, 196
    ministry, 21, 23, 64, 169, 179
    parables, 91
    resurrection, 180, 275
Jesus spent a great deal of time teaching on money, 164
Jethro, 144
Jewish dietetic law, 100
Jewish leaders, 21, 289
Jezebel
    definition, 39
Jezreel, 235
Joanna, the wife of Cuza, 179
Joash, 71
Jochebed, 34, 71, 121
John the Baptist, 16
Jonah's Fish Fry fast-food restaurant, 220
Joppa, 237, 277, 279
Joseph of Arimathea, 265
Josiah, 183, 252, 262, 263, 285
journaling, 90
joy, 46, 47, 154
Judah
    definition, 45, 287

of the squirrel, 18
paralyzed with fear, 167
parenthood, 90, 93
Parent-Teacher Association, 285
Parks, Rosa, 283
Parrott, Les
  on a debt-free marriage, 177
  on a good marriage, 117
Parrott, Leslie, 271
  on a debt-free marriage, 177
  on a good marriage, 117
Partow, Donna 102
passion, 206
pastors and their families live under incredible pressures, 257
patience, 17, 18, 52, 110, 111, 112, 137
patient, 37
patriarchs
  definition, 149
pay off debts, 154
peace
  definition, 123
peace and joy, 157
Peace Corps, 252, 253
peaceful, 19, 140, 141, 146, 147
"peaceful," 18
peasants and kings, 235
perfection, 140, 141, 247, 248
perfect will, 55, 190
persecution
  definition, 91
perseverance
  definition, 51
persistent enemy, 143
personal relationship with God should be your top priority, 174
personality puzzle
  definition, 139, 141
personality traits, 176
personality types
  definition, 139
person of "being" rather than a person of "doing," 228
pessimistic, 140, 141
Pharaoh's edict of death, 138

Pharisees
  definition, 21, 150
philanthropy
  definition, 253
Philemon
  definition, 235
Philippi
  definition, 63
Philistines, 100, 101, 169
phlegmatic, 140, 141, 177
Phoebe
  definition, 251
Phoenician King Hiram of Tyre, 237
physical education, 101
physically abusive relationship, 127
pie chart for your money illustration, 173
pillar of salt, 174
plastic prison of credit card debt, 168
pledges
  definition, 9
plunge men into ruin and destruction, 168
Pool of Siloam, 91
popular, 140, 164, 165
pornography, 295
possessions, 37, 149, 170, 208
postresurrection, 273
Potiphar's wife, 205
poured, 8, 21
poverty, 169, 173
Powell, Colin, 245
powerful, 25, 45, 84, 140, 141
powerful ministry, 67
"practice what you preach," 150
praise
  definition, 9
praiseworthy, 66
prayer
  definition, 24
prayer for a clean heart, 201
prayer shawl, 199
prayers of Bible women, 25, 26
prayer strengthens, 95
prayer walk, a, 25
praying within the will of God, 13

precepts
  definition, 3
pregnancies, 4, 298
prescription medications, 226
pretend vote, 286
priest
  definition, 14
priests in the tabernacle, 138
"princess," 54
Priscilla, 72, 208
Priscilla and Aquila, 36, 122, 209
private prayer chapel, 220
proclamation, 247
procreation
  definition, 93
prodigal
  definition, 91
proof of our faith, 260
proper diet, 5, 17
prophet
  definition, 32, 166, 235
prophetess
  definition, 284
prophet's widow, the, 166, 167
prostitute
  definition, 55
Proverbs, 19, 46
Proverbs 31 woman, 76, 230, 239
provocation
  definition, 137
psalmist
  definition, 5
"psyched up," 70
PTA, 284
  definition, 285
pure gold, 3
purified
  definition, 22
purple
  definition, 199
purple cloths, 199
purpose of the heart found 195 times in scripture, 201
put family feelings over money, 177
put their religion into practice, 150

simple trust, 245
simplify them, 69
sin, 19, 36, 120, 124, 128, 129
sincere, obedient servant, 188
sinful townsmen, 174
single mother, 74, 75, 80, 251
sister, 7, 48, 95, 210, 222, 223
Sister Schubert's Homemade
    Rolls, 191
Sittser, Gerald L.
    on denial, 35
    on suffering, 57
"situational" friends, 196, 198
slanderers
    definition, 89
slave/master relationship, 188
Smalley, Gary
    on forgiveness, 124
    on relationships, 136
    on viewing each other as
        God views us, 119
snails
    definition, 199
soap operas, 205
socially irresponsible
    entertainment, 295
social problem, 5
Sodom and Gomorrah, 129,
    174
solitary place, 68
Solomon
    definition, 19
Solomon, author of
    Ecclesiastes, 189
solutions to broken
    relationships, 120
something blue, 110
something borrowed, 110
something new, 110
something old, 110
"son of encouragement," 288
son of Hur, the, 237
"son of promise," 6
son of Uri, 237
soul, 8, 11, 17, 22, 28, 42
southern hospitality, 234
sovereign
    definition, 32
sovereign will, 151
special blessing, 16

spending behavior, 172, 175, 176
spending time with Jesus, 62,
    177, 296
spikenard
    illustration, 8
spindle, 238
spinning, 61, 237
spirit of sonship, 70
spiritual bankruptcy, 169
spiritual father
    definition, 72
spiritual fitness, 6, 7, 9, 10, 11,
    17, 27
spiritual gifts, 246, 247, 248,
    249
spiritual mentor, 249
spiritual needs, 5, 220
spouse, 114, 115, 122, 123,
    124, 125
stability, 147
staff
    definition, 50
starvation, 40, 217
Statue of Liberty, 304
statutes
    definition, 3
stepping-stones to
    reconciliation, 123, 124
steps you can take to begin
    rebuilding a healthy
    relationship, 124
Stevens, Val, 290
Stewart, Martha, 66, 231
stoning
    definition, 303
stop arguing, 172
stop trying to be perfect, 77
storehouse, 178
stress, 25, 61, 62, 69, 70, 73
"stressed out," 68
stress-free life, 62, 64
stress-related illness, 70
submissive to God's family
    plan, 119
submissive to God's plan, 118
submitted
    definition, 7
successful relationships, 123
succumbing to the influence of
    pagans, 248

suffering is a part of life, 33
sufficiency
    definition, 224
suicide, 44, 166
support of family or friends,
    128
suppressant
    definition, 21
surrender
    definition, 7
surrender everything over to
    God, 123
surrogate mother, 73
surviving a gossip girl, 196
surviving a quarantine queen,
    195
surviving the slander sister, 196
sweeter than honey, 3, 4
Swindoll, Charles R., 148
Swindoll, Luci
    on Christian working
        women, 192
    on true professionalism, 212
symbol of friendship, the, 271,
    272
sympathetic, be, 110, 194
synagogue
    definition, 199
system of hierarchy, 212

T

tabernacle
    definition, 237, 238
Tada, Joni Eareckson
    on an attitude of reverence,
        acknowledging God's
        authority and power, 151
    on being faithful in
        affliction, 42
    on God's plan, 33
    on the healing heart of
        America, 299
"take this cup from me," 36,
    64, 221
tale of two modern women,
    191
Tamar, 139
tambourine, 218
taskmaster, 188
task-oriented, 140

White, Paula
    on predicting your end, 139
    on using what God gave
      you, 256
"who is my neighbor," 264
"whom God hears," 54
"why not be involved in a God-
    ordained government?"
    284
"why should we be involved in
    government?" 285
wickedness, 129, 175
widow, 40, 150
widowed, 73, 142, 153, 278
widow of Nain, 75
widow of Zarephath, 34, 39,
    40, 217, 233
widows, 76, 142, 153, 278
will of God, 13, 36, 190, 201,
    284
Winfrey, Oprah, 87
wisdom
    definition, 11, 19
wise counsel, 92, 247
wise listen and add to their

learning, 208
wise woman, 170, 216, 228,
    232
wise women, 20, 127, 189, 225
withstand the storms of life,
    122
wives and children treated like
    property, 128
wives were never intended to
    be doormats for their hus-
    bands, 118
woman of character, 100
woman who fears the Lord is to
    be praised, 76
women
    at Ephesus, 277
    of faith, 6, 43, 73, 195, 270
    using a spindle, illustration,
    238
    working, 189, 192
workaholism, 212
worldly pleasures, 190
worry
    definition, 24
worrying, 62

worship
    of Baal, 40, 285
    definition, 9
    practiced throughout the
      Old and New Testaments,
      12
wrongs can be confessed, 122

Y

"Y'all come back now, ya
    hear?" 234
Yates, Cynthia, 73
young believers, 224
younger women, 89, 105, 113,
    216, 217, 231
young men were taught how to
    handle money, 165
"your faith has healed you," 4

Z

Zarephath
    definition, 34
Zechariah, 14, 15